The Hidden Feelings *of* Motherhood

Coping with Mothering Stress,
Depression, and Burnout

Second Edition

By

Kathleen Kendall-Tackett, Ph.D., IBCLC
Foreword by Phyllis Klaus, M.F.T., C.S.W. & Marshall H. Klaus, M.D.

Pharmasoft Publishing, L.P.

The Hidden Feelings of Motherhood

Coping with Mothering Stress, Depression,
and Burnout

Second Edition

© Copyright 2005

Pharmasoft Publishing, L.P.
1712 N. Forest St.
Amarillo, TX   79106-7017

806-376-9900
800-378-1317
www.iBreastfeeding.com

Disclaimer
This publication is designed to provide accurate and authoritative information in regard to the subject matter covered. It is sold with the understanding that the publisher is not engaged in rendering psychological, financial, legal, or other professional services. If expert assistance or counseling is needed, the services of a competent professional should be sought.

Library of Congress Control Number: 2005928148

ISBN 0-9729583-8-X

Dedication

This book is dedicated to the mothers who
have shared their stories with me.
You continue to be my best teachers.
May my words encourage you.

TABLE OF CONTENTS

FOREWORD IX

ACKNOWLEDGMENTS XIII

INTRODUCTION
21st Century Mothering: What's Wrong with this Picture?............... 1

CHAPTER 1
Stress: Moving at the Speed of Life 7

CHAPTER 2
Depression: Life without Joy 25

CHAPTER 3
Burnout: When You Can't Give Anymore 45

CHAPTER 4
Hearth and Home: The Fascinating History of Women's Domestic
Work in America.. 69

CHAPTER 5
For Love or Money: Work Arrangements that Work for You 91

CHAPTER 6
Less Work for Mother: Lightening Your Load at Home 115

CHAPTER 7
Tough Beginnings: Making Peace with Your Birth Experience 139

CHAPTER 8
So Tired: Mothers and Fatigue 159

CHAPTER 9
The Long Shadow: Adult Survivors of
Childhood Abuse and Adversity 183

CHAPTER 10
Challenging Child I: Mothering a Child with Behavioral Issues 207

CHAPTER 11
Challenging Child II: Mothering a Child with Health Issues 227

CHAPTER 12
Hello-Goodbye: Mothering and Childbearing Loss 247

EPILOGUE 273

REFERENCES 279

BIOGRAPHY 299

FOREWORD

Phyllis Klaus, MFT, CSW, and Marshall Klaus, MD
authors of *Your Amazing Newborn*

The Hidden Feelings of Motherhood by Kathleen Kendall-Tackett is a unique and caring book on the many real issues women face that are sometimes brought on or activated by birth. This book is about more than birth; it is about being a woman in these modern times and learning to cope with the many unforeseen or unexpected vicissitudes of life and motherhood.

Dr. Kendall-Tackett addresses the enormous load of responsibilities women have to juggle: home, career, infant and child care, and the unrecognized emotional and social changes connected with becoming a mother. No longer does the home scene resemble the typical family of the *Ozzie and Harriet* TV show. Today, the changing face of the family (single mothers, divorced mothers, older mothers, etc.) as well as the expectations women put on themselves means that each family is unique. Women need almost superhuman efforts to make it all work. Not that women haven't always faced rearing children and tending the home, but the demands today and the emotional tenor of expectations often create an overload on the human system that can cause burnout. Dr. Kendall-Tackett not only addresses such important issues facing mothers as isolation, but also discusses unexpected outcomes such as depression, an ill or disabled child, loss, and illness in the mother. She addresses the difficulties that a history of childhood sexual abuse can cause at birth and during the postpartum period.

Dr. Kendall-Tackett not only offers information on what is happening when a woman experiences disturbing events and symptoms, she also describes some causal factors that contribute to stress. In addition, she gives helpful advice, suggestions, and resources on how to meet these distressing events and circumstances. She encourages women to recognize that there are solutions. They do not have to do it all themselves, and they are not alone in facing these challenges. Her ideas for self-awareness and self-help, her bibliography of books and sources for support, and her attitude of caring and hope will help many women in this period of their lives.

Let's step back a little. How women are treated and how becoming a mother is understood right from the beginning moments of the birth of her child can have far-reaching implications, especially if she comes home to the more difficult and lonely scene modern women face a few weeks after the baby's birth. The publication of this book coincides with the discovery of a major principle of the birth process made during recent studies of the perinatal period. This new finding is especially relevant to the major issues discussed by Dr. Kendall-Tackett since altering the care of mother and infant during this early period can significantly prevent some of these problems.

To fully understand the clinical and theoretical significance of this time (from the beginning of labor, birth, and the next several days), it is necessary that it is identified in biology as a sensitive period. It is at this time that the mother is unusually open to major changes in her behavior, especially with her infant dependent on how she is cared for during the process. The more the mother is cared for in a humane manner, the more sensitive and caring she will be with her own infant.

Donald Winnicott reported a special mental state of the mother in the perinatal period that involves a greatly increased sensitivity to the needs of her baby. He noted that this state of primary maternal preoccupation starts near the end of pregnancy and continues for a few weeks after birth. A mother needs nurturing support and a protected environment to develop and maintain this state. He wrote that only if a mother is sensitized in the way we are describing can she feel herself into her infant's place and so meet the infant's needs. In the state of primary maternal preoccupation, the mother is better able to sense and provide what her new infant has signaled. If she senses the needs and responds to them in a sensitive and timely manner, mother and infant establish a pattern of synchronized and mutually rewarding interactions. It is our hypothesis that as the mother-infant pair continues this pattern day after day, the infant more frequently will develop a secure attachment.

Mothers who have continuous emotional and physical support by a doula during labor and birth compared to control mothers without a doula are noted in the immediate neonatal period to be significantly less anxious and to have increased self-esteem. At six weeks after birth, the differences in outcome are even greater. Mothers who had a doula during labor had significantly lower scores on a standard test of depression (50% less than controls) and lower test scores of state anxiety. They had an easier time managing their infants and began to believe the infant was their own on the third day (while controls first felt their baby was their own on the ninth day of life). They felt the labor was less difficult than expected, while controls felt labor was more difficult than expected. When they were asked to compare their infant with a standard infant, women who had a doula felt their infant was stronger, more beautiful, and healthier than the standard infant, while the control mothers felt their infant was almost as beautiful, almost as strong, and almost as healthy.

Other studies reveal that when the child reaches two months of age, women who have had a doula during labor are significantly more sensitive and appropriate to the signals of their babies compared to women who were randomized during labor to an epidural or a control group. These and other observations suggest that some maternity practices do not fit or meet the biological needs of both mother and infant, are harmful to the young dyad, and may actually be inducing some of the problems Dr. Kendall-Tackett is discussing. Thus, as we closely read the many valuable recommendations for helping mothers suffering from depression, severe stress, burnout, and the birth of an infant with a disability or a premature infant, we also must consider the many humane changes to be made in maternity care. Therefore, we need to look at the continuity and thoughtfulness of care needed at birth and, in addition, recognize that women in the weeks after birth also need emotional and physical support, practical help and resources, and a culture that values motherhood.

ACKNOWLEDGMENTS

There are many people who have given generously of their time to share their experiences and expertise with me. This book would not have been possible without their help.

Thanks to Tom Hale and Janet Rourke of Pharmasoft Publishing for making the second edition a reality. I've appreciated your input and support throughout this project. You've been a pleasure to work with.

If writing a book is like having a baby, then these women could be considered the labor assistants. They never knew when a simple "how are you doing?" would result in an earful on whatever topic I had been working on that week. And yet, they continued to ask. My heartfelt thanks to Marcy Alves, Donna Barton, Margaret Jeffers, Marie Goodwin, Mary Beth Magan, Lucie Eldridge, Sue Moulton, Michelle Paquin, Marj Johns, Kathie Martin, and Debbie Rhoades.

In the process of writing a book, sometimes what you really need is a "word in season." These friends spoke encouragement at just the right times, and I am thankful to know them: Martha Vendt, Heather Martin, Annette Dietermann, Nancy Mohrbacher, Ruth Lawrence, Phyllis and Marshall Klaus.

Gerry Koocher, former chief psychologist at Children's Hospital in Boston, now Dean of Health Sciences at Simmons College, deserves special thanks for his collegial and generous spirit. He has many commitments, but made time for me to ask questions and troll for information. His compassion, knowledge, and wisdom are reflected throughout chapters 10-12.

Joan Valk and Kathy Whelan both deserve special mention for their invaluable help in the chapter on childbearing loss. They are both examples of courage and grace under the most difficult of circumstances. Mickey Sperlich and the mothers of the "survivor moms speak out" project added enormously to the chapter on childhood abuse. I was moved by their willingness to help someone they had never met. Brandi Valentine allowed me to share some of her story about life with a son with ADHD. I believe that her story will minister to others facing similar circumstances.

Several years ago, Michelle Winkler former editor of *The Doula* magazine gave me the idea for the book's title and acted as a sounding board for many of the ideas reflected in this book. My thinking has also been shaped by conversations with my friends Maria Tock, Hoke Shirley, Kathy Flannery, Jan Tuxbury, Gerry Ann Dubis, Ted Cross, and the La Leche League leaders of Framingham, Massachusetts: Leslie Simpson, Diane Smith, Sheryl Sacharoff, and Linda Jeffrey.

Kate Pennington, former Area Coordinator for Leaders in La Leche League of Maine and New Hampshire, offered insightful comments on early versions of my history chapter and also helped me locate mothers willing to share their stories with me. Many thanks to her and the La Leche League leaders of Maine and New Hampshire (and other places) for their willingness to share their joys and their sorrows. I also thank Cindy Johnson, Lynn Duffy, Paula Oliveira, Lisa Lamadriz, M.J. Chase, Laurie Geck, and the members of the New Hampshire Breastfeeding Task Force for their suggestions, comments, support, and friendship over the past nine years. They have made working in the field of perinatal health a genuine pleasure. My cousin Connie McLennan shared her insights on raising a child with a chronic illness with me. Her experiences and comments helped shape chapter 11, and by doing so, will help other mothers struggling with similar issues.

I am fortunate to have wonderful colleagues at the Family Research Lab, who have offered me an academic home and been enthusiastic and supportive in my work with mothers. Doreen Cole, who kindly reviewed chapters for me, has also been a faithful ally in the many years we have known each other. I'm always impressed with her wisdom and kindness. Sarah Giacomoni proofed my manuscript and caught all the really embarrassing mistakes that I never seem to see ("we're" vs. "were" vs. "where"). As always, her work was excellent, and she was prompt, cheerful, and a pleasure to work with.

My final thanks go to my family. My husband Doug remains my greatest and most enthusiastic supporter. He was my in-house technical support, always making sure that my computer was backed up and that the batteries for my laptop were charged. He spent many hours fixing my computer when my hard drive crashed. He has also been willing to read drafts (usually with me hovering over him), serve as a sounding board, and generally be a cheerleader throughout. I could never have finished this project without his support.

My sons Ken and Chris are the joys of my life. They have taught me what it means to be a mother, and I continue to learn from them. They also gave me the time and space to work, even though it meant that they were essentially "book orphans" for weeks at a time. I am grateful to have them in my life.

INTRODUCTION

Twenty-First Century Mothering: What's Wrong with this Picture?

Do you remember those puzzles where you looked at a picture and were asked to circle what was wrong? At first glance, nothing seems amiss. But as you look closer, you start to notice some problems.

Well, I find myself looking at 21st century mothers. At first glance, everything seems in order. Mothers in our neighborhoods, in magazines, and on TV look good and seem to function well. Yet, as I look more closely, I see some alarming things. I see mothers who are tired and isolated. They strain under the yoke of too much to do. One mother told me that she hadn't laughed in years. For these mothers, life is joyless drudgery. They are stuck. And, they think they are the only ones.

Mothers are also pressed for time. In response, I see magazine articles promising to help us use *every minute*: How to cram the absolute most into an already too-full day. But no one asks whether we actually need to do all this stuff. And, the time problem seems to be getting progressively worse. In the five years since I wrote the original edition of this book, the term 24/7 has become part of our vocabulary, referring to things you can do 24 hours a day, 7 days a week. I've also seen a dramatic rise in the popularity of liquid foods. While these foods can be convenient, I have to ask what it says about our culture when we no longer have time to chew.

We are paying a price for our constant overload. I see a troubling rise in stress-related illness--even in children. In fact, one study found higher anxiety levels in normal children today than were present in child psychiatric patients of the 1950s (Twenge, 2000). I also believe that

1

our stressed-out lifestyles are largely responsible for the American obesity epidemic. One recent study (Vorona et al., 2005) found that people who slept fewer hours than they needed were significantly more likely to be overweight or obese. Why? Because insufficient sleep is a physiological stressor. Our bodies respond by packing on extra pounds that we might need--just in case. And, time-pressed moms are the ones most likely to be sleep deprived.

Depression is also remarkably common in women in general and in mothers in particular. Whenever I speak on the subject of depression, I mention how the American Psychological Association's Task Force on Women and Depression identified being a mother of young children as an *independent risk factor for depression.* That statement always brings a laugh of recognition. But, we accept it as "normal" and don't stop to question it. Again I ask, "what's wrong with this picture?"

If you picked up this book, chances are you are facing similar challenges. Mothering is a huge job with awesome responsibilities, low pay, and not a lot of respect or support. We all recognize that this is true, yet few seem willing to talk about the difficult parts of mothering. If you are struggling, this book can help.

Who I Am and Why I Wrote This Book

Allow me to introduce myself. I am the mother of two great, teenage sons--and no stranger to mothering stress. I'm writing to you from a wide range of perspectives: mother, wife, health researcher, person with a chronic illness, and author or editor of 11 other books on a variety of women's health issues, including stress and depression in mothers.

In my professional life, I am a health psychologist and researcher at the Family Research Lab at the University of New Hampshire. Some of the topics I study include family violence, depression in mothers, and breastfeeding. I'm also an International Board-Certified Lactation Consultant and La Leche League leader. This work puts me in contact with hundreds of mothers and gives me a chance to get know their stories.

Almost 10 years ago, my life took another turn; I was diagnosed with systemic lupus erythematosus (SLE). Lupus is an autoimmune disease that goes through periods of remission and flares. It is unpredictable and often makes me tired. Even though my illness has been stable for several years, it still affects me every day.

Being ill has forced me to evaluate my role as a mother. Since I have limited energy, I have to make choices and set priorities. What aspects of mothering are essential? What are optional? What is being a good mother anyway? Why do I sometimes feel bad when I can't be on top of everything the way I "should"? Illness has forced me to learn some hard lessons, but has ultimately improved the quality of my life.

And so it is that I approach the topic of mothering stress, depression, and burnout from all these varied perspectives. Now that you have learned about me, let me walk you through the rest of the book.

Book Overview

In chapters 1 to 3, I provide an overview of stress, depression, and burnout. There is a substantial amount of overlap between these three conditions, and they share many symptoms. You might find that portions of all three chapters describe the events and circumstances of your life.

The next three chapters are about one of the biggest sources of stress in your life: work. "Work" includes both tasks mothers do inside the home and paid employment. I have also included a chapter on the history of women's work in America because events that occurred years ago are still influencing women today. Understanding these historical and cultural forces frees you to make better choices for you and your family.

In the remaining chapters, I review some of the specific issues that might be causing difficulties for you. You can read each of these chapters or skip around and read the ones most relevant to your current situation. Each chapter has an overview of the problem I've addressed and some suggestions on what you can do. I've also provided a resource list at the end of each chapter to give you information on Web sites and other publications that may be helpful on the given topic.

You Can Change Your Life

Before we begin, I'd like you to know that whatever you are struggling with, there is a way out. Your situation may seem hopeless. It is not. As you read this book, I want you to recognize the tremendous power that you have. You may not be able change some of your life circumstances, but you can change how you react to them. Reading that, you might think that this strategy only works for people with easy lives. If you feel that way, let me tell you about the life of psychiatrist Victor Frankl. Dr. Frankl, at one point, did have an easy life. And then, the Nazis invaded his country. It was during his experience in a Nazi concentration camp, when all vestiges of his previous life were gone, that he made a key discovery. Although the Nazis could control all the circumstances of his life, they could not control how he reacted to those circumstances. This power to choose became the central focus of his life's work for the next 52 years.

Claudia Panuthos and Cathy Romeo make a similar point. They were writing about one of the most extreme forms of mothering stress--the death of a baby. What they say applies to other situations as well.

> No one who has suffered loss is ever again the same; we are either further enlightened and in harmony with our spiritual beliefs, or we are imprisoned in the darkness of our own bitterness, resentment, and self-pity. However entitled we are to such feelings, they are the spiritual killers of our own souls. Love cannot coexist with bitterness and resentment, nor can we ever grow through self-pity (p. xvi).

Mothering can be richly rewarding: one of life's great joys. Or, it can be an exercise in frustration and despair. You can decide which way it will be for you.

In conclusion, I'd like to invite you to examine your life. Throughout this book, I describe some of the issues and concerns that can drain your life of joy. Assuming that life cannot change is one of the surest roads to misery. Some changes are relatively simple, like cutting down on extra activities. Others are major, like getting out of debt, moving, changing jobs, or finally leaving an abusive relationship. My suggestions are not quick fixes. Rather than tell you how to cram more into each hour, I want you to be able to live according to your priorities and beliefs. My goal is to encourage and empower you. To help you recognize--and overcome--the hidden feelings of motherhood.

CHAPTER I

STRESS: MOVING AT THE SPEED OF LIFE

Does your life feel like a treadmill? Do you run out of day before you run out of items on your to-do list? Do you feel you're on call twenty-four hours a day? If you answered yes to any of these questions, you are not alone. Even a quick perusal of self-help titles will reveal we are a culture under stress. How many times do you hear the word stress in a twenty-four hour period? How often do you use it? When someone asks how you are, do you say "busy," "swamped," or "overwhelmed"? Tina, a single mom with three children, says: "I can't cram another hour of must do into my day." If you are feeling like that, read on. You can live life at a more manageable pace.

A Tale of Two Mothers

Let's take a look at the lives of two mothers. See if either of these stories sounds familiar to you. Mary is employed outside the home and Cindy is home full-time.

Mary begins her day at 6:00 a.m. She must shower, dress, and get ready for the day by 6:30 when she starts preparing breakfast. She assembles all the stuff her kids need to take to school. Do the kids have their lunch money and homework? Are there any permission slips she needs to sign? After the kids are loaded on the bus at 7:00, she hops in the car and heads for the office, just in time to hit traffic. She tears into her office a little after 8:00 only to dash off to a meeting. At the end of the workday, she rushes through traffic to take the kids to lessons or soccer practice. Even though she is married, she does most of the household chores and is responsible for most of the kid stuff. Once home, she begins the nightly ritual of dinner, homework, and housework, that is, if she has no other obligations that night. Maybe there is time to start a load of laundry before dinner. After her nighttime routine, she might try to do some of the work she brought home from the office or bake the cookies for Jimmy's class party tomorrow. She falls into bed exhausted only to start again the next day.

And, that's assuming everything goes according to plan, which it often doesn't. What happens when part of the plan goes awry? She oversleeps. Or, there is no milk. Or, the kids miss the bus. Or, she spills coffee all over her blouse. Or, Tim's mom, who was supposed to drive carpool today, is in bed with the flu. Can she take over? Or, her child is sick, and she also has a tight deadline at work. That's the story for many employed mothers.

Moms at home are also often stressed as Cindy's story illustrates. Cindy also rises early to begin her day. Cindy has three children under the age of six. She home schools her five-year-old so there isn't the morning rush to get kids out the door for school. But, there are plenty of things to do. Tammy was up all night with an ear infection so Cindy is pretty tired. She calls the pediatrician at 8:00 a.m., but gets his answering service. She'll try again after breakfast. She tries to keep the house clean and orderly, but it's hard to do when she is teaching her older child and trying to keep up with the messes of her younger children at the same time. After a morning outing, she is dismayed to discover that she's just walked through the entire grocery store with a big smudge of food on her shirt.

When she attends a social function with her husband, she is frequently asked, "and what do you do"? When she says that she is at home with her children, the questioner quickly moves on to find someone more "interesting" to talk to. Cindy is isolated. She's the only home schooling mother she knows locally, but is glad to be on an e-mail list. Even with that, by the end of the day, she is starved for adult conversation. Since she is "not working," others feel free to ask favors: Would you accept delivery of my package/let the repairman in/pick my sick child up at school/make costumes for the dance recital/bake some cookies/help with the Halloween party? She enjoys some of these activities; they are some of the perks of being at home with her children. But, she'd love a few minutes alone: to take a shower, read more than two pages of a book, or even go to the bathroom. One day it occurs to her that, like her employed counterpart, she has very little control over her schedule and life.

These examples describe a type of stress that researchers refer to as "daily hassles." The accumulation of these small stressors can be overwhelming. But, let's talk for a moment about big stressors. What if your partner leaves, or becomes very ill, or even dies? What would happen then? Or, suppose you are charging through life when one of your children gets very sick or even dies. Do you really want to spend this precious time always being on overload? What if you get sick? I can tell you from personal experience that many things change in a family when mom is sick. Life offers us no guarantees of happy endings. Although we should not live in fear of possible bad things that could happen, occasional reflection on these possibilities can help us keep our life on track.

Why Mothers Are Stressed

I think we'll all agree that mothers are stressed. So the next question we should ask is why. Interestingly, some of our most potent stressors come from the abundance our culture offers. Yes, there can be too much of a good thing; it's the stress of "too much and too many." See if you recognize any of these common sources of stress.

Driving

We've all heard the joke, "a mother's place is in the car." How true it is! The U.S. Department of Transportation (2004a) estimates that a person with children travels fifty-four miles per day. That is *per person* not per family. Mothers drive children to school, extracurricular activities, and appointments, making an average of 4.8 trips per day. And, this number is probably on the low side for many mothers.

Commuting to work is another reason for driving, and commutes are getting longer. Time spent traveling to work has increased 36% since 1983, and commuters spend an average of twenty-five minutes traveling to work (U.S. Department of Transportation, Bureau of Transportation Statistics, 2004b). Yet, this number drastically underestimates the commute time for workers in more urban areas, where commutes of an hour or more are common.

House

In many parts of the country, housing costs are astronomical, and they dictate many other lifestyle choices such as the type of job a person takes, the number of hours she works, and how far she commutes. In areas of the country such as Southern California, New York City, Boston, or Chicago, it is not unusual for a house to cost $500,000 or more. Commutes often expand as families move farther and farther from cities in search of affordable housing.

Houses are substantially larger than they were thirty years ago, and this is true even though our family size has decreased. In 1973, new houses in the U.S. had an average square footage of 1,660 feet. In contrast, by 2003, that number was 2,330 (U.S. Census Bureau, 2005a). Similarly, in 1973, only 19% of new homes had 2 ½ bathrooms, and no one had 3 or more. By 2003, 38% had three or more (U.S. Census Bureau, 2005b). All this extra square footage costs more and gives us more to clean. And, our stuff always manages to expand to fill the empty spaces.

Paper

Global paper use has increased more than six fold since 1950 (Abramovitz & Mattoon, 1999). An average person handles about 300 sheets of paper per day. Included in that number are catalogs, magazines, flyers, newspapers, notes, junk mail, faxes, and school papers. In five days, a family of five can deal with 7,000 pages or 45,000 pages a month (Aslett, 2000). That is a staggering number, one that explains why most households I've been in have at least one large stack of paper laying around. According to some estimates, we spend an average of eight months of our lives sorting through junk mail alone (Davidson, 1991).

Work

Many Americans work too many hours. While the number of hours for the average American has actually slightly decreased since the 1970s (Kirkland, 2000), the number of hours that women work rose steadily through the 1980s. In 1993, women worked 20% more hours than they did in 1976--adding 233 hours to their average work year (U.S. Department of Labor, 1997a). In comparison, men's hours rose only 3% during this same period. Over the course of a year, U.S. workers put in 1,815 hours, tying us in number of hours with the Japanese. In comparison, the average number of yearly hours spent at work in Europe ranged from 1,300 to 1,800 (Armour, 2003). From 1977 to 2002, dual-earning couples added an extra 10 hours a week to their workweeks (Armour, 2003). Lehmkuhl (1999) indicated that there is a similar rise in working hours in Canada. Since 1976, the number of employees working more than 50 hours has increased by 25%.

Another way to measure work time is to compare the number of vacation days Americans take versus citizens of other countries. Italy takes the largest number of vacation days per year--42. The Germans take 35 days, the U.K. and Canada take 28 and 26 days respectively. Interestingly, even the Koreans and Japanese have more vacation days than Americans --each at 25 days. In contrast, Americans take only 13 vacation days a year (Infoplease.com, 2005a).

Time spent at work is time spent away from our families and friends, our homes, and our self-care rituals, such as exercise and relaxation. Some companies are responding by becoming more homelike. The net result is that people spend even more time at work (Hochschild, 1997). Steven Sauter of the National Institute of Occupational Safety and Health describes the problem this way (cited in McGuire, 1999):

> Every day we see reports about the increasing workload shouldered by men and women in this country. Not so long ago, we talked calmly about work overload. And then we started to hear the expression "time poverty." Now, at this meeting we're hearing expressions like "time famine."

Debt

Families are incurring record amounts of debt. Many think that thrift and frugality are quaint vestiges from the past. Why wait when you can have it now? This is a philosophy that Americans and others have adopted with a vengeance. In the U.S., credit-card debt now averages $11,000 per household. American consumer debt including mortgages is now more than the national debt ($6.5 trillion vs. $5.7 trillion respectively; Maranjian, 2004). Consumer credit debt rose from $796 billion in 1990 to $1.4 trillion in 1999--almost double. Perhaps not surprisingly, our personal savings rate is now close to 0% of our income (Maranjian, 2004). In contrast, the Japanese save approximately 16% of their income (Affluenza, 2000).

Other countries are catching up to the U.S. Personal debt in Great Britain hit the £1 trillion mark in 2004 and continues to climb. The average household owes £7,463, not including money owed for their mortgages. And, in Britain, there are now 8 million credit cards more than there are people (Talbot, 2005).

Debt unfortunately severely influences families. It dictates how much both mothers and fathers work, and it is a source of chronic stress. Mothers often feel that they have no choice in whether they seek outside employment, and they sometimes work two jobs. In a study conducted in England, worry about debt was the strongest predictor of depression in mothers of young children at the initial and follow-up contacts (Reading & Reynolds, 2001). Indeed, worrying about debt predicted depression six months later.

Families with large debt loads usually have no financial safety net; even those with middle-class lifestyles know they may be only one or two paychecks from the street. And, this is a continuous source of stress.

Extracurricular Activities

Kids' extracurricular activities can also stress mothers. I mention this with some trepidation. For many middle-class parents, kids' participation in extracurricular activities is the *sine qua non* of good parenting. We all want to do everything possible to ensure that our children have a bright future, even when it means hours and hours in the car.

I'm not mentioning extracurricular activities because I want to knock them; most can be quite worthwhile. Indeed, some of my fondest memories of high school come from my involvement in various activities. Participation on sports teams or in music or arts programs can develop character, help your child excel in school and make new friends, keep your child safe and out of trouble, and look good on a college application. These are some of the many benefits of extracurricular activities. For example, in a recent survey of top CEOs, 90% revealed that they had been in high school band, chorus, or orchestra (Martin, 2004).

However, this is another example of too much of a good thing. Extensive participation in extracurricular activities can be a major source of stress for both you and your child. Pediatricians have noted a rise in stress-related illnesses in children whose lives are heavily programmed (Blum, 2004). Practices and games can take place several nights a week. If there is more than one child in your family, you may be on the road most of the week. Many families I know spend their entire weekends racing from one sporting activity to another. And, their regular chores still need to be done. (If your children aren't doing chores because of their busy schedules, it probably means that you are.)

This type of heavy scheduling doesn't start in high school; it can start practically from birth. Middle schoolers in my town frequently have away games on school nights that last until 10:30 or 11:00 at night. Dinners are eaten in the car on the way to practices or games. Family dinners are rare in some households. Family vacations are almost impossible to schedule. And, sporting seasons seem to be getting longer and longer--meaning this break-neck pace continues throughout the year. Parents who try to cut down often feel guilty because they are not providing every possible advantage to their children.

I think we need to step back and consider whether this current excess in children's activities is really good for our children--or us. Pediatrician Nathan Blum (2004) indicates that we can give our children the benefits of extracurricular activities without making them a full-time job for

13

. He recommends one to three hours a week as sufficient to gain eir benefits. Even the College Board now encourages students not to spread themselves too thin (collegeboard.com, 2005). If you think you'd like to cut down, but aren't sure how to do that, check out the book *Putting Families First* by William Doherty and Barbara Carlson.

The Long Arm of Technology

Modern technology has provided us with items such as cell phones, laptop computers, e-mail, and the Internet. More than half of families go online every day. The numbers are even higher for young adults (74%), those with a household income of more than $75, 000 (86%), those with a college education (82%), and those who live in the suburbs (63%; Infoplease.com, 2005b).

Without a doubt, many of these advances have made some aspects of our lives easier. But, technology has also increased our availability for work. It encourages people to continue to work even after they have left the office and keep in touch with the office on an almost continuous basis (Lemkuhl, 1999). And, it has increased our expectations of an immediate response, even when what we need could wait a few days.

Not too long ago, when we left work, we were gone (that is, unreachable) until the next day--or the next week. Now, we check our e-mail even on vacation and are unwilling to wait even twenty-four hours for information that we can have now. Being available twenty-four hours a day has substantially increased our workloads and the pace of our lives in general.

Stressful Vacations

Whenever I travel, I'm amazed at how stressed families are while on vacation. Some of this stress could be because we have only a few days each year for vacation. We feel pressure to make each day "perfect." The stress we feel could also have to do with the way we, as mothers, prepare for vacations. Theoretically, vacations should be times of relaxation and refreshment. For many mothers, however, they are anything but. Our

14

vacations often take on a more work-like feel. We tend to work right up to the day we leave, then spend a frantic couple of hours packing and preparing the house for our departure. We may drive or fly for hours, and once there, we dash from activity to activity. We return home only to go back to work and our lives the next day. Is it any wonder that we often return from vacation more tired than when we left?

Peer Pressure: It's Not Just for Kids

As an adult woman, you may think that you left peer pressure behind once you left high school. And, in some ways, that's probably true. You probably don't feel the pressure you once did to wear certain things or style your hair a certain way (what else could explain some of those weird hair styles in our yearbooks?). But having spoken with many moms over the last few years, I'm convinced that peer pressure is alive and well. One of the key ways we pressure each other is in our level of busyness. Some mothers view others who are not constantly on the run as somehow "lazy."

Employed mothers, especially of young children, often will go to extraordinary lengths to be at the office and be on top of all the details at home--including baking homemade treats for various school events. The challenges that employed mothers face were described in amusing detail in Allison Pearson's novel, *I Don't Know How She Does It*. In it, working mom Kate is busily pounding on store-bought mince pies to make them look homemade, desperately trying to avoid the tag of "mothers who didn't make the effort." It's a story a lot of moms can relate to. She referred to the coterie of judgmental other moms at her daughter's school as the "muffia."

At-home mothers are not immune to this pressure either. They often feel the pressure to enroll their children in every conceivable activity --pretty much from birth. While these activities can be a nice social outlet for you, you'll be less stressed if you resist pressure to make your children's activities your full-time job. The same can be said for numerous other activities including home decoration, crafts, or elaborate meal preparation. If you enjoy these activities, keep doing them. But if you don't, these might be activities you can trim.

The good news is that once you recognize peer pressure, you can decide whether you want to let it run your life. Take some of that great advice you offer to your kids about resisting peer pressure and apply it yourself. Please stop worrying about whether the "other mommies" will make fun of you!

The Sum Total of Our Stressors

In *Gracious Living in the New World* (1996a), Alexandra Stoddard sums up the malaise of the modern family:

> We are living in a new world, one that challenges our peace of mind and our inner grace. With its frenetic pace and constant state of flux, modern life often feels chaotic and unstable.....
> Technology, while providing us many advantages, encourages us to race through our days so that we no longer know what we'd do if we were to slow down. Many of us feel cut off from life's blessings, from our neighbors, from the wonders of nature, and from our sense of our own significance in the scheme of things. Modern life leaves us feeling spiritually starved (p. xixii).

Throughout the remaining chapters in this book, I will discuss many of the issues Stoddard raises in this quotation. But first, I'd like to describe some of the consequences of the stressed-out life.

The Consequences of Life in the Fast Lane

A stressed-out life does not come cheaply. If you're living this way, you are paying for it with your mental and physical health. A fast-paced lifestyle can negatively affect you, your family, and your community. If you need motivation to make some changes in your life, here it is.

Why Stress Is Bad for Us

Much has been written in the past forty years about the consequences of too much stress. Stress is our body's built-in mechanism to protect us from harm. In response to a perceived threat, our bodies react by pumping out stress hormones such as epinephrine (adrenaline), norepinephrine, and cortisol. This reaction, known as the fight-or-flight response, is designed to save our lives in the face of a threat.

Some stress is necessary for us to survive, but too much is a problem. Many of the negative consequences of chronic stress are associated with cortisol, one of the hormones your body releases when under stress. Cortisol suppresses the immune system making you more likely to get sick and stay sick longer. You are more vulnerable to colds and flu and even more serious illnesses such as cancer. Cortisol inhibits wound healing and can actually increase the amount of time necessary for recovering from surgery or other injury. Chronic stress puts you at risk for diabetes, osteoporosis, heart disease, and hypertension. You may develop eczema or psoriasis. You are more likely to suffer from chronic fatigue. Chronically elevated cortisol can even damage your brain. In sum, it is possible to become very ill when you are always under stress. Your physical health may be affected to the point that you have no choice but to make major life changes.

Chronic stress also has emotional consequences. Ask yourself if being stressed has made you a more cheerful person to be around. Chronic stress can make you more vulnerable to depression. There are a number of similarities between the biochemistry of chronic stress and that of depression (see chapter 2), so this is not surprising.

Unrelieved stress can eventually have bad effects on your relationships. If you are married, you may find yourself fighting more with your spouse. You may not have time to reconnect with each other and nourish your relationship. In a survey by *Working Mother* magazine, 18% of respondents wished for more time with their mates and two-thirds indicated that they didn't even have time for sex (Cassidy, 1999). Adults are not the only ones who suffer; our stress also affects our kids.

Why Stress Is Bad for Our Kids

Let's face it: when you're stressed, you're simply not as available to meet the needs of others--including your kids. And, your kids need you. When you are preoccupied with more work than you can possibly do, can you really find out if your kids are being picked on, if they are struggling with math, or if their teacher yelled at them? Getting to know your kids, or anyone for that matter, takes relaxed time. Spontaneous utterances can occur while we are doing dishes or walking, but they are unlikely to occur during fifteen minutes of scheduled quality time.

Psychologist Shelley Taylor and her colleagues (Taylor et al., 2000) noted that women under chronic stress tend to be less available to their children. Drawing from studies of both animals and humans, they noted that females are more likely to "tend and befriend" when under stress than they are to fight or flee. The fight-or-flight model was developed by studying males. Taylor and colleagues pointed out that if females either fought or fled in the face of danger, their offspring would be much more likely to die. But, by tending their offspring and befriending others, they were able to protect their offspring, and this behavior rewarded them by lowering their stress levels. However, Taylor and colleagues noted one exception to this pattern of tend and befriend: when women were chronically stressed, they were more likely to withdraw from their children and ignore their needs. This is more support for the negative impact of a chronically stressed-out life.

Family mealtimes suffer when families are overloaded. Public service announcements plead with parents to try to have one meal together per week. Suburban teens often eat several meals a week at the local mall because family mealtimes are rapidly becoming a thing of the past. This is expensive and has the potential to be hazardous to these children's health.

Why Stress Is Bad for Our Communities and Culture

And, there's more. For a moment, I encourage you to step back and look beyond the needs of your own family. The stressed-out, overbooked lifestyle is also bad for our communities and the environment. To begin with, the stressed-out life is a wasteful one. Have you ever let food go bad in the refrigerator, bought something new because you couldn't figure out where you put the one you already had, or replaced something you didn't have time to fix? I certainly have. There's nothing wrong with occasionally doing these things. What is worrisome is when a majority of families are doing these things on a regular basis. Our buy-and-dump mentality is having an increasingly negative impact on the environment.

The habits of U.S. culture influence people in other countries. Our demand for cheap, disposable goods fuels some nasty business practices, including the use of sweatshop or even slave labor. Though it is usually impossible to tell whether the goods we are purchasing are made using sweatshop labor, we can decide to stop fueling this market by refusing to adopt the throwaway mentality toward our possessions. But, it is hard to care properly for our things when we're so busy and stressed.

When you are overbooked, volunteerism rapidly declines. Volunteer work is often a logical thing to cut when we have too much to do, but this has an impact on our culture. Schools suffer, for one: parental involvement is directly related to the quality of our schools. For several generations, volunteer labor has held together many charitable organizations; now many of our community organizations have had to stop offering services because there is no one to provide them.

My purpose in outlining some of these problems is not to heap guilt on you or make you add some things to your endless to do list. But, I want you to see that taking steps to reduce the stress in your life is not selfish. Rather, it is something that can benefit you, your family, and your community.

What You Can Do

In this chapter, I've given you an overview of many causes of stress. Several of these stressors will be described in more detail in subsequent chapters along with techniques for handling them. If you are already overwhelmed, you may not know where to start reducing your stress level. Try to think of it as a journey rather than a sprint. Becoming less stressed may take weeks or even months, but here are a few suggestions that will help right now.

Stop Describing Yourself as Busy

When you're swamped, it's easy to tell anyone who will listen that you are very, very busy. As I'll describe in upcoming chapters, your thoughts are powerful. Viewing a situation as negative releases the stress hormone cortisol. This is not good for you! Mentally rehearsing your busyness accomplishes nothing positive and is most likely harmful. So stop describing yourself that way. This is something you can do for yourself right now. Besides, everyone is busy these days. It's actually kind of boring to hear about the busyness of others, and it fuels the peer pressure I mentioned earlier.

Guard Your Mind

Another strategy is to be careful about what you allow in your mind. There is way too much information available on almost any subject and much of it is junk. Pay attention to what you watch, listen to, and read. Even art books or "films" can be excessively negative. Be selective and look for material that builds you up and nourishes your spirit.

One example of possible negative input is the news. Do you need to watch as much news as you do or read the paper as often? News contains lots of negative information, most of which you can do little about. Many health experts suggest you cut back on how much daily news you take in, taking a news' fast. (Having been on a news' fast for years, I can tell you that I rarely miss anything important. Big stories tend to get repeated and talked about.) You can be concerned about the world around you without trying to address every issue. Is there an issue you would like to get involved in? If so, spend your time learning about it rather than trying to cover all the news.

Take Care of Your Body

When you're a passenger on an airplane, you are told that in the event of a change in cabin pressure, you should put your mask on first and then assist your children. You can't help them if you are unconscious. A similar principle applies to your day-to-day health. Mothers tend to put others first. While this is admirable in one sense, it is not a good practice

20

in the long run. You cannot strike a balance between your needs and the needs of your family if you are constantly run down. Therefore, you need to consider it a priority to eat well, exercise, sleep, and get regular physicals. Stop getting up early or going to bed late so you can catch up on a few extra chores. If you're going to dig yourself out of stress, then you must stop abusing your body.

Be Unavailable at Least Some Time Every Day

If you want to de-stress, it is important that you have some time every day, or most days, when you are not available. This means you turn off the cell phone, ignore the fax and phone, and don't check your e-mail. It means that you're available when it is time to work, but that you are not available all the time. This is important for at-home moms as well. Have at least some time during the day or evening when you are not available to anyone, even if it means claiming a half hour to yourself in the bathroom.

Practice Being in the Present

It is amazing how much of our time is devoted to thinking about either the past or the future. Just for fun, make a conscious effort to be in the present for at least a few minutes a day and see if it doesn't refresh your spirit. Instead of wolfing down food, think about each bite. Enjoy the texture, the temperature, the flavor. When you're with your kids, practice really listening to them. So often our bodies are there, but our minds are far away. Practice paying attention and enjoying what's going on now.

Plan Restorative Vacations

Give some thought to your leisure time. Are your vacations restorative or do you return from them exhausted? Every family differs in what they enjoy and what they find relaxing, but here are a few suggestions to make your vacations more enjoyable for you, too.

Stay Within Your Budget

There are many inexpensive getaways. Don't add the stress of paying for your trip over the next year (or more).

Travel Someplace Closer to Home

Go somewhere where you can relax. Don't spend your time cooking and cleaning. While at your destination, try to avoid a manic pace of activities. You might even consider vacationing at home. You can use this time to do the fun things you normally don't have time for. Don't broadcast your plans or you may end up as busy as you normally are, however.

Gradually Re-Enter Your Life

Finally, allow a day before your vacation starts to pack and prepare the house. When you return, allow at least a day to unpack and slowly re-enter normal life.

Be Grateful for What You Have

My final suggestion is to practice being grateful for what you already have. The difficulty of the stressed lifestyle is that it keeps us looking to what we don't have, what we haven't accomplished, and what's wrong with our lives. When we're in the middle of things, it's hard to realize how blessed we really are. How many of us can even fathom what it would be like to have half of our children die before the age of five, or to spend our days doing nothing but hauling water or worrying about getting enough to eat? Even if we feel financially strapped, we are most likely materially better off than women in other times or in other cultures. Sometimes it's really helpful for us to think about all the things we do have and to be truly grateful for them.

Another way to cultivate gratitude is to practice looking at your life the way an outsider would. There is a wonderful scene in the movie *While You Were Sleeping*. Lucy, a character whose parents have died, has no living relatives. After saving the life of a stranger, she is taken in by his gregarious family. Over dinner, the family is talking loudly, interrupting each other, not saying anything particularly brilliant. Yet Lucy is drinking in the entire scene. Rather than thinking that this family is annoying, she is glad to be part of it, even if only on a temporary basis. By standing back and looking at your life, you may start to see the things that are really going well for you and that can also help you reduce your stress.

For Further Reading

There are many wonderful books written for people who want to do something about the stress in their lives or who just want to slow down and simplify their lives. Below are a few of my favorites.

Resources for Stress

Bodger, C. 1999. *The Smart Guide to Relieving Stress.* New York: John Wiley & Sons.

Davis, M., Eshelman, E.R., & McKay, M. 2000. *The Relaxation and Stress Reduction Workbook.* Oakland, CA: New Harbinger Publications.

Doherty, W., & Carlson, B. 2002. *Putting Families First.* New York: Henry Holt & Co.

Hamilton, M. 2001. *Serenity to Go: Calming Techniques for Your Hectic Life.* Oakland, CA: New Harbinger Publications.

Lewis, D. S., with Lewi, G. 1989. *Motherhood Stress: Finding Encouragement in the Ultimate Helping Profession.* Dallas: Word. (This book is out of print, but still available through Amazon. com.)

Luskin, F., & Pelletier, K. 2005. *Stress Free for Good: 10 Scientifically Proven Life Skills for Health and Happiness.* San Francisco: HarperSanFrancisco.

Morgenstern, J. 2000. *Time Management from the Inside Out.* New York: Henry Holt & Co.

Rogak, L. 1999. *The Smart Guide to Managing Your Time.* New York: John Wiley & Sons.

MedlinePlus: National Library of Medicine/National Institutes of Health: www.nlm.nih.gov/medlineplus/stress.html

American Institute of Stress: www.stress.org
Medical Basis for Stress, Depression and Sleep Problems:
    www.teachhealth.com

Resources for Simplifying Life

Kendall-Tackett, K.A. 2003. *The Well-Ordered Home.* Oakland, CA:
    New Harbinger Publications.
St. James, E. 1999. *Living the Simple Life: A Guide to Scaling Down and
    Enjoying More.* New York: Hyperion.
Wright, H. N. 1998. *Simplify Your Life: And Get More Out of It!*
    Wheaton, IL: Tyndale.

Organized Home: www.organizedhome.com

Real Simple magazine: www.realsimple.com

CHAPTER 2

DEPRESSION: LIFE WITHOUT JOY

Is life difficult for you most days? Do you feel sad most of the time? Are things that you used to enjoy no longer fun? If this sounds like you may be suffering from depression. Depression happens to lots of people. In fact, it occurs so often that it is frequently called the "common cold" of mental illnesses. Throughout their lives, women are twice as likely as men to suffer from depression, and mothers of young children are particularly vulnerable (McGrath et al., 1990).

Why Do Mothers Get Depressed?

Why are women especially vulnerable to depression? This question has intrigued researchers. In the popular press, hormones often get the blame. But, the research literature shows this is a truly inadequate explanation. For example, if hormonal fluctuations were to blame for depression, why do more mothers get depressed later in the first postpartum year than in the early days after a baby's birth when hormones fluctuate dramatically? Hormones alone also cannot explain why a mother of school-age children or teens might become depressed. There are often very good reasons why women become depressed, reasons having to do with the circumstances of their lives.

In chapter 1, I described some of the factors that can contribute to stress: feeling out of control of your life, always feeling like there are more tasks than there are hours in a day. These feelings, especially when they are persistent, can also contribute to depression. But, depression can be associated with myriad other factors including fatigue, traumatic events, lack of confidence in your own mothering ability, and lack of help and support from others in your life. Causes of depression vary from woman to woman; what causes one woman to be depressed may not affect another woman at all.

The following pages outline some broad categories of events and circumstances that can lead to or aggravate depression. This is by no means a complete list, but it is a good starting place. Discussions of more specific causes of depression are woven throughout the remaining chapters of this book.

Cost of Depression

In a recent survey by the World Health Organization, researchers found that while depression had little direct impact on death rates worldwide, it accounted for 28% of all disability (Holden, 2000).

Violence Against Women

Violence is perhaps the most potent pathogen to women's mental and physical health, and it remains a fact of life for many (Kendall-Tackett, 2005a). It can impact every aspect of a woman's life, including her current relationship with her partner and her children.

Unfortunately, violence against women is not a rare occurrence. For example, approximately one in five women in the general population has experienced child sexual abuse. And, while sexual abuse has been studied most often, it is not the most common type of child abuse. According to the Third National Incidence Study of Child Abuse and Neglect, both physical abuse and child neglect are even more common (Sedlak & Broadhurst, 1996).

The problem of violence against women doesn't end in childhood. Women continue to be vulnerable to dating violence, rape, and intimate partner violence throughout their lives (Kendall-Tackett, 2005a). Those who have experienced childhood abuse are even more likely to be revictimized, either through sexual assault or domestic abuse.

Depression is a common effect of past and current abuse. For example, the risk of depression is several times higher among adult survivors of childhood sexual abuse than it is among the general population. Studies on physical abuse suggest similar results (Kendall-Tackett, 2003). These effects are described in chapter 9.

Poverty

According to the American Psychological Association's Task Force on Women and Depression, poverty is an independent risk factor for depression in women (McGrath et al., 1990). And, women are more likely than men to be poor. Many factors are related to poverty in women. One example is child abuse and neglect. Several studies have found that women who are survivors of childhood abuse are at increased risk for living in poverty (Kendall-Tackett, 2003a). Marital status is also related to poverty, with single mothers being especially likely to be poor. According to recent census data, poverty rates increased for both single mothers and fathers between 2002 and 2003. However, the poverty rate for single mothers was 28%, more than twice the poverty rate for single fathers (13%). The poverty rates are particularly striking when considered in terms of children. Fifty-three percent of children under age six living with single mothers were poor. In contrast, only 10% of children under age six who live with married couples are poor (DeNavas-Walt, Proctor, & Mills, 2004).

There are many problems related to poverty. Poor women tend to have fewer resources available and less support. They may live in neighborhoods that are unsafe. They may worry about their children's safety at day care or school. They may constantly worry whether child support payments will arrive. In a recent study examining factors related to "nervous breakdowns," women most at risk were poor, young, single mothers with no religious affiliation (Swindle et al., 2000).

Middle-class women may become poor once they divorce. They may need to move from their homes and face new worries about making ends meet. In one recent study, women whose income didn't drop after a divorce were less depressed, more positive in their interactions with their children, and less authoritarian in their discipline style than were

27

women whose divorce made them poor. The children of families with adequate financial resources also fared better socially, behaviorally, and cognitively. The authors speculated that the children did better because their mothers were less likely to be depressed (Murray, 2000).

Fatigue and Sleep Deprivation

Sleep deprivation can wreak havoc on a woman's emotional state. Perhaps because it is so common, its influence on a mother's mental health is often overlooked. A little-known fact is that some children do not consistently sleep through the night for years. Mothers often do not advertise their children's sleep patterns to others because sleeping through the night is regarded as a sign of good parenting. To admit their children do not sleep well is to invite criticism. Even when kids are sleeping through the night, mothers may be using this time to catch up on chores. Sleep deprivation is widespread and has alarming effects on our health. Sleep deprivation and fatigue are described in more detail in chapter 8.

Loss

Hundreds of thousands of women suffer significant losses each year. These losses take many forms: childbearing loss, loss associated with a less-than-perfect birth or a sick child, mothering in the wake of past abuse, or death of a parent. And yet, women are often not given a chance to grieve or even acknowledge these losses. Within a very short period of time, they are expected to "get on with" their normal life. In upcoming chapters, we will talk about several different types of loss.

Social Isolation or Lack of Social Support

Women who have good support are significantly less likely to become depressed than women who don't. Study after study has confirmed this, and we know it's true. But, often our overbooked lifestyles drive away the very support we need. In a recent survey in *Working Mother* magazine, time with husband and time with friends is very often missing from readers' schedules (Cassidy, 1999).

Isolation can be a particular problem for mothers at home with small children. Many mothers live in rural locations and are isolated by geography, some without a car or access to public transit. Sometimes too, mothers become isolated from each other because they fear judgment. Other mothers can be our harshest critics. And, we anticipate that criticism and don't ask each other for help.

Husbands and partners can be significant sources of support. Other times, mothers carry the responsibility for the emotional and physical health of their families all alone. Marianne describes how the many responsibilities that she carried alone contributed to her depression. Her battle with depression began after a series of sleepless nights:

> My husband is a self-employed home builder. Under financial pressure, he had to let his secretary and worker go. He had all the calls from his business directed to the house. My husband was building three large speculative homes, and I was the decorator. We had also started to home-school our five-year-old and I was nursing a baby. I had babysitting for two hours a week, and that's when I would make all these big decorating decisions. I felt like the success of these three expensive homes was on me, and I stopped sleeping at night.

Each of the factors I've described above can contribute to depression. If you are depressed, it's important that you understand depression and know what your treatment options are. The next section gives an overview of depression; the section after that suggests what you can do.

Depression: An Illness of Body and Mind

Depression is an illness that affects both body and mind, and both mind and body contribute to it. You can view depression as an emotional alarm bell that lets you know when something is not right in your life. The underlying cause may be something as straightforward as sleep deprivation or as complex as a history of childhood trauma.

"Better Living Through Chemistry"

One of the giant chemical companies has indicated that their products provide "better living through chemistry." Americans seem to take a similar approach to depression. We state that depression is due to a chemical imbalance, and the way to fix the chemical imbalance is through medication. This, unfortunately, is a pretty simplistic description of depression.

Our best biological theory of depression is that it is due to low levels of the neurotransmitter serotonin. Generally, medications that increase levels of serotonin decrease depression. The newest class of antidepressants: the selective serotonin reuptake inhibitors (SSRIs)--specifically target serotonin. Examples of SSRIs include Prozac, Zoloft, Paxil, and Celexa.

The serotonin explanation seems to be true a majority of the time, but the picture is actually much more complex. For example, we know that some effective antidepressants influence levels of neurotransmitters other than serotonin. If depression was solely related to serotonin levels, why would these medications work? We also know that some antidepressants actually lower serotonin levels and still work as antidepressants. And, there are at least fifteen different kinds of serotonin receptors that we have identified so far. The effectiveness of these various medications also seems related to which type of receptor they work with (Burns, 1999).

Another biological aspect of depression is the elevated level of the stress hormone cortisol in people who are depressed, especially those with major depression. The relationship between serotonin and cortisol levels is not fully understood, but it appears that serotonin helps regulate cortisol. As we discussed in the last chapter, chronically elevated cortisol levels cause all kinds of mischief in the body. Depression seems to leave a biological mark on the body that makes people more vulnerable to future stressors, leading to another bout of depression.

An alternative way of looking at depression is to consider it an illness of both body and mind. The chemical-imbalance perspective is that the body influences the mind. In reality, this relationship is a two-way street.

Our biochemistry can influence our emotional state, and our thoughts, behaviors, and experiences can influence the biochemistry of our brains. What this means, in practical terms, is that there are other things you can do to create favorable changes in the biochemistry of your brain. For example, both exercise and carbohydrates can increase serotonin levels. And, when you think negatively about a situation or event, your body releases cortisol. Thus, a tendency to look at things in a negative way increases your susceptibility to depression.

Why Depression Is Harmful

When you are in the midst of depression, it is often difficult to think about how depression can be harmful. But, it hurts both you and your family.

Why Depression Is Bad for You

Let's start with you. Besides making you miserable, depression can be very bad for your health. This has to do with the effects of chronically elevated levels of cortisol. By elevating cortisol levels, depression suppresses the immune system (Weisse, 1992). You have fewer white blood cells, and the ones you have are less effective in protecting you from pathogens (Avissar et al., 1997). If you have ever taken cortisone-based medications (e.g., prednisone), you know that they are prescribed to temper an overactive immune system, as in the case of allergies, asthma, or autoimmune disease. Naturally occurring cortisol does the same thing.

Depression has some unexpected long-term effects. Depression can increase the risk of heart attacks (Lesperance & Frasure-Smith, 2000). Stress and illness researcher Robert Sapolsky (1996; 2000) noted that depression can lead to atrophy of a structure in the brain called the hippocampus, which is related to learning and memory. Again, cortisol is the culprit. A question that is concerning researchers who study depression is whether it increases the likelihood of Alzheimer's or other memory-related diseases as people age. The jury is still out on that question.

Why Depression Is Bad for Your Family

When you are depressed, you are not the only one who suffers. When one or both partners are depressed, it can sour a relationship and break up a marriage. You may find yourself withdrawing from others who can offer help and support. Or, others may withdraw from you. Depressed people can be irritable and critical and generally not much fun to be around.

But, the most insidious effects may be on your children. Depression can influence the way you interact with your children and many problems children have are related to these interactions. Hundreds of studies have demonstrated the negative effects on babies and children of having a chronically depressed mother. It can influence their brain development and lower their IQ. It can impact their relationships with peers and make them more prone to depression (Kendall-Tackett, 2005b; National Institute of Child Health and Human Development, 1999).

Researchers have noted that depressed mothers interact in one of two styles: avoidant or angry-intrusive. Mothers with an avoidant style spend most of their time disengaged from their babies or children. They often do not make eye contact, and they are oblivious to their children's cues. Mothers with an angry-instrusive style spend more time interacting with their children than avoidant mothers. But, their interactions are tinged with anger and resentment. Both of these styles raise cortisol levels in the children, and these negative effects have been measured even in babies (Radke-Yarrow, 1998).

I'm not trying to make you feel guilty about being depressed. Chances are you've been doing this to yourself. Also understand that it's unlikely you've irreparably harmed your children. Fortunately, children are resilient and do not require perfect parenting. However, I do want to passionately persuade you to take your depression seriously. Sometimes, mothers believe that they are being "selfish" if they take some time to nurture themselves and limit their obligations. But, this type of self-care is essential for your health and the well-being of your family.

What You Can Do

Fortunately, there are many steps you can take to feel better. Available treatments include cognitive therapy, nutrition, supplements, exercise, herbs, and antidepressants. I've outlined these below and also included a reading list for further information. There are things you can start doing today.

Resolve to Do Whatever It Takes to Get Better

Your first step toward getting better is to decide you are no longer willing to be depressed. This resolve is necessary because it may take some trial and error before you find a solution that works for you. Even medications don't automatically work for everyone who tries them and it may take several tries before you and your doctor find the right dosage or combination. Realizing that treatment for depression is not instantaneous gives you a greater chance of success.

Rule Out Physical Causes

It is a good idea to have a physical exam as you begin treatment for depression. Anemia or low thyroid levels can sometimes cause depression. Some basic blood tests can rule these causes out. Since sleep deprivation can trigger depression, you might also start paying attention to your sleeping habits. Try to get a good night's sleep: set regular sleeping times (if possible), try to relax in the hour or so before you go to bed, try not to exercise or drink caffeine in the evening, and be careful about the amount of alcohol you consume before bed. For more information on establishing good sleeping habits, see chapter 8.

Know Your Treatment Options

Our knowledge of how to treat depression has grown significantly over the past twenty-five years. You have lots of options, especially if you have mild to moderate depression. I've listed several options below, which you can either combine or use one at a time. **If your depression is so severe that you cannot function or get out of bed, are thinking of**

killing yourself, or feel that your depression is getting worse, please see your doctor right away. In these more serious situations, you will probably need to be on medication. However, you can also use some of these other approaches as adjuncts to your treatment.

Good Nutrition

Nutrition is the first foundation of good mental health. Naturopathic doctors such as Michael Murray (1996) emphasize a balanced diet as a good foundation for treatment of depression. This diet should be low in fat, refined sugar, and caffeine and high in vegetables, fruits, and whole grains. It's often difficult to eat well when you are stressed, maxed out, or depressed.

Another nutritional alternative involves carbohydrate intake. According to MIT researcher Judith Wurtman, your brain needs carbohydrates to make serotonin, and eating forty-five grams of carbohydrates with little or no fat and with no protein for at least an hour has an antidepressant effect. If you are interested in trying this approach, you might want to get her book *The Serotonin Solution* (1997). This is a diet book, but she has a very interesting discussion of the multiple functions of serotonin. She also has a diet plan specifically for Stressed Moms.

Supplements

Like good nutrition, nutritional supplements help form a good foundation for mental health. Women who are depressed are frequently low in B6, B12, folic acid, choline, and omega-3 fatty acids, and supplementing with these nutrients is helpful in alleviating depression.

Omega-3s are showing particular promise in preventing depression and in treating it (Bratman & Girman, 2003; Kendall-Tackett, 2005b). They can be combined with other treatment modalities. You need to use fish oil as flax seed has not been shown to have an antidepressant effect (Bratman & Girman, 2003). If you are pregnant or breastfeeding, possible mercury contamination in fish-oil products is a concern. To ensure your safety, take supplements that are pharmaceutical grade. Several companies sell pharmaceutical grade fish oil supplements directly to the public. These are tested for mercury, lead, PCBs, and other contaminants (see resource list at the end of this chapter).

Exercise

Exercise is an effective treatment for depression. Daily physical exercise boosts mood by increasing levels of the neurotransmitters serotonin and dopamine and by releasing endorphins. Endorphins relieve pain and create a sense of well-being, and they tend to be low in people who are depressed. A recent clinical trail at Duke University Medical School found that exercise was as effective as Zoloft for patients with major depression (Babyak et al., 2000). As a further benefit, patients who exercised were less likely to become depressed again when treatment ended. The authors of this study felt that this was because they now had a way to cope with life stressors.

The good news is that it doesn't take much exercise to create an antidepressant effect. In these studies, as little as 20 minutes, two to three times a week was enough. That relatively small amount means that it can work into most schedules. Even getting out of the house for a walk can boost your mood.

Cognitive-Behavioral Therapy

Cognitive-behavioral therapy is a highly effective treatment for depression and is as effective as medication for treatment of depression, anxiety, and a host of other conditions. Its central premise is that depression is caused by distortions in thinking. It is not about replacing negative thoughts with "happy" ones. Rather, it is a technique that helps you identify patterns of negative thoughts and asks you to judge whether these thoughts are true. In the book *Feeling Good* (1999), psychiatrist David Burns identifies ten types of cognitive distortions. Some examples of cognitive distortions include the following.

- **All-or-nothing thinking.** All-or-nothing thinking means seeing things in black-or-white categories. If a situation falls short of perfect, you see it as a total failure.

35

- **Over-generalization.** When you over-generalize, you think that one mistake makes everything bad. Whenever you use words like always or never, you may be thinking in this way.

- **Should statements.** Should statements are unrealistic expectations you may have for yourself and others. Mothers seem especially prone to these.

Cognitive therapy helps people identify these distortions and replace them with more accurate (and less self-defeating) cognitions. If you want to try cognitive therapy, I highly recommend *Feeling Good: The New Mood Therapy* (1999) by David Burns. You can also find a therapist who practices cognitive therapy through local psychological associations.

Herbs

Herbal antidepressants have been enjoying a surge of popularity in the United States and are in wide use in other parts of the world. Many people are attracted to them because they are natural, frequently cheaper than prescription medications, and generally have fewer side effects. People also like being able to take them without a prescription, thereby exercising more control over their own mental health care. (Many physicians are uncomfortable with patients self-medicating, however, and may discourage you from trying them.)

Bear in mind that, natural or not, these substances are medications and should be used judiciously. Tell your health care provider if you are taking herbs and don't mix them with prescription medications unless you are under a doctor's care. Also, because herbal medications are gentler than prescription medications, they may take longer to work. Be sure to allow at least two months before you decide whether these medications are working for you.

St. John's Wort. The most widely used of the herbal antidepressants is St. John's wort (SJW). SJW is safe and effective and takes about four to six weeks to alleviate mild to moderate depression. It has been shown to be as effective as tricyclic antidepressants in numerous clinical trials, without the side effects (Kendall-Tackett, 2005b). It should not be used for severe depression, but in at least one study, it was as effective as Zoloft for major depression (van Gurp et al., 2002). SJW is also used for stress and pain, to help with menopausal symptoms, and as an external remedy for wounds, bruises, and burns (Khalsa, 2000).

At this point, St. John's wort appears safe for breastfeeding mothers (Hale, 2004; Humphrey, 2003). However, it can decrease the effectiveness of certain types of drugs such as cyclosporins and oral contraceptives. Be sure to tell your physician that you are taking St. John's wort. And, if you are taking other medications, the safest course is for you to work with a licensed herbalist or a physician knowledgeable about herbal medicine.

Kava. Kava has a long history of use in the Polynesian islands. Kava produces relaxation and is also believed to be antiseptic and anti-inflammatory. Its more common use is for anxiety. It is often mixed in preparations with St. John's wort to treat anxiety and depression; although, some recommend that people with depression avoid Kava (Kuhn & Winston, 2000).

Even with a long history of use in other cultures, there have been some serious concerns about this herb. Although side effects are relatively rare (occurring in approximately 2% of patients), they are serious. Kava interacts with other medications including antidepressants, benzodiazepines, alcohol, and sleeping pills and has potentially dangerous side effects including liver damage (usually with a high dose). The Food and Drug Administration has issued a consumer advisory. **Don't use it if you are breastfeeding** (Hale, 2004; Kuhn & Winston, 2000). Even non-breastfeeding mothers should not try to self-medicate with this herb and should seek assistance from a licensed herbalist if they are interested in using it.

Antidepressants

The final option for the treatment of depression is antidepressant medication. There are basically three types. All work to increase the amount of neurotransmitters (serotonin, norepinephrine, or dopamine) available in the brain.

Tricyclics. The tricyclics are the oldest and cheapest antidepressants. They include medications such as Pamelor (nortriptyline) and Elavil (amitriptyline). They are effective, but tend to have side effects such as dry mouth and constipation so people stop taking them. They are often used to treat chronic pain and insomnia. Most are compatible with breastfeeding.

Monoamine Oxidase (MAO) Inhibitors. These antidepressants are also very effective, but when taking them, you cannot eat or drink anything with tyramine. Tyramine is a by product of fermentation and is common in foods such as red wine and cheese. When they are consumed with a MAO inhibitor, heart attack or death can occur. They are not widely used in the U.S., but may be prescribed if other types have failed. **Avoid these antidepressants if you are breastfeeding.**

Selective Serotonin Reuptake Inhibitors (SSRIs). SSRIs are the newest class of antidepressants and include such well-known medications as Prozac, Zoloft, Paxil, and Celexa. As their name implies, they work specifically on serotonin receptors. While these medications still have side effects, they have fewer than the other antidepressants, and their dosing schedule is less complex. Of these, Paxil and Zoloft have the best profiles for the breastfeeding mother (meaning that the smallest amount of medication gets to your baby.) If you need to take a medication besides Zoloft or Paxil, consult with a local lactation consultant who can give you the most current advice (I also have this information on my website: www.GraniteScientific. com).

Deciding Whether to Take Medications

The decision about whether to take medications is very personal. If you decide to use medication, it does not mean that you have failed or that you are weak. I always feel bad when mothers tell me that none of the other techniques worked for them, so now they'll try medication. You do not need to run through all the other treatment options before you earn the "right" to be on medications. On the other hand, I've also spoken with mothers who had strong feelings against medication and felt forced by their doctor or their family members to take antidepressants.

Please always remember that this is your decision. You are the one who lives in your body and who lives your life. My role, and the role of any health care provider, is to provide information and help you weigh the pros and cons of treatment options. Consider the type of symptoms you have: medications help treat sleep disturbance, especially early morning or frequent awakening that is not related to child care, appetite disturbance (eating too much or too little), fatigue, decreased sex drive, restlessness or agitation, impaired concentration, and pronounced anhedonia or the inability to experience any type of pleasure (Preston & Johnson, 2004). If your depression is severe and/or you have these types of symptoms, medications may be the best approach. Two helpful books that discuss the pros and cons of antidepressants are *Feeling Good* by David Burns (1999) and *When Words Are Not Enough* (1997) by Valerie Raskin.

Melissa describes how medications took awhile to work for her, but eventually helped get her life back on track:

> I'm still on Pamelor. My doctor altered my dosage so it's now triple what he started me on. It took about a month to feel any effects, but for about a month and a half now I have felt great. I'm convinced the medication is helping. I feel I can look a little more objectively at the past year and tell it really was something out of my control to fix, and I wasn't doing it to myself. I'm so grateful to be feeling over the hump. I don't expect a bed of roses, but at least life is starting to be fun again. I'm glad I went ahead with medication. I hope and pray I don't ever have to face depression again.

Medications are probably called for if you have a history of depression that was successfully treated with antidepressants. The medication you used before will probably work for you again. Similarly, if you have a history of bipolar disorder (manic depression), medications are called for, but some antidepressants can trigger a manic episode (see Kendall-Tackett, 2005b).

Special Considerations for the Breastfeeding Mother

Often, when women are breastfeeding, they are concerned about using medications. Sometimes, women will either wean before they want to or refuse to take medications that may be necessary in their treatment. Fortunately, these are not the only two choices. It is important to understand that it is simply too risky not to undergo therapy if you are depressed and breastfeeding. Experts now believe that you can safely take any number of antidepressants while breastfeeding. There are dozens of new studies that suggest that the transfer of various antidepressants into human milk ranges from moderate to negligible. All drugs transfer to a some degree, but the amount is generally quite low. While some doctors suggest trying to withhold breastfeeding shortly after taking the medication to avoid the peak, these products have such long half-lives (25 to 360 hours) that it is probably not worth the effort. Certain drugs have a higher risk and some are virtually without risk. Drugs with potentially higher risk are Prozac, Celexa, and possibly Lexapro. The products with the best safety profile are Zoloft and Paxil. Wellbutrin, Effexor, and others can generally be safely used in most breastfeeding mothers. Hundreds of thousands of infants have been breastfed successfully while their mothers consumed antidepressants, and this is the fact to remember. So far, all long-term studies on neurobehavioral outcome suggest these infants turn out normal.

You do not need to pump your milk to get rid of the medication; it is reabsorbed back into your blood stream and eliminated by your kidneys. For a thorough review of all these medications, refer to Thomas Hale's *Medications and Mothers' Milk* (2004). This book is updated every other year. If you have questions, you might want to get a copy (available on Amazon.com) or log onto his web site (www.ibreastfeeding.com).

Some Final Thoughts

You do not need to feel helpless in the face of depression. There are many options available to you. My prayer is that you will find the technique or combination of techniques that works for you. You are worth it!

For Further Reading

Resources for Depression and Antidepressant Medication

Burns, D. 1999. *Feeling Good: The New Mood Therapy.* New York: Avon. (Approximately 40% of Dr. Burns patients take medications in addition to cognitive therapy. He weighs the pros and cons of medications and also provides a very complete listing of medications, side effects, and drug interactions.)

Hale, T. W. 2004. *Medications and Mothers' Milk. 11th ed.* Amarillo, TX: Pharmasoft Publishing.
(This is the definitive work on medications and the breastfeeding mother. It is available for approximately $30 from Pharmasoft: 800-378-1317. Also, be sure to check Dr. Hale's Web site: www.ibreastfeeding.com.)

Kendall-Tackett, K.A. 2005. *Depression in New Mothers: Causes, Consequences, and Treatment Options.* Binghamton, New York: Haworth.

Nicholson, J., Henry, A.D., Clayfield, J.C., & Phillips, S.M. 2001. *Parenting Well When You're Depressed.* Oakland, CA: New Harbinger Publications.

Preston, J., & Johnson, J. 2004. *Clinical Psychopharmacology Made Ridiculously Simple. 5th ed.* Miami: Medmaster.
(This is one of my personal favorites. This volume is written for physicians, but as the name implies, it concisely summarizes a wide range of information about antidepressants.)

Raskin, V. 1997. *When Words Are Not Enough: The Women's Prescription for Depression and Anxiety.* New York: Broadway.
(A very thorough discussion of medications and side effects, written in a nurturing and helpful style.)

American Psychological Association: www.apa.org

Granite Scientific Press: www.GraniteScientific.com
(This is my website. It has information on depression including two screening tests you can take to see if you are depressed.)

National Mental Health Association: www.nmha.org

National Alliance for the Mentally Ill: www.nami.org

National Institute of Mental Health: www.nimh.nih.gov

Resources for Natural Alternatives to Antidepressants

There is a great deal of information on alternatives to antidepressants, including the options described throughout this chapter. All of these volumes are very helpful.

Balch, J. F., & Balch, P. A. 2000. *Prescription for Nutritional Healing*, 3rd ed. Garden City Park, NY: Avery.

Bloomfield, H.H., Nordfors, M., & McWilliams, P. 1996. *Hypericum and Depression*. Los Angeles: Prelude.

Burns, D.D. 1999. *Feeling Good: The New Mood Therapy*. New York: Avon.

Cass, H. 1997. *St. John's Wort: Nature's Blues Buster*. Garden City Park, NY: Avery.

Humphrey, S. 2003. *The Nursing Mother's Herbal*. Minneapolis: Fairview Press.

Kendall-Tackett, K.A. 2005. *Depression in New Mothers: Causes, Consequences, and Treatment Options*. Binghamton, NY: Haworth.

Murray, M.T. 1996. *Natural Alternatives to Prozac*. New York: William Morrow & Co.

Wurtman, J. J., & Suffes, S. 1997. *The Serotonin Solution to Achieve Permanent Weight Control*. New York: Fawcett Columbine.

Another important source of information on herbs is the *German Commission E Monographs*. These are now available in English from the American Botanical Council at (512) 926-4900, www.herbalgram.org.

American Herbal Pharmacopoeia: www.herbal-ahp.org

National Center for Complementary and Alternative Medicine: www.nccam.nih.gov

Sources for Pharmaceutical-Grade Fish Oil

These are two sources of fish oil that have been tested for contaminants. I have no financial relationship with either company.

Carlson Labs: www.CarlsonLabs.com

Vital Nutrients: www.VitalNutrients.net

Chapter 3
Burnout:
When You Can't Give
Any More

Are you drained? Do you wake up in the morning and wonder how you will get through the day? Are the people in your life exceptionally annoying? Are you withdrawing from others? Do you wonder whether anything you do really matters? There comes a point when you can't give any more. If you are at that point, you may be suffering from mothering burnout. Burnout can be defined as a loss of enthusiasm, energy, idealism, perspective, and purpose. It has been described as trying to run a marathon at full speed. It is a state of total exhaustion--physical, mental, and spiritual--brought on by unrelenting stress (helpguide.org, 2004a).

Burnout is a process during which a person disconnects from work and relationships. In the past twenty years, burnout has been noted in a wide variety of people-intensive professions: teaching, nursing, police work, social work, and medicine. There have been surprisingly few references to burnout in mothers, but as you will see, it's a concept that certainly applies. The self-help organization helpguide.org (2004b) describes burnout as being likely in the following work situations. These could easily apply to mothering. Jobs most likely to lead to burnout are those where employees feel:

- Overworked
- Underappreciated
- Confused about expectations and priorities
- Given responsibilities not commensurate with pay
- Overcommitted with work and home responsibilities (p.1)

Only one characteristic--being insecure about layoffs--does not apply.

Admitting that you are burned out doesn't mean you've failed. On the contrary, it's often the mothers who care the most who are the most prone to burnout. Pediatrician William Sears (1991) states "mothers must be on fire in order to be burned out" (195). Psychologist Avrene Brandt (1998) makes a similar point in an article on the emotional strain of caring for an aging parent.

> Those who are most committed and involved are most likely to become emotionally and physically exhausted. The myth that the harder you work and the more you put in, the better it gets, does not work here. In fact, if you get hooked on this myth, you will neglect other important aspects of your life, put your self-esteem at risk, and find yourself confronted with emotional reactions which add to your stress.

It's not too late for you. Burnout is your mind and body's way of warning you that you need to make some changes. In this chapter, I'll describe some of the symptoms and stages of burnout and the aspects of mothering that may make you vulnerable.

Common Signs of Burnout

A number of signs may indicate that you are burning out. You may experience any one of these or a combination of several (Potter, 1998).

Negative Emotions

Everyone occasionally feels angry or sad. However, when anger or sadness becomes something you experience every day, it may be a sign of burnout. Another aspect of negative feelings is starting to doubt your ability to do what you're supposed to do: "If they knew the real me, they wouldn't think I was a good mother." You begin to feel like an impostor.

Other negative emotions include feeling hopeless, drained, detached from others, bored, and resentful. You may feel stuck in a situation you cannot change and feel little satisfaction from your work. You may wonder if you have made the right choices with regard to your work and your family (helpguide.org, 2004a). Potter (1998) describes this feeling as "emotional tautness."

Some of these negative feelings could be related to unrealistic expectations you place on yourself about what a mother is supposed to be like. You may believe that mothers should give endlessly. You may also feel that you can't say no to anyone, especially your children. The inability to say no is remarkably common. *Working Mother* magazine found that only one-third of the mothers in a recent survey regularly set limits and boundaries with others. A full 54% indicated that they wanted to learn to say no when asked to take on an additional activity (Cassidy, 1999).

Interpersonal Problems

Problems with other people may be an indication you are burning out. You may find yourself withdrawing, feeling frustrated with people, or overreacting to perceived misdeeds. You may become abrasive or harsh. Some of these behaviors can be a way to defend yourself against feelings of vulnerability or helplessness.

People in the helping professions who are burning out find themselves feeling cynical and insensitive to the needs of people in their care. You may find that you are increasingly impatient with your children or partner, and you may disengage or withdraw from the people you care about.

Health Problems

As with stress and depression, burnout can bring a host of health problems. These include aches and pains, colds, headaches, inability to sleep, and chronic fatigue (Potter, 1998). By the end of the day, you may feel so worn out that all you can do is sit slack-jawed in front of the television. This happens to all of us once in a while. But when it gets to be a daily habit, take it as a warning. Exhaustion can also indicate the presence of depression or an underlying physical condition such as hypothyroidism. These possibilities should be considered (see chapter 8). Health problems, especially those that make you overly fatigued, can contribute to or cause burnout (helpguide.org, 2004b).

Loss of Enthusiasm and Feelings of Meaningless

Burnout is often a time of existential crisis. You may find yourself questioning, perhaps for the first time, your role and the work you do. You may have lost interest in your work and your children. Everything seems like too much trouble, and nothing seems to matter. You may find yourself saying, "Why bother?" or "Who cares?"

During this stage, your psychological defenses have worn down. Hurts and painful memories start to break through. You may find yourself overreacting to the smallest upset and feeling miserable most of the time. You may even feel you don't know yourself anymore.

Substance Abuse and Unhealthy Behaviors

To cope with your feelings, you may turn to alcohol or drugs. You may also find yourself eating too much, smoking too much, and drinking way too much coffee. All of these activities are physically depleting and compound the problem.

What Causes Burnout?

A variety of factors can put you at risk for burnout. The self-help organization helpguide.org (2004a) notes, "burnout often arises from excessive demands that are internally imposed (such as having very high expectations of yourself), or externally imposed (by family, job, or society). It occurs when you are unable to meet these demands, become frustrated, and deplete your energy through unrelenting stress" (p. 1). Here is a summary of some of the common causes. I describe many of these in more detail in subsequent chapters.

Unrealistic Expectations

You may have had very little experience with babies or small children before you became a mother. Suddenly, you're in charge of one. Because you haven't had lots of exposure and experience, you may underestimate the amount of work involved in childcare. You may have adopted the view that you can do it alone, not realizing how much you need a good support network.

Mothers internalize beliefs about what they should be and do. Often, these beliefs are unrealistic and even harmful. They often take the form of should statements: "A mother should anticipate all her family's needs"; "Mothers should be able to take care of everything"; "Mothers who take time off are lazy"; "Mothers should never get angry."

Cultural Messages

As children (and parents) of the information age, we are bombarded daily with hundreds of messages. At no other time in history has there been such an onslaught of images designed to sell products. In most families, mothers are the prime consumers, and as such, most of these ads are directed at you. Advertisers try to make you feel bad about yourself as a woman and a mother. That is their goal. These messages are so pervasive that even when we see abundant evidence to the contrary, we believe the lies. Think about it: How many women do you know who have the flawless bodies you see in advertisements or live in perfectly clean, impeccably decorated homes?

The power of image advertising is that we ourselves create the lie. If advertisers came out and said that if we bought their products, we'd have more friends, be more attractive, or be better mothers, we'd recognize it for the lie it is. But when they simply pair their products with symbols of the good life, we create the lie and don't stop to analyze it.

One example of the negative impact of advertising is on women's beliefs about their bodies. Very high percentages of women are unhappy with how they look. And, they will often do things that are quite harmful to their health to meet the unrealistic ideal portrayed in advertisement

49

and elsewhere. Barring that, women may feel secret shame that they are unable to meet such an ideal. Men don't do this, and this may be one of those times when it is good to take a page from them. A highly effective public service announcement had men sitting around complaining about their bodies. A blue-collar man sitting in a diner says: "I have my mother's thighs. I've always had my mother's thighs." You can imagine how ridiculous this sounds. And yet, if it were a group of women, we would probably think it was normal! ("I hear you, honey!")

We also get quite a few messages about what mothers are supposed to do. Rarely on TV or in commercials do you see Cheerios on the floor, piles of unfolded laundry, big stacks of junk mail, or a bathroom that needs attention--unless it is an example of a really bad or incompetent mother. The documentary film *Killing Us Softly* highlights some of the more damaging examples of this type of advertising. In one amusing example, a family was very upset with a mother who made too much cake. This would not have been a problem in most families, I suspect. The ad was funny, but the message was clear: don't mess up or else your family will be mad at you. These advertisements try to create a need for their products. In order to do that, they make us feel bad.

Perfectionism

Perfectionism is a trap that many of us fall into. If you feel you have to do all things well or that your best is never good enough, you are in danger of becoming burned out. I find that mothers who are survivors of childhood abuse are especially prone to perfectionism, especially in regard to their parenting. They try so hard to be good mothers that they feel they can't make any mistakes and that even their thoughts must always be loving and nurturing.

Perfectionism is often due to cognitive distortions described in chapter 2. The most common one is all-or-nothing thinking: if I don't do everything perfectly, I'm a complete failure. Since no one can be perfect, a perfectionist may simply give up, disengaging from relationships, and adopting a cynical, what-difference-does-it-make attitude.

An Impossible Job

Unrealistic expectations are only part of the problem. Another part is that the job of mothering itself, if we do all that our culture implies is necessary, is truly impossible. Our culture sends some amazingly contradictory messages about what an ideal mother is like. Mothers try to live up to these ideals without recognizing the contradictions or the impossibility of the task. Like moths to the flame, mothers keep knocking themselves out trying to do all the things our culture dictates.

As mothers, you are often expected to have a fulfilling career, time for personal interests, a rewarding marriage, involvement in your community, a thorough grasp of current events, and be able to provide baked goods at a moment's notice. Your children should be attractive, smart, athletic, and well mannered. Your homes should be pretty and tastefully appointed, and of course, clean.

Below are some of the implied activities in the job of mother. These are beyond the big responsibilities of childcare and employment. Whenever I present workshops, I find it helpful to actually list and name all these responsibilities. Once you see the list, I think you'll be amazed at the sheer amount of things that you are responsible for doing.

Some of the activities in the list may be ones you enjoy. This listing doesn't mean you should cut activities you like. But, I encourage you to consider whether you need to do them all, or do them all now, and also whether these activities are distributed fairly among members of your family. Are there things that others can do? (We'll revisit this topic in chapters 5 and 6.)

Meal Planning

As mothers, one of your functions is to plan for the sustenance of your family. Even if you don't do the actual cooking, quite frequently you are the one who makes the list, buys the food, and coordinates the whole operation.

Home Decorating and Hospitality

You are often responsible for your surroundings, a job for which you may have little training. The non-stop decorating information on cable TV can leave you feeling overwhelmed and inadequate. But, it doesn't stop there. Once your home is up to snuff, you are also responsible for opening your home to others and planning family events.

School Liaison

Mothers are frequently the ones who meet with teachers, chase after homework, make sure permission slips are signed, and bring cupcakes for birthdays. You may delegate these tasks, but often you are the ones who coordinate them. Mothers are the ones called if there is a problem at school. You make sure that school clothes and supplies are purchased and that your children remember to bring something for sharing, or bring their lunch, or bring their instrument to band practice.

Activity Coordination

In the movie *Baby Boom*, there is a scene where yuppie moms are flipping through thick Filofaxes trying to find a day when their kids can get together and play. Even at three and four years old, the kids in the movie were booked solid. While that depiction is obviously an exaggeration, for some families it is closer to reality than you might be comfortable admitting. There is scouting, soccer, and T-ball; there are lessons and church activities. As I described in chapter 1, no wonder many moms feel like they are always in the car.

Health and Safety

Who in your family makes the doctor and dentist appointments, knows where the vaccination records are, takes the kids for checkups, and remembers to schedule appointments before school starts? Who takes care of the animals, the house plants, and/or the garden? Whose job is it to keep the family supplied with toothpaste, toilet paper, and cold remedies? Who gets prescriptions filled? Who childproofs your home? Who makes sure that fruits and vegetables get eaten? The health and safety of your family is in your hands.

Family Entertainment and Holidays

Who plans your family's outings, vacations, and social engagements? Who buys or makes Halloween costumes? Who cooks and coordinates the Thanksgiving feast? And, let's talk about Christmas! There are gifts, decorations, cards, and family pictures. Who makes sure everyone has appropriate matching outfits and makes the date with the photographer? Several Jewish friends have told me that Hanukkah is getting similarly out of hand. And, some families celebrate both holidays!

Relational Work

When there is an occasion to celebrate, who buys the gift? Who wraps and sends it? Who remembers the birthdays? Who sends the thank-you notes? Who takes the pictures, gets them printed, and puts them in albums? Who keeps the family address book up-to-date?

The role of mother covers a very wide range of activities, many of which are never done. Mothers often feel that life is an endless treadmill. This brings us to the next cause of burnout: overwork.

Overwork

Remember the old expression: "A man works from sun to sun, but a woman's work is never done"? The futility of trying to finish work that is never done puts us at risk for burnout. Do you feel like all you do is work? Do you wish you could have a forty-eight hour day? The sheer number of hours that mothers work during the day depletes the body. As you drag yourself through the day, struggling to meet your daily demands with a tired body, can mental and emotional fatigue be far behind? Work both inside and outside the home is such an important source of mothering stress that I have written the next three chapters about it.

Can We Blame the Protestant Work Ethic?

Over the past few years, I've heard many people attribute our American workaholism to "the Protestant Work Ethic." This is interesting, but not accurate. The Puritans were a source of much of the current work ethic we have in the United States. Protestantism, particularly of the Calvinist variety, had a very particular idea of "vocation." They did not recognize a special category of clergy and laity. Rather, they considered that all work could be God's work. Therefore, they recommended that people work hard and not be idle. This hard work combined with frugality was considered responsible for America's prosperity.

But, there was an important difference between what the Puritans did and what we do. The Puritans, and members of other Christian sects, observed a weekly Sabbath. In colonial America, citizens were prohibited (or strongly discouraged) from working on Sunday. "Work" included cooking and all types of domestic work, hunting, fishing, boating, smoking or chewing tobacco, and using a horse, ox, or wagon if church was within walking distance. Fines, whipping, and time in the stocks enforced the Sabbath. Sunday was to be a time of worship, and the entire day was spent in church. Historian Carl Holliday points out that "modern women" (his work was published in 1922) would balk at spending the whole day in church. However, he concedes that spending one day a week sitting was beneficial for women when the rest of the week involved intense physical labor (Holliday, 1922/1999).

An informal Sabbath was observed for many years in this country even after we cut it from its religious moorings. Stores used to be closed on Sundays. Now we have the ability to work and shop every day of the week. What would the Puritans think about our being able to work and shop 24/7?

Caregiving Overload

Like it or not, fair or not, in most families caregiving becomes the woman's responsibility. Caregiving can take many forms. You care for children, aging parents, and sick partners and friends. While caregiving can enrich you, it can also deplete you if you don't have support and balance it with self-care. Here are some common types of caregiving.

Child Care

Even when employed outside the home, many women still do the bulk of the child and home care. And, it is a source of contention in many relationships. This issue goes well beyond who changes diapers. It involves questions of daily care: Who feeds the children? Who stays home with a sick child? Who handles the nighttime routine? Who schleps to after-school activities? In some families, this type of childcare is equitably divided, or the mother may do most of these activities by choice. In others, it is simply assumed that they are the mother's responsibilities. (I'll discuss this more in chapter 6.)

Children with Special Needs

Not all children are born equal. Some have special needs that may require more time and effort from you. Without help and support, you may be overwhelmed. Some children have difficult or high-need temperaments. These are babies and children who seem to have an especially strong need to be with *you*. They don't separate well, want to be held a lot, and are almost superhuman in their lack of need for sleep. Even one child with a temperament like this can send a mother into caregiving overload. The situation becomes more challenging when a mother has one or more children with high-need temperaments and other children to care for as well.

Children may have difficulties in school in the form of learning disabilities or attention-deficit hyperactivity disorder (ADHD). Parents may find they spend an extraordinary amount of time trying to secure services for their children or helping their children with schoolwork at night. To compound the difficulties, these children may also become targets for bullies because they struggle in school.

Babies or children with chronic illnesses can dramatically increase caregiving responsibilities. Of course, the amount of caregiving varies considerably depending on the condition the child has. But, caring for a child with health concerns takes time and may overwhelm you, bringing you at times to despair as this mother describes.

> On a bad day, I feel like Sisyphus of the Greek myth.... Just when things seem to even out, a new set of daunting challenges presents itself.... At these times, I enter a state beyond fatigue that is akin to despair (Greenspan, 1998, 42).

This is especially true if you have other children at home in addition to your child with health issues. You may feel isolated because it is difficult for others to understand what you are going through. (I'll describe this in more detail in chapters 10 and 11.)

Closely Spaced Children and Multiples

Having children closely spaced in age can lead to caregiving overload since the caregiving tasks are unrelenting. These caregiving responsibilities may be so intense in the early days that everything else goes on hold: the house, the job, friends. According to Karen Gromada, author of *Mothering Multiples* (1999), mothers can get so task focused that they stop thinking of their children as children. Days may disappear into a blur of feeding and diapering, feeding and diapering. And, it's easy to lose yourself in this routine, as Suzanne, a mother of twin infants, describes:

> I'm TOTALLY overwhelmed by these two tiny creatures. Are you people all superhuman or wealthy enough to afford armies of help? How, oh how, do you take care of infant twins by yourself? When they are both crying at the same time, and there's no one else there to pick up one while I pick up the other one, and I am completely sleep deprived, WHAT AM I SUPPOSED TO DO???

When there are several small children in your home to care for, you have no downtime. Sleep deprivation is a particular problem. Sometimes mothers are just overwhelmed by the sheer amount of work involved in baby or childcare. Stress and arguing increase when families have multiples, as this parent describes:

> We've . . . been married for six years, but the last three with the kids have added a depth and craziness I could have never imagined. Sometimes I see a bit too clearly how parents of multiples can get divorced, so it was nice to hear I'm not alone in struggling. I can tell you that being parents of multiples is about the hardest thing on a marriage that I know of.

Chores and taking care of the children are two big sources of arguments. Often, both parents are working so hard and sleeping so little that they snap at each other. Only the most crucial chores get done in the first few months, but other projects start piling up around the house. When families have more than one small child at home, in order to survive, they may need to let go of some of the standards of cleanliness they had before the kids were born.

Another factor complicating the picture for many mothers of multiples, in particular, is that their pregnancy or adoption may have come about after years of infertility treatment. If you adopted your babies, you may also find yourself feeling isolated from other mothers simply due to the differences in your experiences. In either case, you may think "these are babies I really wanted. So how can I complain"? This kind of thinking may not allow you to acknowledge the real difficulties associated with a multiple birth or adoption. The support of others in the same boat can help as this mother discovered:

> I went to my first Mothers of Twins meeting when I was five months pregnant. I didn't feel that I belonged at all. It seemed that everyone was there to complain about how difficult it was to raise twins or triplets. I believed I would be able to become a parent to my twins without voicing a single complaint, frustration, or negative feeling. After all, I put my whole being into trying to become a parent, how could I possibly find anything less than perfect about the experience? Now that I have lived the overwhelming exhaustion of the early months, as every parent of

multiples does, and dealt with the day-to-day logistical issues, I join into these frustration-venting conversations among parents of multiples without a second thought.

Single Parenting

According to the U.S. Census Bureau, there are 10 million single mothers in the United States. This is up from 3 million in 1970 (Fields, 2004). Single mothers often tell me that they did not know the meaning of stress until they started to parent on their own. Single mothers also report having no downtime from relentless child-care activities. Loneliness and isolation can be particular challenges for the single mother. And, as I described in chapter 2, mother-headed households have a higher likelihood of poverty.

These issues are somewhat easier to face if you are a single parent by choice, though the challenges are still very real. But, if you are single against your will either through death, divorce, break up, deployment into the armed services, or your partner's long work hours, single parenting can lead to anger, depression, and burnout. Devon and Elizabeth's husbands left them for other women. Both of them had three young children to raise alone with little or no child support. Devon had to struggle with depression. She had so little money that she sometimes wondered how she would make it through the day. Money was always a problem, and she subsisted for several years just above the poverty level.

Elizabeth also felt depressed and overwhelmed. She found it difficult to care for her children. Some days, their needs were too much for her. She was also very angry: angry at her husband, angry at friends of her husband who seemed unable to make him stay, angry at other women whose husbands had not left them, and angry at God for allowing this to happen to her.

Whether your partner left or died, you may feel all the kinds of anger Elizabeth did and more. Unfortunately, you may also feel the urge to take this anger out on your children. It is especially important that you seek support and find ways to express your anger in healthy ways.

Some examples of this are writing in a journal, speaking to a therapist, or joining a support group.

Anne, a single mother of two teens, describes the total exhaustion that came with caring for her children, one of whom has special needs, and having no time for herself. Even before her divorce, she felt totally overwhelmed by her life. After a long illness, she took her kids to visit her parents. She describes this period as "one of the low points of my life":

> As I lay in bed at my parents' house, I experienced the horrible longing that death would overtake me and my son. I was feeling completely suffocated by my husband and kids. I had nothing else to give them and was getting nothing in return. I was sure that if my son and I were not in anyone's lives, everyone would be better off. I had birthed, breastfed, and cared for my two children for almost six years at this point. I was home-schooling them as well.
>
> Six years and a divorce later, I learned that my son has a form of autism. No wonder I was struggling! Knowing this has changed many aspects of my life. Though he receives help now, my life has been permanently altered and complicated by his condition. As a single parent, I have had to persevere through the trials of getting my son the education he needs, facing the fallout of the teasing and harassment he receives, working full-time at a low-paying job, putting my own career goals on hold, juggling the needs of two very different and high-need children, and finding stolen moments for myself.
>
> I have virtually no social life. I have very little time alone. I am facing the challenges of raising two teenagers at this point. Through all the grieving and loss of dreams, I have learned that we are indeed spiritual beings having a human experience. Each day I need to rediscover this or I simply cannot cope. In the end I want to know that I have, in good conscience, done the best I knew how at the time.

Aging Parents

As our population ages, more women will find themselves caring for aging parents while still raising children. Nearly one in four families is currently providing care for an elderly family member or friend, a number that is expected to increase (U.S. Department of Labor, 1998). Family members are the people most likely to provide this care with 41% of care providers being adult children (National Academy on an Aging Society, 2000). According to the U.S. Department of Labor, 72% of caregivers are women, and women provide the majority of care for aging relatives. For example, women spend an average of 19.9 hours per week in direct and indirect care compared to the 11.8 hours spent by men (U.S. Department of Labor, 1998).

Women between the ages of thirty and fifty are often called the "sandwich generation," in that they must often provide care for both children and parents at the same time. Approximately 41% of women caring for elderly relatives are also caring for children under age eighteen. The Department of Labor put together a profile of the typical caregiver. She is a forty-six-year old woman who is employed and also spends around eighteen hours per week caring for her mother who lives nearby. The number of hours is even higher in some families. Approximately 1.5 million families spend twenty to forty hours a week caring for an elderly family member and another 4 million spend at least 40 hours a week. The study also found that elder caregiving has an impact on work, causing caregivers to come in late, work fewer hours, and even give up work or retire early.

In some cases, providing care for aging parents is voluntary. In other cases, there is no real choice. The amount of work also varies tremendously. Is the parent nearby? Is she living with your family? What is the degree of her impairment? Sometimes people who are chronically ill can become very depressed or have badly impaired cognitive function, making them need that much more care. For example, Mary's father became increasingly verbally abusive each time she spoke with him. Rhonda's mother, on the other hand, became more physically frail each year, requiring more and more assistance on a daily basis.

60

The difficulty of caring for an aging relative is compounded when you don't feel you have a choice in the matter. Anger and resentment are common. If your parent was abusive or neglectful while you were growing up, you might be very angry at having to care for this parent now. The phenomenon of elder abuse and neglect demonstrates that caregivers can get overwhelmed and react in destructive ways. Adult children are the most common abusers of elderly people (Bergeron, 2005).

Codependency and Over-involvement

Codependency is a word that has been so overused it is almost a cliché. Nevertheless, it's often the women who take on everyone else's troubles who are at highest risk for burning out. There is nothing wrong with being concerned about and caring for other people. But, this needs to balanced with self-care. You need wisdom when trying to determine how to spend your limited time and fortitude in putting some limits on how involved you get in problems that are not your own.

The tendency to become too involved may have something to do with your family of origin. In one recent study, women with chronic stressors in their families of origin such as childhood abuse, parental addiction, or parental illness were more likely to be codependent (Fuller & Warner, 2000). Sometimes, too, a significant loss or traumatic event in adulthood can lead to an over-involvement in the problems of others. Lynn's story reflects some of the strain that too many outside commitments can create. Some of these difficulties she relates to her son's death that happened years earlier.

> I am a fifty-two-year old wife and mother of two daughters. I lost a son to SIDS fourteen years ago. My volunteer work includes working with breastfeeding mothers and working as treasurer at the county level of a political party. I work four hours a day as a receptionist in a civil engineering office. I have had breast cancer twice.

Lynn took a helping call from a breastfeeding mother whose baby was not gaining weight. After researching the situation, she realized that the baby might die.

61

That night I couldn't sleep. I was inconsolable. I could not stop crying or thinking about this baby. In the morning, I called the mother back and told her how worried I was and that her baby needed supplements immediately.

Her worry continued through another night of no sleep and crying. She recognized that she needed to turn this situation over to someone else.

It became apparent that I was burning out. I made frantic phone calls trying to find someone who would take care of this mother. I did find relief. I mailed a packet of information to the mother and was in bed for three days after that. I believe this situation tapped into my unresolved grief about my son's SIDS death as an infant. The stress of the past month crashed down on me as I let go of my control and cried. But, I couldn't turn off the tears and that was the sign that I was over the top. I have been exhausted since, but functioning. I know I need to let go of some things, but I value all these aspects of my life highly!

Why do some women cross the line into too much involvement? To understand why this occurs, psychologists Vicki Helgeson and Heidi Fritz's (1999) research on interaction styles is useful. They compared some of the beliefs that underlie healthy and unhealthy involvement in the lives of others. They refer to these styles as communion (healthy) and unmitigated communion (unhealthy) (Fritz & Helgeson, 1998). By identifying when you've fallen into an unhealthy pattern, you can begin to set some realistic limits on how much you do for others.

Healthy and Unhealthy Involvement with Others

Below are some of the characteristics of healthy and unhealthy interaction styles. These characteristics relate to caregiving, attachment style, and relationships. Women in these studies were asked to indicate whether certain beliefs applied to them. Most women will have aspects of both styles, but will lean more heavily toward one or the other.

Caretaking. Healthy and unhealthy interaction styles are both related to caretaking (Helgeson & Fritz, 1998). People with a healthy style help others because they are genuinely concerned and want to increase the other person's well-being. In contrast, those with an unhealthy style help people in order to improve their status in the eyes of others (Helgeson & Fritz, 1998).

Attachment Style. Women with the unhealthy interaction style were more likely to agree with statements such as: "I worry that my partner doesn't really love me" (Helgeson & Fritz, 1998, p. 175). In contrast, the healthy style was associated with secure attachments, as reflected in endorsement of items such as: "I find it easy to get close to others," and "I rarely worry about being abandoned by others."

Relationships. The healthy style is associated with empathy, a positive view of self and others, and the belief that other people are good and valuable. The unhealthy style, in contrast, is associated with depression and a negative view of self. The person with the unhealthy style relies on others for esteem, perceives that others view them negatively, and fears that others do not like them (Helgeson & Fritz, 1998). In addition, those with an unhealthy style often have a history of problems in relationships (Hegleson & Fritz, 1998), are less comfortable receiving help and support from others, and have difficulties asserting themselves in relationships (Fritz & Helgeson, 1998; Helgeson & Fritz, 1998). In sum, they give lots of social support, but rarely receive it from others.

What You Can Do

You have probably noticed that many of the symptoms of burnout are similar to those of depression. One aspect of burnout can be chronic depression. Depending on how bad your symptoms are, you may need to seek the assistance of a mental health professional. But, there are also a number of steps you can take. Burnout is something you should pay attention to. The good news is that you don't have to go through your life in misery.

Stop Denying

When you are burned out, you often don't recognize it. If you are dragging yourself through each day, admit it, and resolve to take some positive action. Acknowledge the stresses and pressures in your life, and start paying attention to all the stress-related symptoms you are probably feeling. It's time to make some changes.

Get Reconnected

People have a natural tendency to withdraw from others when they are under stress. Burnout compounds this by making you irritable and impatient. If you are laboring under perfectionism, you might also withdraw from others for fear that they will discover that you are not perfect, because you are annoyed by their imperfections, or both. When you are burned out, one of the first things you need to do is reconnect with others. Start with your family. Set aside time to be with your partner and children. This is also time to get together with some of the friends you may not have seen for a while. It's important that you reconnect with people who can give back to you.

You might also consider some volunteer work. That may seem a strange suggestion if you are already overwhelmed. And, it may not work for everyone. But, sometimes being involved in the lives of others can expand your perspective beyond your own problems. Caution: If you tend to get too involved in other people's problems, be careful not to take on too much.

Set Some Boundaries

You may find that you have been taking on too much in several areas of your life. Are you the one people always come to with their problems? Do you try to do everything yourself? Do you have trouble saying no? You must learn to set some limits. You are, after all, only human. Stop trying to meet everyone's needs. Does this mean that you should stop caring about others? Of course not! But, you can put some reasonable limits on how you handle their requests. If friends always want to talk about their problems, but never yours, perhaps you can limit the frequency with which this occurs by not always being available to discuss their problems in depth. Or, you can set a time limit on these conversations. You might find that this is better for them, too. By always being there as a shoulder to cry on, you may be enabling some of their problem behaviors. Your saying an occasional "no" will be good for them.

When a request to do something comes in, realistically evaluate whether it will be possible for you at that time. If you freely choose to do something, it will be much more enjoyable than if you feel coerced. If you need some help with saying no, as many women do, check out Henry Cloud and John Townsend's book *Boundaries* (1992).

Get Some Help with Your Work

When you are faced with too much work, try to do less of it. I know that this is easier said than done. For jobs that you decide must be done, start delegating as much as you can. You are not the only one who can do most types of work. Can you get a teenager to give you a hand in the afternoon? Can you swap baby-sitting with another mother? Can you pay someone to do it? Can someone else in your family share the load? Be creative and think of some alternatives to the way you usually work.

That being said, sometimes it really does need to be you. However, there may be some type of respite care available, including adult day care centers and visiting nurses for aging parents. And, don't forget the others living under your roof. All except the youngest children can pick up after themselves and help put stuff away, and this goes for your partner as well. It is essential that you stop trying to do it all yourself (we'll revisit this topic again in chapter 6).

Get Treatment for Depression

Depression can be a significant part of your burnout. If you think that you might be depressed, look into your treatment options (see chapter 2) and take care of it.

Stop Mentally Rehearsing Your Daily Difficulties

As I've mentioned in previous chapters, you need to pay attention to negative self-talk. If you are burned-out, you can make matters worse by going through the day thinking "my life stinks." It may at the moment, but constantly thinking this does not help you at all. Instead, try to think creatively about how you can change the situation.

Some Final Thoughts

Burnout may feel hopeless to you. Fortunately, it is not. Keep reading. Many of the chapters that follow will more specifically address concerns and problems that are making you feel bad. There is a light at the end of this tunnel.

For Further Reading

There have been a number of good books written about burnout. They provide a good overview of burnout and offer a number of helpful suggestions.

Books/Web Sites on Burnout

Berglas, S. 2001. *Reclaiming the Fire: How Successful People Overcome Burnout.* New York: Random House.
Glouberman, D. 2003. *The Joy of Burnout: How the End of the World Can Be a New Beginning.* Maui, HI: Inner Ocean Publishing.
Potter, B. 1998. *Overcoming Job Burnout: How to Renew Enthusiasm for Work.* Berkeley, CA: Ronin.
Reinhold, B.B. 1997. *Toxic Work: How to Overcome Stress, Overload, and Burnout, and Revitalize Your Career.* New York: Plume.
See www.helpguide.org for articles and self-administered tests on burnout.

Books on Perfectionism

These are two of the best books for dealing with perfectionism. They are written on depression, but both address the faulty cognitions that underlie perfectionism. In *Feeling Good,* there are chapters on perfectionism and approval addiction, challenging readers to "dare to be average."

Burns, D. 1999. *Feeling Good: The New Mood Therapy.* New York: Avon. (See especially chapters 10-14).

Burns, D. 1999. *The Feeling Good Handbook.* New York: Plume. (See chapters 9-10.)

Resources for Caregiving Overload

Card, E., with Watts Kelly, C. 1996. *The Single Parent's Money Guide.* New York: Macmillan Spectrum.

Ginsburg, B.G. 2003. *50 Wonderful Ways to be a Single Parent Family.* Oakland, CA: New Harbinger Publications.

Gromada, K. 1999. *Mothering Multiples.* Schaumburg, IL: La Leche League International.

Lebow, G., & Kane, B. 1999. *Coping with Your Difficult Older Parent: A Guide for Stressed Out Children.* New York: Perennial Currents.

Morris, V., & Butler, R.M. 2004. *How to Care for Aging Parents.* New York: Workman.

Nelsen, J., Erwin, C., & Delzer, C. 1994. *Positive Discipline for Single Parents: A Practical Guide to Raising Children Who Are Responsible, Respectful, and Resourceful.* Rocklin, CA: Prima Publishing.

Noel, J. B., with Klein, A. 1998. *The Single Parent Resource.* Beverly Hills, CA: Champion Press.

Weishett, E. 1994. *Aging Parents: When Mom and Dad Can't Live Alone Anymore.* Elgin, IL: Lion Publishing.

Web Sites for Single Mothers

M.O.M.S.: Single Moms on a Mission: www.singlemoms.org

Parents Without Partners: www.parentswithoutpartners.org

Single Parents Association: www.singleparents.org

Web Sites for Mothers of Multiples

Mothers of Supertwins (MOST): www.mostonline.org

National Organization of Mothers of Twins Clubs: www.nomotc.org

Triplet Connection: www.tripletconnection.org

Web Sites for Elder Care

Aging Network Services: 301-657-4329 or www.agingnets.com

American Association of Retired Persons: 202-434-2277 or www.aarp.com

Children of Aging Parents (CAPS): 800-227-7294 or www.careguide.com

ElderCare Online: www.ec-online.net

CHAPTER 4

Hearth and Home: The Fascinating History of Women's Domestic Work in America

As mothers, we are bombarded every day with advice and cultural messages about everything from how to clean our houses to how to raise our children. These messages always imply that we can do more--and do it better. Most mothers fall short of this mark. If you find yourself feeling guilty without understanding why, read on. There are historical and cultural forces that you may not be aware of that are probably shaping your beliefs about who you are and what you should be accomplishing. Ruth Schwartz Cowan (1983) in her classic book *More Work for Mother* describes the influence of these cultural forces this way:

> Many of the rules that tyrannize housewives are unconscious and, therefore, potent. By exploring their history, we can bring these rules into consciousness and, thereby, dilute their potency... If we can learn to select among the rules only those that make sense for us in the present, we can begin to control household technology instead of letting it control us (p. 219).

History can be wonderfully informative, giving a perspective that few other things can. And, history is a common reference point. In order to understand where we are now, we need a historical context. Many of the events that are shaping us now date back to the period of time before the American Civil War known as the antebellum period. Although many of the events I describe took place in America, they have influenced mothers all over the world.

In this chapter, I provide a brief history of women's work both inside and outside the home. I've used three primary historical texts: *Domestic Revolutions: A Social History of American Family Life* (Mintz & Kellogg, 1988), *More Work for Mother* (Schwartz Cowan, 1983), and *"Just a Housewife": The Rise and Fall of Domesticity in America* (Matthews, 1987). Inevitably, my discussion will have some limitations. Within any of the eras I cover, there have, of course, been mothers who were able to carve out for themselves satisfying lives even when the broader culture was against them. Further, there are vast differences in the experiences of mothers based not only on when they lived, but their social class and ethnic heritage. Finally, I want to acknowledge that even when a culture did support mothers, there were women who felt confined by their role and were unhappy. Culture alone cannot govern relationships that occur in individual families. But, I hope this information will help you recognize the cultural forces that may be influencing your own life.

Women of the Antebellum Period

From 1830 to 1860, the status of the American housewife was at its peak. Historian Glenna Matthews outlines several reasons for this. In the years following the Revolutionary War, home began to become a place of emotional attachment, a haven in a harsh world where children and adults were nurtured. These changes represented a fundamental cultural shift. Prior to the Revolutionary War, fathers were considered responsible for raising children. In custody disputes with few exceptions, fathers were granted custody. The few parenting books that existed during this time were addressed to fathers. It was many years before mothers were considered better nurturers of children "of tender years."

With the rise in the status of the home, the role of the mother was elevated. In a young country, embarking on the grand experiment of democracy, mothers came to be seen as the moral center of the culture. There was much emphasis on mothers being the trainers of the citizenry. As such, they needed to be educated and thoroughly knowledgeable about the issues and concerns of the day. For the first time, the literacy rate of boys and girls was about equal (Matthews, 1987).

Domesticity had a high place in the broader culture. The "notable housewife" was a frequent theme in fiction, and she was positively portrayed. Her role required a great deal of skill. Female craft traditions such as cooking, baking, and stitchery became jealously guarded family treasures that were passed from mother to daughter.

It is the correct thing to remember that the lady who rules the household must have absolute authority in it and rule as absolute queen. No comfort or order can be obtained without this…. The lady who holds this position must remember that the every-day happiness of those in the home circle is in her hands; that she has the greatest power of anyone to make the home a place of peace and happiness, or a place to avoid."

Everybody's Book of Correct Conduct, Being the Etiquette of Every-day Life, 1893

This is not to romanticize the work of mothers during this time. Much of the work in housewifery was grueling and unrelenting. There were limited opportunities for women. Women could not vote, and married women could not own property. Looking at the lives of these women through modern eyes, we would note that their work was largely segregated by sex and limited to the domestic realm. Some individual women wrote in letters and journals that they were overwhelmed with the responsibilities of childcare and running a household.

As difficult as it was, however, women's domestic work was infused with transcendent meaning that came from both religious and secular sources. Although aspects of their work were hard and tedious, they were constantly told that they were making a significant contribution to their country. Women of the antebellum period were raising citizens for the new republic. The importance of this role was extolled from the pulpits. According to Matthews (1987), religious beliefs were moving away from the more rigid Calvinism of the Puritans to an emphasis on God's grace. This influenced how children were treated within the home. Mothers and fathers were supposed to be living examples to their children of God's love.

71

Many of the ideas about the notable housewife may, in fact, have come from the Bible. In the Old Testament book of Proverbs, we see an example of a notable housewife in the virtuous woman of chapter 31 (verses 10 to 31). Her primary sphere is domestic, yet she has interest in the wider world. She works hard, is competent, handles money, buys and sells land, manufactures goods for herself, her family, and to sell, provides for her family, and helps the poor and needy. Her husband has status in the community because of her efforts. Both her husband and children praise her and call her "blessed."

> Who can find a virtuous woman? For her worth is far above rubies.
> The heart of her husband safely trusts her; so he will have no lack of gain.
> She does him good and not evil all the days of her life.
> She seeks wool and flax and willingly works with her hands.
> She is like the merchant ships, she brings food from afar.
> She also rises while it is yet night and provides food for her household and a portion for her maid servants.
> She considers a field and buys it; from her profits she plants a vineyard.
> She girds herself with strength and strengthens her arms.
> She perceives that her merchandise is good, and her lamp does not go out by night.
> She stretches out her hands to the distaff, and her hand holds the spindle.
> She extends her hand to the poor, yes, she reaches out her hands to the needy.
> She is not afraid of snow for her household for all her household is clothed with scarlet.
> She makes tapestry for herself; her clothing is fine linen and purple.
> Her husband is known in the gates when he sits among the elders of the land.
> She makes linen garments and sells them and supplies sashes for the merchants.
> Strength and honor are her clothing; she shall rejoice in time to come.

She opens her mouth with wisdom, and on her tongue is the law of kindness.
She watches over the ways of her household and does not eat the bread of idleness.
Her children rise up and call her blessed; her husband also, and he praises her: "Many daughters have done well, but you excel them all."
Charm is deceitful and beauty is vain, but a woman who fears the Lord, she shall be praised."
Give her the fruit of her hands, and let her own works praise her in the gates.

Proverbs 31: 10-31

Mothers were also extolled beyond the pulpit. Secular support of the notable housewife came from nineteenth-century philosophers such as Ralph Waldo Emerson, one of the most important intellectuals of his time. Domestic themes were also present in the works of Nathaniel Hawthorne. For both Hawthorne and Emerson, the model American home was loving, welcoming for visitors, free of social caste, and inhabited by a family that could be emulated.

The importance of mothers and other domestic themes were also key in the growing movements for the abolition of slavery and for women's suffrage. As Matthews (1987) states: . . . "The domestic sphere was not viewed as an a historical enclave where people could meet basic needs... but rather as a dynamic scene of actions that could affect the outcome of history" (p. 57). Women reformers used the moral authority of the home to highlight the plight of the less fortunate. One of the most famous exemplars of this is Harriet Beecher Stowe. We all know her as the author of the remarkable *Uncle Tom's Cabin*, a book that Abraham Lincoln credited with ultimately bringing about the end of slavery. What you may not know is that prior to writing *Uncle Tom's Cabin*, she was best known for her writings on domesticity. *Uncle Tom's Cabin* prominently features themes of home and motherhood throughout.

Uncle Tom's Cabin also drew from her own experiences as a mother. Beecher Stowe wrote *Uncle Tom's Cabin* shortly after the death of her infant son Charley. At the urging of a relative, she wrote a book that addressed the issue of slavery--the first book to do so. She used her experience of mourning for a child to give her empathy for the slave mother who could lose her children by having them sold away from her. Eliza, one of her main characters, is a slave who runs away with her young son to keep him from being sold. In a letter to Eliza Cabot Follen (December 16, 1852), she makes the connection between her personal experience and the experience of her character Eliza.

> I have been the mother of seven children, the most beautiful and most loved of whom lies buried near my Cincinnati residence. It was at his dying bed and at his grave that I learned what a poor slave mother may feel when her child is torn away from her. In those depths of sorrow which seemed to me immeasurable, it was my only prayer to God that such anguish might not be suffered in vain. There were circumstances about his death of such peculiar bitterness, of what seemed almost cruel suffering that I felt I could never be consoled for it unless this crushing of my own heart might enable me to work out some great good to others.

> I allude to this here because I have often felt that much that is in that book had its root in the awful scenes and bitter sorrow of that summer. It has left now, I trust, no trace on my mind except a deep compassion for the sorrowful, especially for mothers who are separated from their children.

In *Uncle Tom's Cabin*, the homes of the characters are also evidence of their moral stature. The home of the Quaker couple that offers refuge to Eliza is cheerful, neat, and warm--the embodiment of Beecher Stowe's most deeply held beliefs. In contrast, the home of the villainous Simon Legree is filthy, ragged, and slovenly. But merely keeping house well was not enough; notable housewives needed to be of good character as well. An example here is the character of the cousin who comes to take over the household. She handles her duties well, but it is not until she overcomes her prejudice that she is granted notable housewife status.

The importance of women using their influence for good was something Beecher Stowe believed throughout her life. She also emphasized that women must be knowledgeable citizens, particularly in regard to slavery. In a letter to Charles Sumner written after the publication of *Uncle Tom's Cabin*, she wrote:

> The first duty of every American woman is to thoroughly understand the subject for herself and to feel that she is bound to use her influence for the right (cited in Matthews, 1987, p. 56).

In later years, we would see how the perception of women's role in the broader culture had changed.

The Decline of Domesticity: 1865 to 1920

The decline of domesticity began in the years after the Civil War, which ended in 1865. The notable housewife was no longer a theme in literature. Rather, she was gradually replaced with the overbearing mother or "housewife bitch," which soon became prominent in literature. Matthews (1987) cites numerous examples from the writings of Sinclair Lewis and George Peck, author of the *Peck's Bad Boy* series. No longer the moral center of the family and the culture, mothers were seen as the problem.

Matthews hypothesizes that these negative images of housewives started to appear because of the perception that the housewife/activist had, in fact, gained too much power. Many women's groups, such as the powerful Women's Christian Temperance Union (WCTU), used their activism to try to curb traditionally male behaviors such as drinking and gambling. A backlash was perhaps inevitable: "Politicizing the home and then turning this to female advantage inevitably made enemies for domestic values, enemies who would welcome a diminution in the sanctity of home" (Matthews, 1987, p. 91). But negative portrayals in literature of housewives were only the beginning of change in how mothers were perceived. Soon, industrialization and modern science would also change the role of the housewife and change it forever.

Industrialization, Consumerism, and Women's Work: 1920 to 1960

Several cultural forces severely eroded the status of the American housewife during the early and mid-twentieth century. Certainly one of the most pervasive was industrialization. One of its first changes in the household was that it created an even more marked division of labor between the sexes than had existed previously as men left the home to work in offices and factories. And, its influence did not stop there.

The Laborsaving Device

Industrialization had a large influence on women's work with the invention of the laborsaving device. Such devices--washing machines, sewing machines, and vacuum cleaners--were designed to make the onerous tasks of taking care of a home less burdensome. They were also designed to eliminate the need for servants. These intentions were not bad, but the devices had unforeseen long-term effects on the work women did.

First, laborsaving devices clearly did make some tasks easier, but they simultaneously raised the standards. For example, since cleaning now took less time, the yardstick of cleanliness rose. Since it was easier to wash clothing with a washing machine, women could now wash clothes more often. As family diets became more varied, cooking became more complex. Larger homes meant more to clean. Finally, work that had traditionally been hired out (at least in middle-class homes) returned home and became the job of the housewife. These tasks included laundry, rug and drapery cleaning, and floor polishing (Schwartz Cowan, 1983).

Before the advent of laborsaving devices, most middle-class homes had at least some domestic help. With machines, women did most of these chores alone. Indeed, Schwartz Cowan describes how the housewife of the 1950s could single-handedly produce what her counterpart in the 1850s needed a staff of three or four to produce: middle-class standards of health and cleanliness for her family. Laborsaving devices eliminated much drudgery, but not the labor or time needed for household tasks:

"even with the new products and machines, women were still working the same number of hours as women in previous generations. There was more work for a mother to do in a modern home because there was no one left to help her with it" (Schwartz Cowan, 1983, p. 201).

Laborsaving devices had another insidious effect. Since the technology was new, kitchens and households were now redesigned to accommodate these machines. Women had to rely on outside experts rather than their mothers or each other to help them use, manage, and repair the new technology. What had traditionally been their sphere of expertise suddenly became foreign.

Finally, many tasks that required skill were eliminated. In fact, time management experts told women to make their household tasks as automatic and brainless as possible. "The problem no one had foreseen was that housework continued to fill women's time while it starved their brains" (Matthews, 1987, p. 195). Dr. Abraham Myerson first identified the malaise of the housewife in 1920 in a book entitled *The Nervous Housewife*. He also identified isolation as a particular problem for the housewife, in addition to the de-skilling and devaluation of her job. In 1930 in *Ladies' Home Journal*, he added one more problem to the list: the devaluation of motherhood itself (cited in Matthews, 1987).

The Army of Experts

Knowledge that was traditionally transmitted woman to woman began to be considered obsolete. We now needed to be taught by experts how to cook, raise our children, and run our households. Immigrant families were told to shed their traditions in favor of modern techniques. When groups resisted and continued to practice their old ways, they were often objects of derision and pity.

During this time, home economists such as Charlotte Perkins Gilman became exasperated with the inefficiency of the American housewife. She argued that women must be freed from domestic work so that they could do more important things. She proposed community kitchens where all families in a community could eat together, communal child rearing, and provision of outside services, such as laundry, for the family.

She believed that professionals instead of amateurs at home should do housework. Economist Juliet Schor (1992) describes Gilman's proposed solutions in positive terms, making the broader point that the reason most homes and home appliances are not designed with ease of care in mind is that we don't value women's time. (A more likely explanation is that many product designers are male, and they may not actually use the products they design.) Whatever the case, we should be careful not to adopt our culture's negative attitude about women or domestic work that is evident when we speak of housewives' "inefficiency" or the unimportance of their work.

Industrialization also turned women from producers of goods to consumers. As more items were mass-produced, fewer were created at home. Women were no longer responsible for making cloth or clothing, soap or candles. And clearly, many women (if not most) relished being released from these tasks. Yet, something was lost when women's domestic work was de-skilled. Women in the past had concrete evidence of their productivity and contribution to the family. They could point to vegetables grown, jars of preserves put up, clothing sewn, and cloth woven. Many of these household tasks were also outlets for women's creativity.

Sewing, quilting, lace-making, stitchery, and some kinds of cooking became dramatically less common during the twentieth century as mass-produced items came to be considered better than what women could produce themselves. Many of the daily tasks women now performed lacked any kind of permanency. Cleaning, diapering, and driving were all tasks that had to be done over and over, and there was often no evidence that they had ever been done at all. In *Motherhood Stress* (1989), Debbie Lewis describes this lack of permanent products and speculates that this is why so many at-home mothers enjoy various types of needlework: they know the product they create will last for more than five minutes.

Scientific Eating

Eating, too, did not escape the encroachment of science. Home economists and other experts told women that they could no longer rely on their families' palates to tell them what food was good. Instead, women needed to rely on nutritionists to tell them what their families should eat. Scientifically engineered food substitutes began finding their way into American homes. These were widely touted in women's magazines which described those who resisted as ridiculous when they failed to embrace the modern way. Interestingly, the native cuisines of many immigrant families were not so easy to change. These families ignored the pitch for scientifically engineered foods and continued to eat their traditional diets.

Commercially baked bread did not catch on until the early 1900s, and other substitutes for homemade food did not really catch on until there were food shortages during World War II. Curiously, after the war, these foods were marketed as better than the foods they were designed to replace. Canned, packaged, and mass-marketed foods eventually took over the market, and have become so much the norm that foods prepared from fresh ingredients taste strange, especially to kids. Matthews (1987) describes her dismay at this development:

> Arguably, the nadir of American cookery came in the fifties. This was the heyday of prepared foods and the cream-of-mushroom-soup cuisine whereby the cook could pour a can of this product over anything that was not dessert and create a culinary treat according to the standards of the day (p. 211).

Cream-of-mushroom cuisine appears to be making a comeback as advertisers capitalize on baby boomers' nostalgia for their youth.

We are still reaping the consequences of the marketing campaigns that brought scientifically engineered foods into our homes. Consider the campaign to promote margarine as being healthier than butter. Now we have learned that trans fatty acids (which are in both margarine and most commercial baked goods) are as bad or even worse for you than the saturated fat and cholesterol in butter. I wonder if the chemically laden fat-free products now flooding the market will have a similar history. We're eating more and more of these foods and finding ourselves, as a country, fatter than ever. A growing body of research evidence indicates there is a connection.

As with other forms of fake food, breastmilk substitutes appeared on the scene in the 1920s. These substitutes were called "formula" in reference to their scientific origin. Formula was marketed for decades as being better for the health of babies. Studies from that era demonstrated the tragic error of this claim; for instance, one study found that babies who were fed formula had a mortality rate that was three to six times higher than babies who were breastfed (Woodbury, 1925). Eighty years later, hundreds of scientific studies have confirmed the inferiority of this scientifically engineered product. Nancy Mohrbacher and I describe this sordid history in more detail in our book, *Breastfeeding Made Simple* (2005).

Scientific Mothering

A parallel development occurred with regard to child rearing. Rather than feeding babies when they appeared hungry, women were no longer to trust these cues. Instead, they were to rely on outside experts to determine when and how often babies should eat. This approach had a disastrous impact on breastfeeding. When feedings are rigidly scheduled, a mother's milk supply decreases. But, that was okay according to the experts of the day since bottle-feeding allowed a much more scientific approach. Intake could now be accurately measured. Unfortunately, variations of this advice still exist today.

According to psychologists such as John B. Watson, parents were to mold children's behavior through a process of positive and negative reinforcements. In fact, Watson openly questioned whether mothers were the best ones to be raising children given their lack of a scientific education. (I often wonder if John Watson knew any actual children.)

> It is a serious question in my mind whether children should know their parents. There are undoubtedly much more scientific ways of bringing up children which will probably mean finer and happier children. (Cited in Matthews, 1987, p. 183)

His comments have an eerily modern ring to them. In a 1997 book about overbearing social welfare policies and their negative effects on families, Dana Mack observes:

> Our family policy, it seems, has been based upon a long-standing conviction on the part of educators, psychologists, and social service professionals that parents really should not be too heavily engaged in the child-rearing process, but rather should abandon it to professionals (p. 21).

Mothers of the twentieth century were warned that they must abandon the child-rearing techniques of previous generations whereby mothers kissed and coddled their young children. Parents were advised to let their babies cry. They were told to adopt a strict regimen for feeding, sleeping, and toileting so that they conditioned a child to be polite and cleanly. Mothers were told that they could start bowel training at age one month by inserting a tapered soap stick into the rectum for three to five minutes (Mintz & Kellogg, 1988). Much of this child-rearing advice now seems ridiculous if not cruel.

Consumerism

Industrialization brought us another aspect of modern life: consumerism. By the 1920s, large numbers of mass-produced consumer goods were within the financial reach of the average family. In order to create a market for these items, the advertising industry was born. With it came the marketing of obsolescence and creative waste. The idea was to train women to buy new items rather than use everything to the very end. Consumerism has as its foundation the chronic need to purchase new goods without considering whether the item is really needed, whether it's durable, or how it was produced. Consumerism is a trend that continues to this day and whose impact is felt not only in our overflowing homes, but also in our overflowing planet.

As I described in chapter 3, advertising erodes women's self-esteem. Mothers were (and are) repeatedly told that if their families were not healthy, attractive, and popular and if they themselves were haggard-looking or tired, it was *their fault* since the means to remedy these problems were easily available. Guilt continues to be one of the most common appeals used in advertising to women (Schwartz Cowan, 1983).

Industrialization and the growth of consumer culture had an impact on community life in general. As more and more products became available for purchase, the value of neighbor helping neighbor began to fade. In a work published in 1898, Alice Morse Earle spoke of the decline in community:

> We nowadays have generalized our sentiments; we have more philanthropy and less neighborliness; we have more love for mankind and less for men. We are independent of our neighbors, but infinitely more dependent on the world at large. The personal element has been removed to a large extent from our social ethics. We buy nursing and catering, just as we hire our houses built and buy our corn ready ground. Doubtless everything we buy is infinitely better; nevertheless, our loss in affectionate zeal is great (p. 390).

No doubt, purchasing services from professionals rather than having them come via relationships would appeal to many who opted for the scientific approach. But, others realized that a great deal was also lost.

The Automobile

Another impact of industrialization was the advent and increasing availability of the automobile. As early as 1925, it was in widespread use. The car became the means by which the American housewife did most of her work and where she spent most of her time (Schwartz Cowan, 1983). Mothers spent a large part of their day chauffeuring other members of the family, a situation that has only gotten worse. But, there were problems associated with the car being women's primary place of work. First, by the end of the day, they could not point to something tangible that they had accomplished. In addition, driving also had the effect of isolating women from each other. Rather than having a place where they could gather, they were encased in their individual automobiles.

The Low Status of Housewives

The popular literature of the day also continued to attack American housewives in several ways. Some plays, novels, and films presented the idea of home being a place of emotional attachment as a joke and women at home were portrayed as idle or even as parasites. At the same time, women's magazines and advertisements advised women to create a haven for their husbands at home. But, unlike their counterparts of 100 years earlier, creating this haven entailed being deliberately dumb about the goings-on in the outside world. During the 1930s and 1940s, the *Ladies' Home Journal* repeatedly told women not to be concerned or involved in the world outside their homes. In an article published in September 1938, Bruce and Beatrice Gould issued the following advice:

> Be glad you're dumb about all these earth-shaking questions. They don't affect you nearly so much as a lot of other things much nearer home. . . . The great problems of the world are all Greek to you, but the problems of your home and family and community are right down your alley. Be glad you're dumb while your husband is saving the world. Be brave and you can save the home. (Cited in Matthews, 1987, p. 198.)

Contrast this with the mother who was responsible for the education of citizens of the new republic 100 years previously.

While the technological advances of the first half of the twentieth century did free women from some of their most challenging tasks, our culture didn't stop to ask questions about these developments. Did all these changes really constitute progress? What happens to the way women feel about homemaking when they change from producers of the family's products to consumers? What happens when women must rely on outside experts for advice on everything from what we should eat to how we should treat our children? What happens when we are told to make our routine jobs brainless and we spend the majority of our time in our cars? We were to see.

The Problem That Has No Name: Betty Friedan and The Feminine Mystique

In 1963, Betty Friedan fired the opening salvo of the modern women's movement with the publication of her book *The Feminine Mystique*. In this book, she put into words "the problem that has no name": that women were largely unhappy with the role that our culture prescribed for them. She stated that women needed to be liberated from housework in order to fulfill their potential through paid employment. This was a message that resonated with millions of women.

What Friedan articulated was the growing discontent of the American housewife. Interestingly, writer and Nobel Prize laureate Pearl S. Buck made many of the same points about the plight of the American housewife in a book written in 1941. Returning to the United States from China where she lived for many years, she was astonished to observe that the status of the American woman was so low. Isolated, discouraged from using their minds for anything outside the narrow sphere of the home, and cut off from aspects of homemaking that had taken considerable skill, Buck concluded that American women were "starving at the source." She went on to describe how women had almost no influence on American national life and how feminine qualities were despised. She also noted with some alarm, that women were passing this disdain for all things female on to the next generation. She wrote: "What is one to think of women who deliberately teach their sons to despise women?" (Buck, 1941, p. 44)

However, as historian Glenna Matthews suggests, the time was not yet right for women to openly discuss their unhappiness with the changing role of the housewife. America was just recovering from the Great Depression and was soon to enter World War II. Further, the forces that had devalued the work of the housewife didn't reach their full flower until the 1950s.

The 1950s: The Golden Era for Families?

The 1950s have often been described as the golden era of the American family. It is true that the majority of women during this time did

84

stay home with their children. But as we have seen, the culture itself did not have positive things to say about women at home. Negative or unattainably perfect stereotypes were reinforced by yet another technological invention: television.

In the meantime, the destruction of mother-to-mother transmission of skills and the constant messages of advertisers had another insidious effect: the loss of skills became real. Women were forced to rely on goods and services provided by other people, putting them even more firmly in the role of consumers rather than producers. And, if we were to believe advertisers, fairly dumb consumers at that. To me, the most troubling aspect of this decline in skills is the financial bondage it places on families. Purchased alternatives are almost always more expensive than what you can make at home. But, since mothers feel they don't have any choice, they continue to purchase expensive goods and services, sometimes teetering at the brink of poverty to do so.

Traditionalists often blame Betty Friedan and other feminists for devaluing homemaking and creating women's unhappiness. This is neither fair nor accurate. Many other forces led to the unhappiness of American housewives. Friedan simply named the problem. However, as Matthews, a feminist historian, points out, the early women's movement did make the mistake of adopting our culture's contempt for all things domestic.

Two generations later, women are questioning whether simply shedding all vestiges of the housewife role is really the solution. Many women are working full-time and still doing the bulk of child and home care. Many are asking whether we have traded the bondage of one cultural tradition for another. Can caring for children and tending a home be rewarding activities? Have we, in fact, thrown the baby out with the bath water?

The Rise of Modern Domesticity

Interest in domesticity is once again on the rise. Books on the joys of mothering and making a warm, beautiful home are hitting the best seller list. Some examples include Sarah Ban Breathnach's *Simple Abundance*

(1995), Victoria Moran's *Shelter for the Spirit* (1997), and Alexandra Stoddard's many titles, including *Creating a Beautiful Home* (1992). But, the rise of domesticity is perhaps best personified in a single woman.

Martha Stewart: The Return of the Notable Housewife

Before her spectacular fall from grace, *Business Week* magazine dubbed Martha Stewart America's lifestyle queen, noting that "even those who scoff at Stewart's perfect-housewife image admit that she's a stunningly savvy entrepreneur" (Brady, 2000). Her various business enterprises include *Martha Stewart Living* magazine, a television show, and products for garden and home. Even as she was sent to prison, the domestic movement she started continued to grow and will live past her. There are many contenders waiting in the wings hoping to be America's next domestic goddess. Diane Fisher (1996) describes why she thinks Stewart's brand of domesticity is catching on:

> Perhaps many of us raised in a generation geared up to juggle all the balls, the cellular phone, briefcase, hand weights, and diaper bag, perhaps we're finally getting ready to opt out of an inhuman scenario: this idea of doing it all . . . As unreal and perfect as Martha Stewart can be, she reminds us of the joy in arranging flowers, gardening, lovingly setting a table. We almost are ready to admit that we miss the domestic arts! (p. 133)

What I've also found telling, however, is the viciousness of many of the attacks against her, including people's glee in her prison sentence and public disgrace. One spoof called her the "dominatrix of domesticity." Given what we know about history, we should be somewhat troubled by the appearance, once again, of the housewife bitch.

Of course, many people joke about her because she sets the bar so high. I like the fact that she puts a positive face on domesticity, shows women how to live with style and beauty, and encourages women to learn new skills. While few mortals could even come close to doing all she does, it is good to know that we don't have to. I hope that as mothers become more confident in our their choices, they can use Martha and the wannabes as the resources they are rather than feeling inferior because they are not just like them.

Women's Ways of Knowing

Interestingly, another movement may also positively change how we think about home and childcare. Scientists have recently begun to question whether male ways of conceptualizing the world are really best. Or at the very least, do these models best describe the experiences of women? To address the limitations of male-centered models, there has been a movement to conceptualize women's ways of knowing. One of the most influential books on this topic is *Toward a New Psychology of Women* (1995) by Jean Baker Miller. The premise of this book and others that followed it is that women approach life differently than men. Women's growth and psychological development occur in relationships with others, including our families and friends. Men tend to be independent; women are more likely to seek relationships. Rather than despising our femaleness, we should embrace it. Relational theory resonates with thousands of women.

Along these same lines as I described in chapter 1, psychologist Shelley Taylor and her colleagues (Taylor et al., 2000) have put forth an intriguing alternative to the fight-or-flight response. They hypothesize that women under stress are more likely to respond relationally--to "tend and befriend." In a recent volume that I edited, *The Handbook of Women, Stress and Trauma*, I also noted that women's primary sources of both stress and trauma--and their greatest sources of strength--were grounded in their relationships (Kendall-Tackett, 2005a).

This willingness to embrace women's history and culture has also led to a resurgence of interest in women's craft traditions such as quilting, stitchery, and cooking. Indeed, quilts made by traditional groups such as the Amish are now recognized as works of art and sell for hundreds or even thousands of dollars. Interestingly, Wellesley College's Centers for Research on Women (former academic home to Jean Baker Miller), uses quilt motifs on many of their brochures and materials.

Environmental Concerns

Change may be coming from another source that has little to do with domesticity per se, but could have a large impact on families. With an increasing concern about the environment, many have been calling for a change in the way we consume goods. According to Vicki Robins of the New Road Map Foundation, overconsumption is bad for us in a number of ways. It leads to a declining quality of life. As I described in chapter 1, we work longer hours in jobs we may hate so we can buy more stuff. Overconsumption leads to debt, economic weakness, and the lowest savings rate in the industrialized world. Finally, overconsumption leads to problems for the environment including the accumulation of toxic waste and garbage, water and air pollution, and the depletion of renewable resources (Robins, 1994).

Waste is another direct result of consumerism. The business practice of "planned obsolescence" generates an enormous amount of waste as manufacturers change colors or styles frequently to get you to continue to buy. This applies to everything from clothing, to plastic containers, to household appliances (think avocado-green refrigerators).

Noting that massive consumerism has a negative impact on the environment, some have argued for policies that may have a dramatic impact on our spending habits. These policies could include eliminating subsidies for fossil fuels, foods, and other products allowing the true (much higher) price of these items to surface. The new higher prices would curb consumerism and encourage families to abandon the buy-and-dump mentality that is still prevalent in the U.S. and other parts of the world.

The Reappearance of the Mother/Activist

As with her counterparts in the 1850s, mothers are once-again using the moral authority of their role to call for social changes. There are numerous examples of mother/activists. One example is Mothers Against Drunk Drivers (MADD). This organization was founded in 1980 by a group of mothers after a drunk driver killed a 13-year-old girl. At the time this organization was formed, sentences for drunk drivers were lenient. This organization has managed to change public opinion about the seriousness of drunk driving. Like Harriet Beecher Stowe before them, mothers in this organization turned their personal pain into social action. And, they did so specifically referring to their role as mothers.

Discourse on Work Options for Mothers

Finally, some have argued that it's time for our culture to offer mothers more options for combining work and family. Which brings us full circle. You will recall that we started this discussion by acknowledging that women often feel a vague sense of guilt. As you can see, there have been a variety of cultural forces shaping how we live and the choices we make. And, not all of these have been benign with our best interests at heart.

As mothers, you must feel free to evaluate your options and make choices based on what's best for your family. Shortly after her election to the Senate, former First Lady Hillary Rodham Clinton acknowledged that women should be free to choose whether they stay home with children or seek employment outside the home (Stan, 2000). I found her comments interesting since she's been the icon for the "working mother" since the 1992 presidential election.

> I think we should do everything possible to give families real choices about whether or when one or both parents should work during a child's young years because there isn't any doubt in my mind that the most important job any of us have is caring for children (p. 63).

I hope that by discussing our past, you will feel free to examine the "shoulds" in your life. Many of the tasks we do and standards we have adopted were not freely chosen, but "given" to us by the advertising industry and an army of experts. To realize the goal of bringing our workload down to a more manageable level, we must begin to make conscious choices about our work at home and in the marketplace--the topic of the next two chapters.

CHAPTER 5

For Love or Money: Work Arrangements That Work for You

Employment continues to be a controversial topic among mothers. The popular media has been quick to dub this tension as "the mommy wars." To tell the truth, I initially approached this topic with some hesitation. Everyone it seems has an opinion on this subject, and the discussion can get ugly. But, employment is a potentially major source of mothering stress, and it's important to talk about.

I enter this discussion as someone who has done it all. Since having my kids, I've worked full-time and part-time, I've had a home-based business, and I have been home full-time. After having all these different roles, I've observed two things.

1. **No choice is perfect.** There are advantages and drawbacks to any arrangement you make.

2. **No matter which one you choose, someone will probably think you made the wrong choice.**

If your current work arrangement is working for you, you can probably skip ahead to the next chapter. But, if you want to explore your options, read on. You might be in search of a schedule with more sanity. You may want to use your skills while being available to your children or find a way to stay home for a few years. Or, you may be a mother at home who is thinking about re-entering the workforce. Recognize that while a perfect solution is an illusion, a good solution is entirely possible.

Why Mothers Work

Mothers work for a variety of reasons. Before we explore the different possible work options available to you, I would encourage you to think about what you get (or would get) by being employed. Money is just one of several reasons to work. Understanding why you work can help you find an arrangement that is best for you.

To Earn Money

Money is the most obvious reason to work, and it is not a trivial issue. If you are single, you work to support your children. The choice is work or public assistance, particularly if child support is sporadic or nonexistent. Even when two members of a family work, you may need both salaries just to make ends meet.

For families with lower incomes, your wages may mean the difference between "making it" and poverty. For example, according to the U.S. Department of Labor (1997b), in families of Hispanic origin, the median income for single mothers was $13,474. For households with only a father, the median income is $22,257. For married-couple families, the median family income is $29,861. The statistics are even more striking for black families where family income varies greatly according to whether the wife is employed. When both husbands and wives were employed, the median family income is $48,533; when the wife was not in the labor force, it is only $25,507. For female-headed households, the median income is $15,004 (U.S. Department of Labor, 1997c). Even if your family is not near the poverty level, the second salary gives you a financial buffer that provides security, especially in this era of downsizing. In many parts of the country, a second salary may also be necessary if you want to purchase a house.

From a psychological standpoint, money is important, too. Money often equals power in a family. Women may experience a subtle, or not so subtle, shift in the balance of power in their families when they step out of the workforce. Extra home and childcare responsibilities often fall upon the person who makes the least amount of money. Given our culture's lack of respect for at-home mothers, this is hardly surprising.

To Pay Off Debts

An issue related to money is debt. Many mothers work to pay off large debts. Some of these debts were from student loans. Mothers with advanced or professional degrees often feel that they must work to justify the large amount of debt they incurred, or the loans may be their partners'. Credit card and other consumer debt is another source of strain in families. Interest on this type of debt is so expensive that it is often difficult to pay it off. Families can be in bondage to consumer debt for years. Unfortunately, advertisers continue to encourage families to live beyond their means.

To Keep Health Insurance

Another reason to work is health insurance. Some mothers work because their job has health insurance. To quit their jobs, or even to go part-time, would mean losing their coverage. In families where someone has a pre-existing condition, mothers may be afraid to leave an insurer for fear that person won't be covered by a new insurer.

To Experience Satisfaction from a Job Well Done

As I described in chapter 3, mothering is notoriously lacking in indicators of job performance; it may take years before you know whether you did a good job as a mother. In contrast, there are often more tangible rewards from paid employment. The tasks involved for most jobs are more concrete, with obvious beginnings and endings. Also, depending on the type of job you have and how long you've been doing it, you may have developed a high level of skill. It's wonderful to have skills and use them. You may not feel very skillful as a mother, whether or not that is actually true.

Because You Love Your Work

You may work because you love what you do for a living. It may be something that is an integral part of who you are. You work because you couldn't imagine not being able to do the work you love. This was very

93

much an issue for me, and it is for many other mothers I meet. I just wanted to be able to do it while still being available for my children.

Because You Crave Intellectual Stimulation

Full-time childcare is demanding work, and you may find yourself starved for adult conversation. You may long to continue to learn things, keep up on current events, and pursue culture. Sometimes work can give you these things.

Because Other People Expect You to Work

You may also work because that is what your friends and family expect of you. The pressure to work can be subtle or overt. Some may have told you that you are letting other women down or that you are wasting your education. You may get pressure from your own mother who didn't like being home or from your husband or partner who wants a higher standard of living.

To Be Different from Your Mother

Growing up, if you had an at-home mother, you may have observed her being unhappy at home and were determined not to follow in her footsteps. Even if your mother enjoyed her time at home, you may have unconsciously adopted our culture's contempt for housewives in general and decided not to do as she did.

To Follow a Career Path

You may work to keep up with a career. Perhaps you have worked hard to become a member of a profession. You might be a year or two from a specific goal such as finishing a residency, making partner, or getting tenure. You may also have a license that you worked hard to get and that you want to keep current.

To Escape from Home

You may work because there is chaos at home. You may be overwhelmed by care giving responsibilities. Maybe your children are difficult to be around. Susan returned to work not only because she was feeling overwhelmed with taking care of her children and aging mother, but also because her house was isolated and dark much of the day. Being inside all day, especially during the winter, made her feel trapped.

Because You Want to Make a Difference

Finally, mothers work outside the home because they want to make a difference in the world. You may have a cause that you feel strongly about and don't think you can wait five or ten years to do something about it. Perhaps you have the type of job (such as being a medical doctor or nurse) where the fruits of your labor are dramatic, and you see that you are saving lives. Your job may be less dramatic, but one that still touches people's lives. This is not to say that being home with children doesn't make a difference, for it certainly does. But, the results of your efforts at home are long-term and may not have the immediate results that working in your field does.

How Much Does It Cost You to Work?

Once you have considered what you get out of working, the next thing to consider is how much it costs you to work. Sometimes we only take into account the most obvious expenses, such as day care. But, there are many other expenses you may not have thought of. On the surface, it may seem you are getting ahead. But, as you calculate your true cost of working, you might find that you are actually losing money when you work.

The figure you need to know is how much you have left after you have covered all your work-related expenses. In other words, how much you are netting. When you know this figure, you may become open to more options. As we just discussed, there are lots of reasons for working, and money is only one of them. But, if you realize you are actually losing money, perhaps you can come up with an arrangement that is less costly in terms of both money and your physical and mental energy.

If there are two of you working, consider how much it costs each of you to work. You and your partner might decide that it makes more sense for you to stay in your job while your partner stays home with the kids. If you want some help in calculating how much the second income brings in, check out the second income calculator at MSN Money (http://moneycentral.msn.com/investor/calcs/n_spwk/main.asp).

Increase in Tax Rate

You might be surprised to learn that this can be your biggest expense. Your full-time salary might be just enough to push you into a higher tax bracket. When we lived in Massachusetts, I was stunned to learn that 48% of my full-time salary went to taxes. From the money that was left, we still had to pay all the other expenses, like day care for two kids. However, when I worked part-time, my salary did not raise our tax rate. By working part-time, I was netting almost the same that I would have for full-time work, but with a greatly reduced level of stress.

Child Care

Child care is the next-largest expense. Child care can be cost-effective when you have one child. But, child care costs for two or more children can be prohibitively expensive. Finding quality day care that you can afford continues to be one of the toughest challenges employed mothers face.

Commuting

In chapter 1, I described the costs of commuting in terms of time and stress. Now, let's talk money. The IRS allows $.375 a mile as the cost of business travel. Use this figure to calculate how much your commute costs, realizing that it is probably on the low side. Be sure to include any tolls and parking fees that you pay. Also, recognize that commuting costs are going to keep going up as fuel costs continue to rise. If you use public transit, calculate the amount you pay on a weekly or monthly basis.

Clothing

No question about it, when you are employed outside the home, you will probably need nicer clothes than when you are at home. Different occupations have different standards. Someone working in a law office will have to dress up more than someone in a manufacturing job. Be sure to include any hosiery, makeup, salon, or accessory expenses here, too.

Purchase of Services

When mothers are employed, families purchase more services. The obvious one is day care. You may also purchase more meals out and more convenience and take-out foods. You might hire out house cleaning, gardening, car washing, and dog walking. There is nothing wrong with hiring the help you need. In fact, I suggest it in the next chapter. But, when calculating the costs of employment outside the home, these costs must be included.

Purchase of Treats

When you feel stressed, it is often easy to justify the purchase of treats for yourself, your partner, or your children because you are working so hard. These treats can range from large to small, from snack foods to jewelry to a really nice car. How you spend your money is, of course, your business. But, you should realize that you are more likely to make expensive purchases when you are employed and include these purchases in your tally of work-related expenses.

Are Men the Best Role Models?

We tend to think that work and family dilemmas are only for women. Men, we feel, never have to make these kinds of choices and sacrifices. But, is that really true? Would our lives be better if we had a "wife" at home to take care of things?

In his book *The Paradox of Success*, former businessman John O'Neil describes his climb up the corporate ladder. He was always traveling, making big deals, being really important. One morning, as he was leaving for a trip, his young daughter was clinging to his legs, begging him not to go. The limo driver who had come to pick him up didn't say a word, but was giving him a look of disapproval in the rearview mirror. Even years later, that look still got under his skin. He cites that incident as when he first started to question his "success-at-any price" mentality and whether he really had his priorities straight. I found the subtitle of his book telling: "When winning at work means losing at life." Before we uncritically adopt a male model of success, we should at least consider what men who have done it that way have to say about their lives.

Creating Work That's Right for You

In this section, I describe some basic types of work options, thinking mostly about flexibility of schedules. Sometimes mothers don't want to explore other options because they don't want to ask for "special" schedules that will allow them to meet the needs of their children. If this is you, there may be viable options that you have never considered. I ask you to temporarily suspend your objections and stand back and look at the big picture.

More and more people are calling for work options and not just for reasons of parenting. People are asking for reduced hours to improve the quality of their lives through volunteering or returning to school. People are asking for flexible work options so that they can care for aging parents or be with a child who is having difficulties. People with disabilities find that work options allow them to participate in the workforce rather than relying totally on public assistance.

Working from home, flexible schedules, and compressed work weeks lead to less traffic in congested areas and are generally better for the environment. Telecommuting and Web-based businesses are opening up opportunities for people in small or geographically isolated communities, many of which have costs of living that are substantially less than living in a city. Virtual work boosts local economies in small towns and rural areas as telecommuters and people with Web-based businesses move to these areas. Our little state of New Hampshire (population 1.3 million) has the highest per capita rate of high-tech workers in the country. Work alternatives are catching on.

The Demographic Imperative

In *Breaking with Tradition: Women and Work, the New Facts of Life* (1992), Felice Schwartz describes the demographic imperative that will force companies to make some changes in the work options they offer. The future workforce will have fewer white males than ever before, so companies that want to hire and retain competent staff will have to look to women, minorities, and (I would add) people with disabilities. Schwartz sees greater opportunities for these disenfranchised parts of the workforce than ever before. And, if companies want to include women of childbearing age, they'll need to recognize and make some practical adaptations.

Below, I've listed some of the major types of work options. These can be combined any number of ways in a two-adult household. My husband and I both telecommute and have for many years. I've also had a variety of nontraditional work arrangements.

Flextime and Compressed Work Weeks

Flextime refers to starting and finishing work at non-standard times. It might mean starting early and leaving early, or starting late and working later in the day. For some types of jobs, this type of scheduling is not possible. But, when it is, it might let you meet the school bus, get to

99

work before commuter traffic is in full swing, or accommodate a longer morning routine.

A similar concept is the compressed workweek, wherein a full workweek is compressed into four ten-hour days, or three twelve-hour days. This allows for more full days at home, but with full-time benefits.

Part-time

Part-time work is another popular option. The number of hours can vary tremendously, from a few hours a week to almost full-time. Sometimes, employees share their jobs with another person or function as independent contractors who are employed hourly or on a contract basis. Part-time positions are generally not advertised, but many types of work can be adapted to fit a part-time schedule. Part-time work is also attractive to employers since it is often cheaper to hire a part-time worker or independent contractor than a full-time employee.

Telecommuting

Telecommuting is an increasingly popular alternative work arrangement. It can be full- or part-time and involves working at home while communicating with your employer via telephone, fax, and e-mail. You can telecommute for all or part of your work week. My husband, Doug, has telecommuted full-time for over 17 years. He works for a high-tech company in southern California. We live in New Hampshire in a town of 3,900. Both of us started telecommuting before it was trendy, and people told us that it would never work. It does.

Home- or Web-based Business

You can start almost any type of business: you can make things to sell, publish information, or be involved with a reputable multilevel marketing business. If you have professional skills, you can also sell your time as a consultant and provide training to people in your field. If you have office or computer skills, you may hire yourself out as a virtual assistant. There is increasing demand for people who will help other entrepreneurs from remote locations, usually via the Internet. Check out some of the resources at the end of this chapter for other ideas on home-based businesses.

Sequencing

Sequencing is another option for making a manageable lifestyle. Its name is taken from a book entitled (oddly enough) *Sequencing* (1996) by Arlene Cardozo. Sequencing takes that long view of your life and says you can have it all, but not all at the same time. The idea is that you have a time when you concentrate on your career. Then, you step out of the workforce for a few years to raise your children.

When your children are in school or are a little more independent, you return to the workforce. Of all the books I've read, this one offers the most specific, practical suggestions for keeping up your career while tending your children. For example, Cardozo advises mothers to keep up their professional licenses, stay involved in their professional organizations, and stay up on their fields. While you have young children at home, she suggests that you limit your workweek to ten hours and that you don't take assignments with tight deadlines. That way, you still have the flexibility you need to respond to your children's needs.

Sequencing can also be a helpful approach if you need to take an extended leave due to a health or other crisis in your family. On two separate occasions, I have had to take a six-month leave due to lupus flares. On both of these occasions, I could not work at all. Using the sequencing model, I kept up with my reading and some limited professional activities. As an added psychological benefit, sequencing kept me from becoming depressed and gave me a vision of life beyond being sick. Both times, I was able to successfully transition back to my work with relative ease.

Home Full Time

This is another option that you have. You may have been employed all your life and now have decided to stay home and focus on the needs of your family. An increasing number of women are selecting this option.

If you are considering it, realize that going from the world of work to home full time can be a huge culture shock. Everything about it is different from being employed. While at first the change might be a relief, after a while you may long for your old life. Social isolation, the competition among mothers and the perceived decrease in social standing can all be hard to cope with if you are not prepared for them. Most of these challenges can be overcome, but forewarned is forearmed. Here are some suggestions to help you cope.

First, I recommend that you give yourself at least six months until you make a decision about whether it is working for you. The first two to three months can be the hardest, but if you hang in there, you can probably make it work. Second, get support! Find a group of mothers you enjoy and don't feel like you are in competition with. Women you become friends with during this phase in your life often become lifelong friends. But, it may take several tries to find them. Don't be discouraged. They are out there.

Finally, find ways to use your mind. The need to exercise our brains is every bit as important as exercising our bodies. Take a class. Study a language. Join a discussion group. And read, read, read. Give yourself the chance to do things that renew you that you never had time to do before. While undoubtedly challenging, this can be a great time in your life. Try to make the most of it.

Advantages of Alternative Work Arrangements

Alternative work arrangements can be a win-win for all involved. Besides giving you more control over your schedule, alternative work arrangements offer some advantages that you might not have considered.

Tax Advantages

Both telecommuting and home-based businesses offer a lot of nice tax advantages. Your home office must be your primary workspace. If it is, you can take a percentage of all home expenses you incur over the year off your taxes. For example, if your home office is about 20% of your home, you can deduct 20% of your electric bill, gas bill, and other home maintenance costs from your taxes. While your apparent take-home pay may be substantially less when you work for yourself, you should be sure to include these hefty tax savings when comparing how much you are netting at home versus outside work.

Caution, however, is in order. If you are self-employed in the U.S., you will have to pay self-employment tax--the portion of Social Security your employer would normally cover. This can be a substantial cost. Be sure to check with your accountant or tax preparer to find out the most current tax laws regarding home offices before taking any deductions. Home-office deductions can also flag you for an audit, so keep all receipts related to home care.

Reduced Costs of Working

Alternative work arrangements allow you to substantially cut your cost of working. Your commuting costs will often be less and, if you work at home, your clothing cost will usually be substantially less. You can also reduce the cost of restaurant lunches.

One cost that you will probably reduce, but not entirely eliminate, is childcare. If you are working at home, you will probably still need some childcare. Even a few hours every week can give you a chance to concentrate on paperwork or return phone calls without the accompaniment of screaming children (been there, done that). And, you can often have your provider right in your home so you are available if needed.

More Flexibility

Alternative working arrangements give you a chance to be more involved in your children's lives. If the school nurse calls, you can go retrieve your child from school. You can take an afternoon off to see a school play or help in a classroom. You can run errands or schedule appointments during the day so that these are not all left for the weekend. These work arrangements offer you a lot more control over your life.

Modeling for Your Children

If you work at home, your children can actually see what you do for a living. It gets them more involved in your life and shows them work in action. It also shows them someone who is successfully balancing work and family. As they get older, you might even hire them to do some work for you.

Alternative Work Arrangements Are Good for Business

Companies that allow flexible work options also benefit. Employees are happier on the job and are, therefore, less susceptible to stress-related illness. This lowers health care costs. Employees with alternative arrangements are often more productive. Companies are better able to retain employees, reducing costly turnover. When the job market is tight, companies that are truly family-friendly will have an advantage in attracting new talent.

Some Drawbacks of Alternative Work Arrangements

As I mentioned earlier, there are drawbacks to almost any arrangement you can make. There is no perfect arrangement, but by anticipating some of the possible problems, you can often head them off. Even if you can't, the pluses may still outweigh the minuses.

Invisibility

When you are not in your office every day or at normal times, you can become invisible to your coworkers. You may get passed over for assignments, miss meeting announcements, and generally feel out of the loop. This can be a problem, especially if you are on a specific career path.

There are several approaches you can take. First, be sure that your boss is aware of what you are doing with regular contacts and progress reports. Keeping the lines of communication open with coworkers really helps. Perhaps a colleague feels that he or she must pick up the slack for you.

If that is true, see what you can do to remedy this situation. Having a contact in your office can keep you abreast of what's going on and remind others of your existence. Try to cultivate such allies, and let them know that you appreciate them on a regular basis.

You might also need to go to your office periodically. David, a local computer programmer, works at home four days a week and spends a fifth day in his main office. My husband goes to his office in California about four times a year. (Note: If you do have two regular offices, it can affect your home-office status with regard to tax deductions.)

Perception of Others

In some corporate cultures, someone who wants to work less than sixty (or seventy or eighty) hours a week is suspect. In *The Time Bind* (1997), Arlie Hochschild's respondents indicated that even in a company with family-friendly policies in place, there was often subtle, or even overt, pressure not to take advantage of these policies.

In my own life, I was surprised to learn that even serious illness was not an adequate reason in some people's minds for not working "enough." When I realized that I could never work enough to please some people, it was surprisingly freeing. This realization allowed me to make decisions that worked best for my family and me.

With a compressed workweek or flextime arrangement, you may find that people don't approve when you leave earlier than they do or don't come in one or two days a week. Your boss may call meetings after your normal quitting time. You may feel pressured to stay even though you started your day hours before everyone else. If you have an alternative work arrangement, you may find yourself taken off of projects or "mommy-tracked." Julie, a junior faculty member at a major university, was told that her department expected long hours from her if she was to get tenure. Her work was excellent, but she wanted to be home with her family in the evening. Her solution? She slipped over to her office each evening, turned on the light, locked her office door and went home! She was recently awarded tenure.

You may not want to resort to that kind of subterfuge. And, only you can determine how seriously you want to take other people's attempts to track you. Keep in mind that eventually people get used to these arrangements. If you keep turning in excellent work, most people in your office will get the message that you are working hard, too. But, if you are getting seriously undermined, try to fix the situation if you can. If you can't fix it, either ignore it or consider leaving. Being constantly undermined will eventually affect your well-being.

Finally, realize that some people will be jealous of your work arrangements and will let you know it. If people make snide remarks, it's best to respond in a non-defensive but honest way. When people say, "It must be nice," say "It is." When they say, "You're lucky," say "Luck had very little to do with it." When people say, "I wish I had that kind of job," say "I'm confident that you could." These kinds of answers deflect sarcastic remarks without justifying your arrangements to others. Remember, you don't owe every nosy person an explanation about your work. If someone sincerely wants to know, I'll share information. Otherwise, I consider particulars about my working arrangements to be private. And, so should you.

Isolation

Just as isolation is a problem for the at-home mother, it also can be a problem for someone working at home. It's important that you get out of the house occasionally, even if it is just to take a walk or run some errands. Make sure that you are not sitting in front of your computer every day with no outside human contact. When you start losing your social skills or spending all day in your pajamas, it may be time to get more involved in the outside world.

You must also realistically consider your temperament. Are you someone who likes to work alone? Do you mind being by yourself for long stretches of time? If you like to have other people around, working at home full-time may not be for you.

Lack of Demarcation between Home and Work

Another real danger is that you may actually end up working more with an alternative work situation. Part-timers know that hours can multiply until they are working close to full-time (often for part-time pay). Having your work at home especially makes it difficult to draw a line between the two. It's very easy to slip into a home office at all hours of the day or night. You may work through mealtimes and into the wee hours of the morning. My husband's company is in California (meaning a three-hour time difference), and it's not unusual for us to receive phone calls at eight or even nine o'clock at night. If at all possible, have separate home and office telephone lines. When it's time to quit for the day, close the door and turn off the phone ringer. Sometimes that's hard to do, but you must draw this line if you want your arrangement to continue to work for you.

Another work/family line is teaching family members to respect your working time. While you want to be available, you also need to let people know that there are times when you need to concentrate on work. Having a separate space to work that is off limits to others can be a challenge if you live in a small apartment or house. Space is one more factor to consider if you are contemplating an alternative working arrangement.

What You Can Do

Since I have an unusual working situation, I'm often asked how I arranged it. Both my husband and I have learned some things through trial and error. Here are some suggestions I often give to mothers who are looking for work alternatives.

Imagine Your Ideal Job

Approach the question of employment with an open mind. Over the years, I've been amazed at the creative choices that families have made, including different shifts, fathers home full-time, and both partners working part-time. I've heard of mothers who are mail carriers whose day care facility is on their route. This allows them to see their children at lunch or at other times during the day.

If you approach every possibility with a "yes, but. . . ," you dramatically limit your ability to come up with a solution. Take a moment and think about what your ideal life would look like and don't stop yourself with "yes, buts . . ." In your ideal life, what type of work and how much of it would you do? How would you get to and from work? What type of child-care arrangements would you make (including staying home yourself)? Consider writing these ideas down. Often, this exercise can help you come up with some options.

Be sure to go back to the list earlier in this chapter about why we work. Which of these reasons are important to you? Are there ways that you can incorporate them into a new working arrangement?

Realistically Assess How Much You Are Netting Now

Figure out how much you are actually netting in your current job. Even if money is your primary reason for working, you might find that you can gross a lot less than you are now and still be netting the same. Also, consider whether you can live on less. Two great books to help you do that are Amy Dacyczyn's *The Complete Tightwad Gazette* (1998) and Dominguez and Robin's *Your Money or Your Life* (1992). These books will give you lots of suggestions about really saving money and improving the quality of your life at the same time.

Consider Leaving Your Current Company

You may find that your current employer is unwilling to make accommodations for you. If that is true, you might consider seeking another job. Again, research your options and try not to quit without knowing your next step. If you don't know where to begin, take a look at *Working Mother* magazine. Each year they publish a listing of family-friendly companies, complete with contact information. The library is also a great source for books on all types of working arrangements. Sometimes, just knowing that you could leave may make your current situation more bearable.

Develop a Plan

If you want a livable working arrangement, assume that you will have to take the initiative. While companies may eventually catch on and offer these options on their own, it may take years. Research your options and present a plan. Try to anticipate the concerns of current or prospective employers, and tell them how you will address those concerns. For example, my husband's current employer was concerned about hiring someone who lived so far away. He offered to work for them on a trial basis for three months. That was 13 years ago.

Don't Rush into Change

In some cases, the change you make may be dramatic. Your plan has a much higher probability of success if it's not one that was made on impulse. Cautionary tales abound of men and women leaving their high-powered jobs to open a little store or country inn--only to be miserable in their new lives. Even with a plan, you might still find yourself in culture shock. But, chances are you'll be happier with your new arrangement if you've had some time to think it through and weigh your many, possible options.

Be Confident

Confidence is contagious. Project it to prospective or current employers, even if you have to fake it at first. You don't have to apologize for wanting special arrangements. Many other people want them, too. You could be a role model for other women. Be confident that you have unique skills to offer. Be honest about your needs and limitations, and present a positive plan for how you will deal with them. Realize, too, that not everyone will be willing to make these types of accommodations. If they don't, talk to someone else. Remember, alternative work arrangements are good for employers, too.

Conclusion

You may be ready to make a change and find a more livable work arrangement. As you make the transition, it can be helpful to keep your goals in mind. In closing, I'd like to share one of the best things I've read on this topic in recent years. It's from a novel, *I Don't Know How She Does It*, by Allison Pearson (2002). In this book, Kate, a career woman with a highly demanding job and two small children, finally decides that she has had enough. She makes a list of her reasons to make a change. This book has resonated with many employed mothers. What she wrote may inspire you, too.

Reasons to give up work

1. Because I have got two lives and I don't have time to enjoy either of them.
2. Because twenty-four hours are not enough.
3. Because my children will be young for only a short time.
4. Because becoming a man is the waste of a woman.
5. Because I am too tired to think of another reason (p. 325)

You *can* find a work arrangement that will help you balance work with the rest of your life. I wish you great success in your efforts!

For Further Reading

Resources for Alternative Work Arrangements

These books are full of ideas on different work arrangements. Read them with an open mind. You might be amazed at what you come up with.

Arden, L., Moyle, J.T., & Hurwitz, B. 1999. *The Work-at-Home Sourcebook*. Palo Alto, CA: Live Oak Publications.
Bredim, A., & Lagatree, K.K. 1998. *The Home-office Solution: How to Balance your Professional and Personal Lives While Working at Home*. New York: John Wiley & Sons.
Cardozo, A.R. 1996. *Sequencing: A New Solution for Women Who Want Marriage, Career and Family*. San Bernardino, CA: Borgo Press.

Edwards, P., & Edwards, S. 1999. *Working from Home: Everything You Need to Know about Living and Working Under the Same Roof.* East Rutherford, NJ: Jeremy P. Tarcher (Penguin USA).

Folger, L. 2000. *The Stay-at-Home Mom's Guide to Making Money.* Roseville, CA: Prima Communications.

Igbaria, M., & Tan, M. 1998. *The Virtual Workplace.* Hershey, PA: Idea Group Publishing.

Kendall-Tackett, K.A. 2005. *The Well-Ordered Office: How to Create an Efficient and Serene Workspace.* Oakland, CA: New Harbinger Publications.

Levin, M.R. 1998. *Teleworking and Urban Development Patterns: Goodbye Uglyville, Hello Paradise.* Lanham, MD: University Press of America.

Nilles, J.M. 1998. *Managing Telework: Strategies for Managing the Virtual Workforce.* New York: John Wiley & Sons.

Parlapiano, E.H., & Cobe, C.P. 1996. *Mompreneur: A Mother's Step-by-Step Guide to Work-at-Home Success.* New York: Berkley Publishing.

Roberts, L.M. 1997. *How to Raise a Family and a Career Under One Roof.* Moon Township, PA: Bookhaven Press.

Tamsevicius, K. 2003. *I Love My Life: A Mom's Guide to Working from Home.* Deadwood, OR: Wyatt-MacKenzie Publishing

Families and Work Institute: www.familiesandwork.org

Independent Home Workers' Alliance: www.homeworkers.org

Mothers' Home Business Network: www.homeworkingmom.com

Books Describing the Work/Family Dilemma

These books do a good job of summarizing the issues and dilemmas for employed and at-home mothers. They both offer information on alternative work arrangements and present lots of mothers' stories.

Crittenden, A. 2001. *The Price of Motherhood: Why the Most Important Job in the World is Still the Least Valued.* New York: Henry Holt & Co.

Lewis, D.S., & Yoest, C.C. 1996. *Mother in the Middle: Searching for Peace in the Mommy Wars.* New York: HarperCollins.

Marshall, M.M. 1991. *Good Enough Mothers.* Princeton, NJ: Peterson's.

Pearson, A. 2002. *I Don't Know How She Does It.* New York: Anchor Books. (This is an entertaining novel with a story many employed mothers can relate to).

Resources for Money and Debt

If you are thinking you'd like to stay home or explore working fewer hours, these books will give very specific suggestions on how to live on less--usually with greatly increased satisfaction. *Your Money or Your Life* has a great guide to calculating what your real hourly wage is.

Dacyczyn, A. 1998. *The Complete Tightwad Gazette.* New York: Villard Books.

Dominguez, J., & Robin, V. 1992. *Your Money or Your Life: Transforming Your Relationship with Money and Achieving Financial Independence.* New York: Viking.

Strauss, S.D., & Sande, P. 2000. *The Complete Idiot's Guide to Beating Debt.* New York: MacMillan

Simple Living Network: www.slnet.com

National Foundation for Credit Counseling: www.nfcc.org

National Center for Financial Education: www.ncfe.org

Resources for Employed Mothers

These books offer support and advice to mothers who are employed. Guilt for employed mothers is described, as are strategies to counteract it. Alternative work arrangements are also described.

Galinsky, E. 1999. *Ask the Children: What America's Children Really Think about Working Parents.* New York: William Morrow & Company.

Garey, A.L. 1999. *Weaving Work and Motherhood.* Philadelphia: Temple University Press.

Goldman, K.W. 1998. *Working Mothers 101: How to Organize Your Life, Your Children, and Your Career to Stop Feeling Guilty and Start Enjoying It All.* New York: HarperTrade.

Marshall, M.M. 1991. *Good Enough Mothers.* Princeton, NJ: Petersons.

Pryor, G. 1996. *Nursing Mother, Working Mother.* Boston: The Harvard Common Press.

Weisberg, A.C., & Buckler, C.A. 1994. *Everything a Working Mother Needs to Know.* New York: Doubleday.

Families and Work Institute: www.familiesandwork.org

Working Mother magazine: www.workingmother.com

Resources for At-Home Mothers

Unfortunately, many women who are home full-time feel the sting of societal disapproval. Here are some books, publications, and organizations that can help women at home feel confident in their choice.

Hunter, B. 1991. *Home by Choice: Understanding the Enduring Effects of a Mother's Love.* Sisters, OR: Multnomah Books.

Fox, I., & Lobsenz, N.M. 1996. *Being There: The Benefits of a Stay-at-Home Parent.* Hauppauge, NY: Barron's Educational Services.

Friberg, S. 1979. *Every Child's Birthright: In Defense of Mothering.* New York: Bantam Books. (This wonderful book is out of print, but many libraries have it.)

Jones, F., & Jones, A. 1998. *Come Home to Your Family: How Families Can Survive and Thrive on One Income.* Buffalo, NY: General Distribution Services, Inc.

Ramming, C. 1996. *A Mother's Work: A Guilt-Free Guide for the Stay-at-Home Mom.* New York: Avon Books.

Family and Home Network (Publishers of *Welcome Home*): www.familyandhome.org

La Leche League International: www.lalecheleague.org

Mothering magazine: www.mothering.com

CHAPTER 6

Less Work for Mother: Lightening Your Load at Home

Forty years ago, Betty Friedan wrote that women need to be liberated from housework. Looking at our lives now, I have to ask: Have women been liberated from housework? I think you know the answer. The type of work mothers do has dramatically changed over the past 100 years. However, the sheer number of hours that women devote to child and home care has remained constant, ranging from forty-nine to fifty-six hours a week (Schor, 1992). What's going on? Why are mothers continuing to work so hard?

In some ways, it's easy to see why mothers work hard at home. Home is where you feed and clothe your family, nurture your relationships, exercise and sleep, and entertain yourself. Home is where you handle the mountain of paperwork that comes through your hands each day. It is where you launch projects, celebrate special occasions, and offer hospitality to guests. And, you are probably shouldering most of this load.

Since the original edition of this book came out, I've had lots of conversations with mothers about housework. Based on these conversations, I ended up writing two books on organization--*The Well-Ordered Home* and *The Well-Ordered Office*--in an attempt to lessen the amount of work that women do. I've noticed that when women make their household work easier, their stress levels go way down. In this chapter, I'll describe some basic organization techniques and other strategies to help lighten your load at home. But first, I want to discuss why household work tends to be thought of as mothers' work.

Mothers and the Second Shift

When I was an undergraduate, I remember having impassioned class discussions about how men and women should share child and home care. Nobody thought this was a bad idea; in fact, my classmates, would probably still say the same thing. The reality in many homes, however, is much different. In many families, men do far less work at home than women, even when the women are employed outside the home. Sometimes couples start out equally sharing the work, only to fall into rigid sex roles after having children (Crittenden, 2001).

Sociologist Arlie Hochshild (1989) refers to the work women do at home as the "second shift" (the first shift is their jobs). Mothers who are employed often come home to dirty houses, piles of laundry, and hungry families. A recent study demonstrated that this is a substantial source of stress for women. The researchers in this study compared the blood pressure of employed men with children and employed women with children. Men's blood pressure dropped once they got home, but women's blood pressure did not. Home functioned as a haven for men in the study, but not for women (Marco et al., 2000).

At-home mothers can also face a second shift. They spend much of their day tending to their kids' needs. Some days, it's an accomplishment just to take a shower and get dressed. When their partners come home, at-home moms often use this time to prepare dinner, do the laundry, go grocery shopping, or clean the house.

Single mothers have an even larger second shift. They face raising children, being the breadwinner, and caring for a home alone. Single mothers, in particular, can feel overwhelmed by all the tasks that need to be done.

The Paradox of the Laborsaving Device

In chapter 4, I described what the advent of laborsaving devices did to women's work at home. These machines were supposed to free up lots of time for mothers. What we now realize, of course, is that these devices simply changed the nature of the work without necessarily reducing the time it takes to accomplish the task. Ruth Schwartz Cowan, in *More Work for Mother* (1983), gives perhaps the best analysis of why machines do not necessarily free up time and why mothers continue to work so hard. Below are three of her examples.

The first example is the stove. She noted that when women cooked on an open hearth, meals were relatively simple. Women did the cooking, but men and children split and gathered the firewood. "When wood cook stoves became the norm, women still cooked, but men only needed to provide half the amount wood. Stoves were laborsaving devices, but the labor they saved was male" (p. 61). Once gas and electric stoves were introduced, men's participation in cooking completely disappeared, but women still cooked. Moreover, since it was now possible to cook several things at once, meals became more complex and women spent more time overall cooking.

The second example Schwartz Cowan gave was clothing. The advent of mass-produced cloth meant that women no longer needed to spin, men no longer needed to weave, nor children to card. But, women still needed to sew. Middle-class women hired seamstresses or had servants who assisted in sewing. But, with the advent of the sewing machine, middle-class women began sewing for their families alone. Once manufactured clothing was widely available, women were still the ones primarily responsible for the purchase and upkeep of their families' clothing. Now, time is spent shopping, washing, mending, taking items to the dry cleaners, and, sometimes, ironing.

The refrigerator also had an impact on women's daily work. Women no longer needed to shop every day and men no longer needed to haul ice. But, the refrigerator put door-to-door vendors out of business. Women began going to large self-service supermarkets, spending more time shopping and traveling to and from the store. Large stores mean many more choices and much further to walk. The net result is that shopping for food takes substantially more time than it did when food was delivered to women's doors.

Schwartz Cowan points out that although some of women's tasks have changed, women are still responsible for cooking meals, tending children, nursing the sick, and buying and maintaining clothing--a fact little changed by the forces of industrialization. Laborsaving devices do not necessarily save time, but they increase our expectations of what mothers should accomplish.

Strategies to Lighten Your Load

Chances are, you put in many hours on home and childcare. Throughout the rest of this chapter, I'll offer some suggestions to help bring your workload to a more manageable level. I recommend three strategies: analyze what you are doing and eliminate any unnecessary tasks; streamline tasks that remain; and share the load with other people, including your partner, your children, and professionals.

Analyze and Eliminate Tasks

Let's start at the beginning by examining how you spend your time at home. Are there any tasks you can eliminate? Before you say "no," I'd encourage you to keep an open mind. Creative solutions often come after a period of brainstorming when you uncritically consider all possible ideas. Allow for the possibility that you could actually drop some tasks.

Inventory Your Activities

In order for you to be able to drop some tasks, you first need to have a realistic sense of how much you do. Start by paying attention to all the activities that fill your days. You might find it helpful to write down everything that you do for at least one week. If you're not sure where to start, take a look at the list in chapter 3 (under Impossible Job). You may feel that your to-do list never gets any shorter and that what you've actually accomplished is never quite enough. But, when you write it down, I suspect you will be amazed at how much you actually do accomplish.

Once you have your list in hand, consider each activity and ask yourself whether it needs to be done. If you are saying yes to every item, try another approach. Ask yourself what would be the worst thing that could happen if you didn't do it. The answers may surprise you.

You should also include kid things on this list. As I described in chapter 1, you may want to let your children participate in activities that will make them well-rounded and give them future opportunities. But, in many communities, extracurricular activities have gotten way out of hand. Mothers can spend every night of the week driving to lessons, sport practices and games, and other activities. The amount of time involved grows as you add children. Consider limiting the number of outside activities your children participate in. It will save you time and help your children learn to strike a balance between enough and too much. Relationships in your family tend to improve when you actually have time to talk with each other instead of rushing off each afternoon or evening.

The choices you make are personal. The solution that works well for my family may not work for yours. I've even found that what worked for me five years ago no longer works because the needs of my family have changed. Realize, too, that deciding to eliminate an obligation from your list doesn't necessarily mean that you have to eliminate it today; for example, your children may need to finish out the season before they withdraw. Whatever you decide, I encourage you to be flexible and experiment to find solutions you can live with.

Develop Realistic Standards: Aim for "Clean Enough"

Another area where you can probably eliminate some tasks is in housecleaning. Like anything else, cleanliness can be taken too far. Your home is for you and your family to live in. I recommend that you aim for the goal of "clean enough." What does that mean? After a certain point, cleanliness is largely a matter of preference. I suggest you use two criteria to hit a level that is good for you. The first criterion is level of organization. Can you find what you need without thrashing around? Do bills get paid on time? Is there an orderly flow of mail and other paper? Do you have a way to track appointments for your family? Can you consistently find your keys, clean underwear, or your glasses? Are you usually well stocked on items like toilet paper, toothpaste, or milk? If not, becoming more organized will help a lot.

The second criterion is level of cleanliness. A certain minimum standard is necessary for health and safety. After that, "clean" is also subjective. If you invite people over, are you able to relax and enjoy them, or do you wish they would turn around so you can vacuum the rug? Does it take days to get your home in shape for guests? If so, you are unlikely to have company (and you'll be too exhausted to enjoy them). Think about how you can get your home to be clean enough for you to enjoy without exhausting yourself. Don Aslett's book *No Time to Clean* (2000) has a lot of great suggestions including a list of cleaning tasks you can eliminate.

If you are cleaning and organizing beyond the point of "clean enough," you can probably do less. I'll give you some suggestions in the next section to get you started. And, you might want to read my other book, *The Well-Ordered Home* (Kendall-Tackett, 2003b).

Streamline Your Tasks

Once you have eliminated some tasks, consider whether the ones that are left could be done more efficiently. In most cases, the answer is probably yes. The good news is that organizational skills can be learned. I spent many years of my adult life being domestically challenged. If I can learn, so can you. Below are some steps to get you started. I would also encourage you to read some of the books listed at the end of this chapter for more detailed suggestions.

Analyze the Situation

According to professional organizer Julie Morgenstern (1998), the first step in any organizational scheme is to figure out where you're having problems. Are you always losing keys? Is your morning routine a disaster? Do you buy duplicates when you can't find stuff or because you don't realize what you have? Pick your worst situation, and start there first. Resist the temptation to say "everything."

Once you've figured out what you want to change, try mentally walking through the problem to see if you can come up with a solution. If you lose your keys, think about what door you usually use when you come into your home. Would it help if you had a key rack right next to that door? If you tend to have lots of books and magazines next to your bed, would a bookshelf or end table with drawers help? Think about what you actually do now rather than what you "should" do. If your organizational efforts are based on shoulds, it will be much harder to develop a system that works for you.

Get Rid of Clutter

Once you've identified some challenging areas, it's time to get rid of some stuff that may be clogging your home. Clutter can dramatically increase the time you spend cleaning. It takes longer to clean if every surface is covered with knickknacks, and your rooms are overflowing with furniture. Other tasks take longer too. Working in a crammed kitchen is unpleasant and wastes time. Trying to put clothes away in a too-full dresser drawer is a pain. Adding more toys to the three-foot mound is frustrating.

Look around. Is it time to get rid of some possessions? I'm not suggesting you give away your favorite things or your memories. But, are there items that are broken? Can they be fixed, or do they need to be replaced or even eliminated? Are there items you don't need that someone else can use? Do you have clothing in four different sizes in your closet?

As you get rid of clutter, I want to alert you to a pitfall that can undermine your efforts. Julie Morgenstern calls it "zigzagging." Here's an example of what she means. You start going through a drawer, only to find a book that belongs on the bookshelf. You discover the bookshelf is a mess. You start working on it, only to discover something that belongs upstairs. So, you return that item to where it belongs. Next thing you know, you're working on the closet in your bedroom. By day's end, you have half-completed projects all over the house, but haven't finished anything! Instead, try tackling one project at a time. When you find stuff that belongs elsewhere, set it aside in a box or a pile. When you have finished the project you are working on, take the accumulated items and put them away. In the process, note any other areas that need your attention. One of these areas might be your next organization project. There are many excellent books to help you declutter, but my all-time favorite is Don Aslett's *Clutter's Last Stand* (1984).

Respect Your Work Spaces

Respecting your workspaces will make it faster and easier for you to work, and will encourage others to work, too. Pay particular attention to the kitchen and laundry areas, but the principles apply to any area of your home. Respecting your work spaces means thinking through the kind of work that takes place there and then making any changes you need to make your workspaces more suited to your needs.

The first step in respecting your workspaces is to eliminate all clutter from your work areas. This, all by itself, will make a real difference. The kitchen is often a place that gets really decorated. Resist this temptation, and try to limit your decorations--especially on your counter tops. Try to keep your counters clear, and be judicious about wall decorations. The kitchen and bath have a lot of moist heat that combines with dust to make gunk. Everything in these rooms should be very cleanable. The fewer items laying about, the fewer you have to clean.

Your laundry area can also be a trouble spot. The laundry area often becomes the depository of loose change, missing socks, odds and ends of clothing, and pocket contents. To make this space more workable, have a trash can handy and a bin for transporting loose articles to other places in the house. Also, try to arrange this space so you have somewhere to fold clothes if you can, it will make laundry much easier for you.

Second, make sure everything you need is at hand. Any job becomes more onerous when it is accompanied by frantic searching. It's also easier to procrastinate or never do something if you have to go to another room to get what you need. Think about the supplies and tools you need in each area, and make sure that they are available.

Third, think about your physical comfort. Is there enough light? We think about lighting a lot more in kitchens, but laundry areas frequently have very poor light. Adequate light will make your work area more pleasant and your work easier to do. Consider temperature. Is the area too hot or too cold? Your work will seem much more pleasant if the temperature is comfortable. Also, if you are doing a lot of standing, especially on a cement slab or tiled floor, think about getting an anti-fatigue mat from a janitor supply store. This can make a very big difference in how your legs and back feel.

Make It Easy to Clean

Since cleaning can occupy a significant portion of your time, you owe it to yourself to make it as easy as possible. One strategy is to keep your cleaning supplies where you need them. If, for example, you have to make a special trip to the cleaning closet, guess what happens? You put it off. But, if you have your supplies handy, you can take a quick pass and be finished in a few minutes. Having your supplies where you need them will help you use little odd bits of time, like during commercials, rather than needing to dedicate special time to, say, cleaning the bathroom. Similarly, keep vacuum cleaners near where you need them. If you live in a multistory house, you might consider a vacuum cleaner for each floor. I also keep cleaning supplies I use for my car in my car. I can use little bits of time to keep the inside of my car clean and rarely have to set aside a special time for this purpose.

Having your supplies handy is only one half of the equation. The second is to use good quality cleaning supplies. Good-quality cleaning supplies make an amazing difference. For very little money, you can get supplies that will save you hours, including concentrated cleaners you mix yourself, window squeegees, a good vacuum cleaner, and decent cleaning rags. This is another way to respect your workspace. Your time is too valuable to waste it using substandard tools, especially for tasks you do every day. Fortunately, well-made cleaning tools are relatively inexpensive in janitor supply or home improvement stores or online (try Don Aslett's Clean Report, www.cleanreport.com) and they will pay you back many fold.

Finally, consider whether you really need to clean as much as you do. Truth be told, cleaning too much is generally not our problem. But, there might be areas where you do too much. Sometimes, the best solution is not to clean at all or to do it less frequently. You might even think about replacing things in your home that seem to require a lot of care.

Is Housework Beneath You?

One final barrier to becoming more organized at home might have to do with your thoughts about housework. A century's worth of denigrating domestic work has had an insidious effect; many young women I meet are of the opinion that housework is beneath them. They assume that housework is not for "smart" women, and one way to show that you are smart is to be domestically challenged. These young women rightly reject the image of the woman at home who obsesses about whether her sheets are white enough. Yet, they overlook the fact that everyone needs to eat and have their clothes cleaned occasionally. Unless you are very wealthy and can pay for all of these services, it is in your best interest to develop at least basic proficiency in domestic tasks. Having a home that runs smoothly can have a positive impact on every member of your family. In her book *The Time Bind* (1997), Arlie Hochschild observes, with some alarm, that many women she interviewed were working longer hours to avoid going home! A smoothly running home can even increase your willingness to be around members of your own family.

And, there are other benefits. Let's think about your morning routine. Instead of frantically running around and looking for lost keys/ schoolbooks/shoes, how would it be if everyone ate breakfast and calmly went out for the day? Do you think that this might influence the quality of your children's day? How about yours? A smoothly running home can do this.

Order also makes it easier, and more likely, that your family will clean up after themselves. People are more apt to put things away when there is a place to put them, and if they don't have to fight with the contents of a drawer or cupboard every time they open it. Even young children can learn where to put things away if you clearly mark locations (such as drawers or shelves). And with that said, we now move to my final suggestion: sharing the load.

Share the Load

You'll notice the title of this section is not "Getting Others to Help." That would imply that child and home care are your sole responsibility and that others are helping you out.

As I mentioned, in most families, mothers do take on the majority of the domestic work. Sometimes that is by conscious choice. You may be a mother at home, and you and your partner may have decided that it makes sense for you to handle things on the home front. If that is working for you, then by all means keep doing it. However, many times mothers do the majority of the domestic work because it is *assumed* that they should. This is where problems start for it is not a fair arrangement. I firmly believe that everyone who lives in your home should participate in its upkeep. But, that's often easier said than done. Trying to get others to participate does not happen overnight. I wish I could tell you some magic phrase that would make everyone want to pitch in right now. Of course, there is none.

You might wonder why you have to initiate this change. The most obvious reason is that your own behavior is the only behavior that you can completely control. Another is that if you've been doing most or all of the work, others have no stake in changing the status quo; change means more work for them. In this section, I describe three ways others can share the load, including your partner, your children, and outside help.

Chore Wars: The Gender Gap in Child and Home Care

Women at home full-time spend approximately fifty hours a week in child and home care. Employed women spend about thirty-five hours a week in these same activities. In contrast, men on average spend slightly less than eleven hours per week, with husbands of employed women spending approximately ten minutes extra per day and men with small children another ten minutes (Schwartz Cowan, 1983). A commentary in *Business Week* indicates that this may have changed slightly, with men putting in around fourteen hours a week (Hammonds, 1998). Crittenden (2001) noted that men rarely do more than 30% of the household work--even when they are unemployed.

The gender gap in housework is often fodder for comedians. Men, we're told, have an impaired cleaning gene. Their idea of cleaning the bathroom might include flushing the toilet and picking up a few things. All kidding aside, the issue of who cleans the house and takes care of the kids is a major source of family strife. Relationships have ended over who takes out the garbage.

A survey in *Ladies' Home Journal* online asked: "Given the chance to improve your husband, would you opt to make him a better lover, or would you rather he did more around the house?" Sixteen percent of respondents wanted a husband who performed better in bed. A full 46% wanted a husband who would make the bed (Johnson, 2000).

Sometimes, men think that they are doing half the work. That's what Arlie Hochschild found in *The Second Shift* (1989). Men in her study thought that their responsibilities included taking care of the car, yard, and money, killing spiders, and barbecuing. Their wives' responsibilities were basically everything else. The men honestly believed they were doing half.

Schwartz Cowan (1983) made a similar observation. She found that men's self-assigned jobs included taking out the trash, mowing the lawn, playing with the children, painting or fixing things, and occasionally shopping for household durables. Men typically do not do laundry, clean, or cook. They also frequently do not feed, clothe, bathe, or transport children—the very tasks that can eat up a lot of your time. The good news is that most of these tasks can be shared with a partner.

Sometimes, lack of willingness to share chores reflects a deeper problem in the relationship. In this case, it's time to consider professional counseling. But, the chore wars can become a major issue in any family. Below, I've listed some suggestions for seeking detente.

Recognize Expectations and Cognitive Distortions

Everyone operates under assumptions that they probably aren't aware of, and these can color your views of domestic work. These assumptions include your sense of fairness, what you believe about men's versus women's work, your religious and cultural beliefs, and your memories of the way things were done in your family of origin. Not only do you probably have expectations about sex roles for various tasks, but you have ideas about the way things are done. You may honestly believe that "everyone" does a particular task the way you do and that any other way is "stupid." Your partner may have the same beliefs about his approach. There may have been certain routines or rituals in your family of origin that you assumed were common to everyone. When your partner unwittingly violates one of these rules, you may then read too much into his behavior.

These issues may have come up before you had children. But, they may be particularly salient now that you have children and the workload has dramatically increased, as Ron describes:

> The biggest roadblock Sarah and I ever hit was the difference in styles when doing chores. My mother-in-law did things differently than my mom. They weren't necessarily wrong or bad, but I did find them difficult to adjust to.

Sometimes issues like leaving the cap off the toothpaste are blown massively out of proportion because of our expectations. As I described in chapter 2, cognitive distortions can lead to a wide variety of problems. For example, a messy room may become "proof" that your partner does not care about you. Kate describes her and her husband's different standards of cleanliness:

> Some things are important to me and not to him. He can sit and read on a bed where the sheets haven't been washed for three months. And, he never buys shampoo; if we run out, he just uses soap.

Stefan, her husband, describes the household tasks he is responsible for:

> Kate would probably eat Cheerios every night, so I usually cook. If I crave pasta, I buy the stuff and make it (Johnson, 2000).

127

It's important to be aware of situations when you might be influenced by cognitive distortions. For example, anytime you find yourself saying "never" or "always" (as in "he never helps"), it is a clue that you might be engaging in all-or-nothing thinking. When you are feeling calmer, ask yourself if it is really true that he "never helps." Perhaps he doesn't help enough, but it is rarely helpful to discount the work that he is already doing.

Seek a Solution or Compromise

Sometimes you really do have different standards and are going to have to come to a compromise to bring peace to your home. Have a conversation about a particular issue when you are calm, and try to adopt a problem-solving approach. For example, if leaving the lid off the toothpaste tube drives you crazy, can you get toothpaste that has a built-in lid? If dirty clothes on the bathroom floor are a problem, can you put a hamper in that room? If the dining room table gets covered with junk mail and other stuff, can you put a container near where your family comes into your home to collect these items? Try to be concrete about what is bothering each of you and what you each need. If you and your partner are clear about what your needs and expectations are, then you are in a better position to find a solution.

Corral the Mess

Corralling the mess is one strategy that can work well in areas that need compromise. Basically, you let someone be as messy as they want-- within a confined space. For example, you may agree to not touch each other's home offices. You may request that he put clothes on a single chair in your room rather than on the floor. You may agree to keep the living room tidy most of the time, but let the family room have a more lived-in look. It's also helpful to have a container or basket available in places where odds and ends accumulate, such as the kitchen, laundry area, entryway, or (in our house) the top of the stairs.

Beware the Witching Hour

Whether you are home full-time or are employed, one of the most challenging hours of the day is the hour before dinner. At-home moms often long for adult conversation after taking care of young children all day. Or, they may yearn for some quiet time alone. Employed moms come home to mountains of chores, dinner that needs to be prepared, and homework that needs to be supervised. Partners returning from work at this time may also desperately want some time to decompress. Children are often at their most needy during this time as well. Efforts toward preventing family strife during the witching hour will pay big dividends. Every family must come up with a plan that works for them, but here are some possibilities.

If you are employed, you might find that it works well for you to sit and relax when you first get home. Even twenty minutes can help. Use this time to reconnect with your children or have some quiet time alone or with your partner. If you are an at-home mother, you might find it helpful to do most of the dinner preparations earlier in the day so that you will not be dealing with cranky children when you feel most frazzled. Have snacks ready to keep everyone from dissolving with hunger. Perhaps you can hire a teenager to help for a couple of hours, or trade dinner preparations with another mother. Think about keeping a stock of easy-to-prepare meals available so that others can pitch in. Be creative and try some different approaches. Every little bit helps.

Getting Kids to Do Their Chores

It's important to involve children from a young age in caring for your home. Again, there is no magic formula here, but two of the best plans I've seen are in Stephen Covey's *The Seven Habits of Highly Effective People* (1989) and Don Aslett's *No Time to Clean* (2000). Both authors are fathers of large families and obviously speak from a wealth of experience. I will summarize their suggestions here, but if you would like additional information, I encourage you to read their books.

Teach by Example

Perhaps the best way to encourage kids to do their chores is through example. Instead of simply telling them to do something, offer to do it with them. Perhaps they are dawdling because they don't know what they are supposed to do. Maybe they are resisting because there is no place to put anything away. Or, perhaps being sent to clean their rooms just seems too isolating and feels like a punishment. You could probably do your kids' chores faster yourself, but in the long run, it is better to teach them to do the work themselves. And, they are more likely to comply when doing chores means they have some one-on-one time with you or dad.

Make Chores Easy and Fun

Children are more likely to do chores if they are easy to do. Isn't this true for all of us? Making chores easy means having supplies they need at hand and making sure they have a place to put things away. For young children, clearly indicate where they are supposed to put their possessions. Use pictures if they cannot yet read. Also, make sure that they have a convenient trash can, one large enough that it doesn't tip over, and an accessible laundry hamper.

Consider whether any of the chores you want your child to do are too hard. For example, if you want your child to make his bed, ask yourself whether there are too many blankets and pillows. Is the bedspread heavy? Is the bed hard to get to because it is too close to the wall or other furniture? If you want him to put away his clothes, ask yourself whether the bar in the closet is too high? Is it difficult for him to use hangers, and would pegs work better? Are the drawers clearly marked? (This is more important for younger children.) Is there a place for dirty clothes? Try to look at each job from your child's perspective.

Making chores easy for your child might also mean that you have to sort some possessions. I once read that by the time American children are five, they will have five times their body weight in toys. Most kids can part with some toys, especially those they have outgrown. When they are young, you'll probably need to do the sorting yourself, since young children rarely want to part with anything. As children mature, involve them in the act of giving to others who may not have as much. This is a wonderful opportunity for a life lesson. You might also consider letting them have a yard sale, from which they keep the proceeds. Your initial or periodic investment of time making chores easier for children will pay off with faster subsequent cleanups that the children can do themselves.

Finally, think creatively about making each chore fun. One mother used to toss a handful of change in the dishwater each night. The child whose turn it was to wash dishes got to keep the change at the bottom of the sink. Her children could hardly wait until it was their turn to help with the dishes. Think about how fun might be helpful at your house.

Let Them Experience the Consequences

Sometimes, children don't learn to take responsibility for their chores because their mothers bail them out and do the job for them. For example, mothers may continue to do their children's laundry even after they agree that their children should take this task over. If you let your children experience a day with no clean socks or underwear, they'll be more likely to make sure their laundry is done in the future (although some kids won't mind at all!). This strategy especially works for older children or teens.

Counselor Kevin Leman (1987) describes the effective use of consequences in a case of a single mother and her teenage son and daughter. After a family meeting, mom and the teens agreed that the teens should start dinner each night. But, she kept coming home, night after night, to kids on the phone or playing video games, and no dinner started. Her counselor then suggested that if dinner was not started when she returned home, she was to pick up her purse and go out to dinner-- alone. There was adequate food in the house, so she knew her children would not starve. After three nights of this, her children got the message and started preparing dinner every night.

Some Mistakes We Make

As mothers, we can make it less likely that our children will participate in home care by our actions. For example, you may labor under the belief that you must do everything for your children. Sometimes, this belief comes from your particular cultural or ethnic heritage or the way that you were raised. Your mother may have done everything for you, so you try to emulate her. Conversely, your home life growing up may have been chaotic, so you do everything for your kids in an attempt to be different. Mothers at home may do it all because "what else do they have to do"? Employed mothers may do it all because they feel guilty about not being around more.

Some mothers even think that it is bad for children to have to do chores. If you feel this way, let me propose an alternative view. Eventually, your children will leave your home. Are you doing them a service by letting them think that clean laundry appears in their drawers as if by magic? That food automatically appears in the cupboard? Won't they be better prepared for life if they know how to take care of themselves? If that doesn't persuade you, consider this: What do your actions tell your children about women if you are always the one who picks up after others?

Another common mistake mothers make is to be too critical of their children's efforts. If you did something, only to have someone come along and do it over, would it make you more or less likely to offer to do it in the future? While it is nice to have standards, you have to be careful about how you enforce them. This is your home, not Marine boot camp. If a job is not done to your satisfaction, see if you can figure out why. Perhaps you need to more fully explain what you want. Perhaps it is too hard to do. Remember that you have a dual focus when you ask a child to work around the house: getting the work done and training the child.

Trading Money for Time: Paying for Help

This final suggestion can be a great adjunct to your work at home. My husband and I are avid do-it-yourselfers. Living in a house that is almost

200 years old gives us lots of opportunities to do things ourselves. But, we have discovered that there are many times when it makes sense to pay someone else to do a job. Over the years, we have paid for services ranging from housecleaning to meal preparation to shopping to home improvement. We have also done all these things ourselves.

By purchasing services, you are trading money for time. Sometimes, paying for services can cost many times more than it would if you did the job yourself. But, the cost can be equal or even less when the person providing the service has the equipment and/or the skill to do the job faster and better than you could. Make conscious choices about buying services, and you'll most likely find that doing so can really help in lightening your load.

Paying for help may involve either hiring a person or paying for a service that other people have provided. I would even include things like prepared food in this category, whether it is frozen, canned, or from a restaurant. During one lengthy lupus flare, I learned to keep some prepared foods on hand for days when I am not feeling well. Although prepared foods are more expensive than those I could make myself, they are still substantially cheaper than going out to eat. And, they are easier for someone else to make.

When considering whether to purchase a service, think not only about its cost, but about the time involved in acquiring the service. The time you save may not be significant if you must drive to drop off and pick up people or items. Similarly, if you must wait around for a person you hired, the time you save may be negligible. Consider also what your feelings are about the task. You or your partner may hate a task so much that you want to hire it out. Even if it costs more and doesn't save a lot of time, hiring a professional might still be worth it. These are decisions that you will have to make.

When we first moved into our old house, I was overwhelmed by the huge amount of painting we needed to do. I decided to hire someone to do part of it, then the rest seemed much more manageable. One of my friends is home with four small children. She has recently decided to pay someone to clean her house once a month since it is almost impossible for her to get any housework done during the day. I think it is a great idea! Here's a partial list of services you can purchase. New services are available all the time.

Prepared foods
Cleaning (maintenance or big job)
Child or elder care
Boxing and shipping packages
Yard care
Laundry
Pet care
Personal shopping
Home repair or maintenance
Sewing
Carpool
Errands
Clerical work
Money services (banking, bookkeeping, paying bills, figuring taxes)
Organization

What You Can Do

Throughout this chapter, I've offered specific suggestions to help you lighten your load at home. In closing, I'd like to offer a few more that will help you bring all this information together.

Start Small

If you have never tried to change your work at home before, you may find that you are overwhelmed by the information in this chapter. Don't be discouraged. Rome was not built in a day; it can take weeks or even months to get a good organization plan in place. As your needs change, you may find that you have to periodically update what you have done.

You can't do it all at once, but you can start by fixing one problem. It may take some time before things seem different for you, but every step you take moves you closer to your goal. Start with a task you do every day. Then, you will see that your efforts are paying off.

Be Flexible

As you think about dividing up some of your work, try not to think within the parameters of strict sex roles. For example, don't assume that handling money or home repair (or killing spiders) are jobs for men. You might be much better at these tasks than your partner. Along these lines, think about tasks that you like, are neutral about, or hate. You may have jobs you hate that your partner doesn't mind. A swap makes good sense. If you both hate a task, this might be a good one to hire out. Use talent and preference as your criteria rather than rules about who "should" be doing the task.

Take Time to Enjoy the Fruits of Your Labors

Sometimes, we start living for our homes rather than in them. With limited time and a crushing workload, this is easy to do. One of the reasons to lighten your load at home is to give you more time to spend with people you love. Make sure that you are not freeing up time just so you can do more work. Take the time to enjoy yourself.

For Further Reading

A number of very helpful books on the market will help you lighten your load at home. Here are some favorites organized by type. Happy reading!

Books about Making Your Home a More Inviting Place

These wonderful books all have great suggestions that cost little money.

Breathnach, S.B. 1995. *Simple Abundance: A Daybook of Comfort and Joy.* New York: Warner Books.

Kendall-Tackett, K.A. 2003. *The Well-Ordered Home: Organizing Tips for Inviting Serenity into Your Life.* Oakland, CA: New Harbinger Publications.

Moran, V. 1997. *Shelter for the Spirit.* New York: HarperPerennial.

Schaeffer, E. 1971. *The Hidden Art of Homemaking: Creative Ideas for Enriching Everyday Life.* Wheaton, IL: Tyndale House.

Stoddard, A. 1992. *Creating a Beautiful Home.* New York: Avon Books.

Stoddard, A. 1988. *Living a Beautiful Life: 500 Ways to Add Elegance, Order, Beauty and Joy to Every Day of Your Life.* New York: Morrow.

Resources for Household Organization

These resources have excellent strategies for becoming more organized and thinking through the best solutions for you.

Hemphill, B. 1998. *Taming the Paper Tiger at Home.* Washington, D.C.: Kiplinger Books.

Kendall-Tackett, K.A. 2003. *The Well-Ordered Home: Organizing Tips for Inviting Serenity into Your Life.* Oakland, CA: New Harbinger Publications.

Kendall-Tackett, K.A. 2005. *The Well-Ordered Office: How to Create an Efficient and Serene Workspace.* Oakland, CA: New Harbinger Publications.

Morgenstern, J. 1998. *Organizing from the Inside Out.* New York: Henry Holt and Company.

Editors of Real Simple. 2004. *Real Simple: The Organized Home.* New York: Time Inc.

Starr, M. 2003. *Home Organizing Workbook: Clearing Clutter, Step by Step.* San Francisco: Chronicle Books.

Essortment: http://www.essortment.com/in/Home.Organizing/

Fly Lady: http://www.flylady.net/

Home & Garden TV:
www.hgtv.com/hgtv/ah_organizing_storage/0,1800,HGTV_
3142,00.html_

MommyTips: www.mommytips.com/mt/Moms/Home/Organizing/

Organized Home: www.organizedhome.com

Resources for Streamlining Home Care

For helpful books on how to cut down on cleaning, Don Aslett is king. These books can save you hours. They are inspiring, funny, and very practical. He also has a mail-order cleaning-supply business (The Clean Report), and you can order his books from there, too.

Aslett, D. 1984. *Clutter's Last Stand.* Cincinnati: Writer's Digest Books.
Aslett, D. 1992. *Is There Life After Housework?* Cincinnati: Writer's Digest Books.
Aslett, D. 2000. *No Time To Clean.* Pocatello, ID: Marsh Creek Press.
Aslett, D., & Aslett Simons, L. 1995. *Make Your House Do the Housework.* Cincinnati: Better Way Books.
Don Aslett's Clean Report: www.cleanreport.com

Resources for Involving Children in Home Care

These two books have great advice on involving children in the care of your home. Both are good reading in any case. These web sites also have good information and products.

Aslett, D. 2000. *No Time to Clean.* Pocatello, ID: Marsh Creek Press.
Covey, S.R. 1989. *The Seven Habits of Highly Effective People.* New York: Fireside.
OrganizedHome.com: www.organizedhome.com
   (This site has some great information on how to get kids to do chores)
The Well-Ordered Life: www.theWellOrderedLife.com

CHAPTER 7
Tough Beginnings: Making Peace With Your Birth Experience

I often make presentations to health care providers about how birth can affect women's emotional health. These presentations always strike a chord with the women in the audience, and many wait afterwards to tell me about their experiences. Invariably, at least one woman will tell me about a highly traumatic birth, often comparing her experience to rape. These conversations tell me that women not only remember their births, but that these experiences, especially if negative, have long-lasting effects.

I first noticed the connection between birth experiences and depression when interviewing women for a book on postpartum depression. Even though many women were relating stories to me of difficult births, a surprising number of health care professionals minimize the impact of birth experiences. An editor of a prestigious journal in obstetrics once told me that negative birth experiences were a thing of the past, especially with the recent implementation of "family-centered care." One week after our conversation, I interviewed a mother who had had a cesarean section with failed epidural anesthesia. She could feel everything and screamed through the entire operation. Since talking with her, I've talked with several other women who have had similar experiences. Nursing researcher Cheryl Beck also noted a similar disconnect between what women in her study on birth trauma experienced and their doctors' perceptions of events.

Portions of this chapter appeared in a magazine article entitled Making Peace with Your Birth Experience, 2002, *New Beginnings*, 19, 44-47.

> Whereas some of the mothers in this study felt as if they had been raped, the clinicians appeared to the women as oblivious to their plight. The mothers perceived that the clinicians focused only on the successful outcomes of clinical efficiency and live, healthy infants (Beck, 2004a, p. 34).

Given the potential negative impact of a difficult birth, you might be wondering how often they occur. One study tried to find out. The researchers found that negative birth experiences were remarkably common. In a national survey of over 1,100 American mothers ages 18 to 80, 60% described their births in mostly positive terms or in terms such as "difficult, but worth it." More troubling were the 40% who described their births in predominantly negative terms. Fourteen percent of these women described their births as "peak negative experiences"--one of the worst experiences of their lives. The narrative accounts painted an even more vivid picture. Some of these mothers wrote that their experiences had been so bad that they decided not to have any more children (Genevie & Margolies, 1985).

Recently, several studies have noted that women can develop post-traumatic stress disorder (PTSD) after birth. Beck (2004b) reviewed this literature and noted that the PTSD rates ranged from 1.5% to 6% of women in the samples. Those are appalling statistics! By way of comparison, the rate of PTSD in citizens of lower Manhattan after September 11th was 7.5%. This means that the percentage of women who had PTSD after birth was only slightly lower than those who had been close bystanders to a terrorist attack (Galea et al., 2003). You should also know that the study with the 1.5% rate excluded women who had had previous episodes of either depression or PTSD--the women most vulnerable to having PTSD after birth.

What Makes an Experience Negative?

Some births seem really bad to outside observers and yet mothers feel positively about them. Other women have births that seem "perfect" on paper, yet the mothers are deeply troubled. What makes the difference?

Health care providers are often mystified about why this occurs. An obstetrician at one of my recent talks asked this very question, giving examples of two women in his practice. The first woman had a "crash C-section" following placenta previa--a potentially life-threatening obstetric complication. Despite the emergency nature of her birth, she felt positively about the experience. The second mother had a birth that the OB thought was great. Yet, she thought it was bad.

I believe part of the reason for this confusion is that providers are often seeking to define "good" and "bad" in terms of objective characteristics: length of labor, use of pain medications, medical interventions, and type of delivery. Researchers, by and large, have done the same thing. Indeed, the most typical way that researchers have considered the question of negative birth experiences is to compare women's reactions to cesarean versus vaginal births. They assume that vaginal deliveries are usually positive, which is certainly not always the case and that cesareans are usually negative (also not always the case). Objective factors do have some influence, but they cannot fully explain women's reactions to birth.

Cesarean versus Vaginal Deliveries

Women's reactions to cesarean births vary a great deal, but we can make some general statements. First, women are more likely to perceive cesarean births negatively than vaginal deliveries, but not in every case. Among women who have had cesarean births, the reactions are more likely to be negative if a woman was under general anesthesia, if it was an emergency (versus planned) operation, and if no support person was present (see Kendall-Tackett, 2005a & b for more detailed descriptions of this research).

Studies about whether cesarean births cause negative reactions in women have had contradictory findings. One study (Durik, Hyde, & Clark, 2000) compared women who had planned cesareans, unplanned cesareans, or vaginal deliveries, looking at quality of mother-infant interactions at 4 and 12 months postpartum. The researchers found no significant differences based on delivery type (cesarean versus vaginal). The authors concluded that cesarean births appeared to have no negative impact on women.

141

In contrast, Fisher, Astbury, and Smith (1997) found significant differences based on type of delivery in a prospective study of 272 Australian women. They found that women who had cesareans were significantly more likely to have negative moods and low self-esteem than women who delivered vaginally. The authors concluded that cesarean childbirth carries "significant psychological risks rendering those who experience these procedures vulnerable to a grief reaction or to post-traumatic distress and depression" (p. 728). The research design they used allowed them to determine that birth caused these negative reactions, and these reactions were not related to any symptoms the mothers had before they had their babies.

The Importance of Your Interpretation of Events

Rather than group women's birth experiences by objective factors, such as vaginal versus cesarean, I have found it more useful to consider women's subjective experience of events. These can help us predict who is going to have a negative reaction and what aspect of birth may have caused it. Trauma researcher Charles Figley in his book *Trauma and Its Wake* described the aspects of an event that will make it traumatic. He noted that an experience would be troubling to the extent that it is sudden, overwhelming, and dangerous. Your birth experience may have had one or more of these characteristics, and they could be influencing how you are feeling now. These same characteristics can also affect your partner.

Sudden: Did things happen quickly? Did it change from "fine" to dangerous in a short time? Did anyone have time to explain what was happening to you?

Overwhelming: Did you feel swept away by the hospital routine? Did you feel disconnected from what was happening? Did you have general anesthesia?

Dangerous: Was your delivery a medical emergency? Did you develop a life-threatening complication? Did you think you or your baby would die?

Cheryl Beck in her study of women who had traumatic deliveries also found that danger was an important predictor of negative reactions. She noted that birth trauma was likely to occur when the women perceived that they or their babies were in danger and the birthing women themselves experienced "overwhelming fear, helplessness, loss of control, or horror" (2004a, p. 28).

Researchers have identified some other subjective factors that influenced how women felt after birth. For example, Beck (2004a) found that women's perceived level of care was an important factor. If women felt cared for during their births, they were more likely to perceive them positively. In contrast, women in Beck's study described their care providers as cold, mechanical, or uncaring, and they felt degraded or raped after their experiences.

A related factor was women's sense of power and control. Women who felt like they had no control were more likely to react negatively. Perceived control can also explain why women can feel positively about an objectively difficult birth if they felt they had a say in what happened to them versus others making the decisions about their care (Kendall-Tackett, 2005a).

Beck (2004a) also noted how women in her sample were terrified by the hospital experience itself. These women trusted the hospital staff to provide safe care--trusting them not only with their lives, but the lives of their babies. They felt the doctors and nurses provided unsafe care. In summarizing these women's experiences, Beck (2004a) noted the following.

> Women who perceived that they had experienced traumatic births viewed the site of their labor and delivery as a battlefield. While engaged in battle, their protective layers were stripped away, leaving them exposed to the onslaught of birth trauma. Stripped from these women were their individuality, dignity, control, communication, caring, trust, support, and reassurance (p. 34).

143

A Tale of Two Births: One Woman's Story

In this next section, I share the story of two of Kathy's births. Each birth was difficult, but for different reasons. Both of these stories have elements that I described above. There is a fear of dying, overwhelming pain, and experiences that overpowered her. She also experienced a replaying of events after her births. Memories were often triggered by talking with other couples who had similar experiences.

When Peter was born, the birth itself was pain free. He was small, especially his head and shoulders, and it truly didn't hurt at all. I kept insisting I wasn't really in labor up until two minutes before he was born when the doctor told me to lie down, shut up, and push! He was born at 9:30 a.m. They told us he had Down syndrome at noon. By 4 p.m., I was hemorrhaging so badly that I came within two minutes of death. I had to have an emergency D & C with no anesthesia (talk about PAIN!!) and a big blood transfusion.

That night, they told us Peter needed immediate surgery and had to go to a hospital in another city--a very traumatic day, to say the least. And, then they sent me home the next day with no mention at all that I might want to talk to somebody about any of this--the Down syndrome, the near-death experience, nothing. I can still call up those memories with crystal clarity. Whenever we hear about another couple, I have to re-process those feelings. Interestingly, most of them relate to the hemorrhaging and D & C, not to the Down syndrome "news." They're all tied up together. Maybe it's good to remind myself every so often of how precious life is.

My third birth was excruciatingly painful--the baby was 9 pounds 3 ounces with severe shoulder dystocia--his head was delivered 20 minutes before his shoulders. I had some Stadol in the IV line right before transition, but that's all the pain relief I had. I thought I was going to die and lost all perspective on the fact that I was having a baby. I just tried to live through each contraction. Of course, I was flat on my back, with my feet up in stirrups, and watching the fetal monitor as I charted each contraction--I think those things should be outlawed! I know now that if I had been squatting or on my hands and knees I probably could have gotten him out much easier. I'm the one who has the giant shoulders and incredibly long arms, so I can't blame anyone else for my two babies with broad shoulders (Miranda, the first, also took several extra pushes to get her shoulders out, but she was "only" 8 pounds 1 ounce).

That night, (Alex was born at 9:00 a.m. in the morning), I could not sleep at all because every time I tried to go to sleep my brain would start re-running the tape of labor, and I would feel the pain and the fright and the fears of dying all over again. I stayed up all that night and the next day. I didn't sleep until I was home in my own bed.

In Kathy's stories, we see some classic symptoms of a post-traumatic stress response: the fear of dying, the re-experiencing of her birth, the sleeplessness. She did eventually come to a place of peace over her experiences, but the memories of those two episodes of labor have remained vivid.

Some Common Reactions

People who experience traumatic events of any kind often have similar types of reactions. After a difficult birth, you may experience a range of responses. Below are some common reactions.

Fear/Anxiety

During your labor and delivery, you may have become convinced that you or your baby would die. This reaction is remarkably common even when health care providers think your delivery is normal. A study conducted in Sweden (Ryding, Wijma & Wijma, 1998) found that 55% of the mothers in their study who had emergency cesarean deliveries intensely feared that they or their babies might die.

145

In the months immediately following your troubling birth, you may have feared anything that reminded you of your birth experience or your health care provider. You might have missed your six-week appointment and felt uncomfortable with routine medical exams. You might have trouble sleeping, or you might startle easily.

Fear can manifest as deliberately seeking out circumstances similar to your birth so you can do it "right" this time. This is a way for you to have mastery of an event that was beyond your control. You might find yourself planning "the next time" while your baby is only a few days or weeks old.

Replaying of Events

In the weeks and months following your difficult birth, you may find that you keep replaying events over and over again and that you think about your birth experience all the time. You might experience this symptom as daytime flashbacks of your birth or as nightmares. If you are experiencing this symptom, especially if it is interfering with your sleep, there are medications that can help. Talk with you doctor about it or see my book *Depression in New Mothers* (Kendall-Tackett, 2005b) for a complete description of the treatment regimen for PTSD.

You may need to talk about your experience over and over again as a way of dealing with your feelings. Beck (2004b) found that both replaying events and needing to talk were very common in the women in her study. She also found that other people in these women's lives did not want to hear about their births anymore—or at all.

Anger

Anger is another very common reaction. You may be angry at your doctor who didn't listen to what you said or who treated you in a callused way. One friend told me that her doctor sat beside her and read a book during the most difficult part of her labor. You might also be angry with some of the nurses or other hospital staff, your insurer, or the hospital. And, your birth experience may have created angry feelings between you and your partner (more on this in a moment).

Finally, you may be very angry with yourself. After a difficult experience, it is easy to play the "if only" game. You might spend a long time berating yourself for not knowing enough about the doctor or hospital, not taking the right childbirth education class, going along with routines that were not in your best interest, or not fighting harder to get the kind of birth you wanted.

Denial

Sometimes, in the wake of a negative birth, you may deny that your experience was bad. There can be many reasons for this. You may have worked hard to have a vaginal birth after cesarean (VBAC), for example, only to find that it too had aspects that were less than perfect. You may have bonded with your doctor or the nurses and don't want to consider that they did some bad things. You may have had a premature baby or one with an illness or disability. You may have had enough to cope with right then and couldn't take the time to reflect on your birth. These feelings may hit you months or even years after the fact.

Depression

Depending on the severity of your experience, you might have become depressed in the weeks or months following your traumatic birth. If you have had other traumatic events in your life such as childhood abuse, you are at increased risk for becoming depressed or having PTSD in the wake of a difficult birth.

Even without a history of other traumatic events, however, you still have a risk for depression after a difficult birth. In Kelly's story, we see a number of different factors that contributed to her reaction following her birth experience. She had a midwife-attended birth and told herself for months that she had had a wonderful experience. It wasn't until much later that she allowed herself to realize that there were some less-than-perfect aspects of her experience.

What if I want to go back to her if I have another baby? I didn't realize until a month ago that it was a negative experience. It was too important for me to think of it as a good experience. That really set me up for depression, trying to deceive myself. I blame myself for what happened. I was conditioned. The whole prenatal experience conditioned me...I don't want to make trouble. I know I got the best care available. I don't want to make enemies or waves.

If you had a negative birth experience, even if it was many years ago, it may be contributing to some of the feelings you are experiencing right now. Be assured that you are not going crazy. It is important for you to get closure on your birth experience so that you can move on with the rest of your life.

How Birth Experiences Can Influence Your Relationships

Your birth experience might be influencing how you feel about others including your child, your partner, and your doctors. Elizabeth, one mother I interviewed, told me that she still couldn't travel by airplane because the hot stuffy environment of the cabin reminded her of her labor and delivery experience. This negative experience was still influencing her several years, and one subsequently positive birth experience, later.

Your Relationship with Your Baby

You are probably well aware that a difficult birth experience can have a negative impact on you. But, you may be surprised to learn that this experience can also affect your relationship with your baby. The studies below describe how this might happen.

The first study was a randomized clinical trial looking at the effect of labor support. The researchers were interested to know how an optimum birth experience influenced women's reactions. In this study, women were randomly assigned to a "doula" or "no doula" group when they arrived at the hospital (a doula is an experienced woman who provides emotional and physical support during labor). This support was in addition to any they might have received from husbands or other labor companions. Women in the no-doula group received standard obstetric care.

The women who had doulas had objectively better births, including significantly shorter labors and fewer medical interventions (i.e., pain medications, assisted births, or cesarean sections). These findings were not too surprising. More interesting (at least to me) were the mothers' perceptions of their infants at six weeks postpartum. The mothers who had doulas were significantly more likely to describe their babies as beautiful, clever, and easy to manage; they cried less and were "better" when compared to a "standard baby." They also perceived themselves as closer to their babies, communicating better with them. They were pleased to have their babies and found that becoming a mother was easy. Women who had doula support during labor felt more positively about themselves after their births. Specifically, they showed "significantly less anxiety, fewer signs of depression, and a higher level of self-esteem" than women who did not have doulas (Klaus, Kennell, & Klaus, 1993, p. 45).

In contrast, the no-doula mothers were more likely to describe their baby as "just slightly less good" or "not as good" as a "standard baby." They were more likely to describe their adaptation to motherhood as difficult and were likely to think that anyone could care for their babies as well as they could. They were also more likely to be depressed. These women's birth were not necessarily traumatic. Even so, simply not having emotional support during labor influenced their perceptions of their infants six weeks later (Klaus, Kennell, & Klaus, 1993).

An older, but still important, study had similar findings. Judith Trowell (1983), in her three-year longitudinal study in the U.K., compared women who had cesarean births with women who had vaginal births on their perceptions of their infants at one month, one year, and three years postpartum. At one month, the mothers who had cesarean births were significantly more likely to be depressed and to express doubts about their ability to care for their infants. At one year, the mothers who had cesareans were more likely to describe motherhood as negative and to describe themselves as resentful, overwhelmed, or angry. They were significantly less likely to have positive interactions with their children on the Strange Situation assessment (a measure of mother-child attachment). At three years, the mothers who had cesareans were more likely to report serious problems in their relationship with their children and to describe them as "unmanageable," "out of control," or "nasty." The mothers were also more likely to report the use of physical punishment, but almost all of the mothers in the study used physical punishment. In addition, the children born via cesarean section were less likely to have completed their full course of vaccinations. This was not because the mother made a conscious choice to avoid vaccinations. It was because the mothers hadn't been able to manage it.

While the results of the Trowell (1983) study are certainly striking, the results should be interpreted with caution. First, the sample size was small. Second, the women in the cesarean group had cesareans that were emergencies (versus planned) and were conducted under general anesthesia. Both of these conditions increase the likelihood of a negative psychological response. However, even with these cautions, the findings of the two studies described above suggest that your birth can have a significant influence on how you feel about your baby and yourself as a mother.

One reason you may have had a hard time relating to your baby after a difficult birth is your post-traumatic stress response. Cheryl Beck (2004b), in her study of birth trauma, found that many of the women in her study described themselves as being "numb" after their traumatic deliveries. Numbness is a common response after traumatic events in general. She also found that the women were often convinced that their babies were going to die. When they didn't, the women had a difficult time reorienting themselves to the fact that their babies had indeed survived, and they felt disconnected from their babies as a result. Even if you didn't think your baby would die, you may have felt so numb from your experience that you found it hard to emotionally connect with anyone.

Reactions of Other People

Unfortunately, a difficult birth can have a negative impact on your relationships with other adults in your life, including your partner. In one study (Allen 1998), women with PTSD after birth reported being angry at their doctors and their partners, feeling less close to their partners, feeling emotionally detached from their babies, and having less patience with their other children.

You might find that no one lets you talk about your experience. You may feel isolated because you can't relate to mothers who didn't have a difficult birth (Beck 2004b). People will often blame you, or some presumed deficit in your character, for the experience you had: "You didn't try hard enough/exercise/eat the right foods/attend the right class," "You're such a negative person anyway," or "You had such unrealistic expectations." Because some people may blame you (whether they say this directly or not), they do not want to hear what you have to say.

I've noticed that some people are blinded by their own experiences-- either positive or negative. A lot of women have unresolved issues about their births. When you talk about yours, it might bring up some of the negative feelings from their own experiences. By dismissing your feelings, they are also dismissing their own. Conversely, if a woman has had a positive experience, she may have a hard time relating to your experience and wonder what the big deal is. This gets back to the issue of blaming you or some deficit in your personality for your experience.

Finally, people might be uncomfortable with the fact that you are unhappy. They want to say something that will make you feel better. Some people think that they can make you feel better by giving you a "count-your-blessings" lecture. As you already know, this approach generally does not work.

What You Can Do

If you have already had a negative birth experience, you cannot change that fact. There are, however, a number of positive steps that you can take to help you resolve your experience and heal from it. Here are some things that other mothers have found useful. As I offer these suggestions, I would like for you to keep in mind that coming to terms with a negative birth experience is a process that can take months. Don't be discouraged if it doesn't happen overnight or if you seem to have bad days. You can overcome this!

Know That You Have The Right To Your Reaction About Your Birth Experience

Many people will try to talk you out of feeling bad about your birth experience (if they haven't already tried). They may tell you that "it wasn't so bad," or they may point to your healthy baby (if indeed you had a healthy baby). While a healthy baby is important, having one should not take away from what has happened to you.

Process Your Experience

You may find it helpful to talk with a person who will not try to minimize your feelings or give you a pep talk. It may take several tries until you find a person who is willing to just listen, but keep trying. You probably need to grieve over your experience. You might also find it useful to contact one of the support organizations (see resource list) that can validate your feelings and help you come to terms with what happened. Other women have found that going to a therapist helps.

Another option is to write about your experience. Some women find writing in a journal to be very therapeutic. If you'd like to give that I try, I'd suggest that you get *Writing to Heal* by James Pennebaker to help you get the most out of this activity. Others might write letters to the people involved (whether or not they are ever mailed). In either case, writing gives you a chance to express your feelings without fear of censure.

Learn As Much As You Can About Your Experience

I always encourage women to get copies of their medical records and try to understand what happened. If possible (and if you feel comfortable) talk with your health care provider or someone else who can help you understand the events that occurred during your birth. It also helps to read books that might put your birth experience in a broader perspective (see the listing at the end of this chapter). This type of reading will do much to validate your experience and help you understand it. You may still be angry (or you may get angry for the first time), but eventually the experience will not dominate your thoughts. If you plan to have another baby, the information you gain during this stage will make you a much more informed consumer.

Understand That Your Partner May Have Also Been Traumatized

As I described earlier, a negative birth experience can create problems between you and your partner. Your partner may have also felt powerless and swept away by the experience. He might feel as though he failed to protect you and might react to his bad feelings about himself by being angry with you. Because of his negative feelings, he might not be able to provide effective emotional support for you as you try to work through your feelings. In this case, the best thing you can do is be honest about your feelings toward one another and try to find outside support together. If, however, your partner is not willing to work with you to resolve your birth experience, you must seek help alone.

Sometimes, your partner may have been partly or directly responsible for your negative experience. Some women's partners are disengaged from them during labor. Rather than offering support, they watched television, slept, made phone calls, or stared blankly into space. They may have made cutting or insensitive remarks, either during labor or later. Lorraine's husband was a physician at the hospital where she gave birth. During her labor, he chatted with his colleagues as she handled contractions alone. Later, he told her that she had "embarrassed" him by the way she handled contractions. She was devastated by his remarks. They eventually divorced.

Recognize That Birth Is Only The Beginning Of A Life-Long Relationship With Your Baby

Underlying many of the feelings women have following a difficult birth is a deep sense of failure or guilt. You may feel bad that you "allowed" this to happen or somehow were not strong enough. Your feelings following a difficult birth may compound your already shaky confidence as a mother.

You need to realize that motherhood is a role you gradually grow into. The difficult beginning you had does not need to be the blueprint for the rest of your mothering career. It is important to realize that a negative birth experience can affect your relationship with your baby, but it does not have to. This is why it is vital for you to get the support you need as soon as possible. I have seen mothers who have had difficult births try to make up for it by being "Super-mom"--to everyone's detriment. It is difficult for anyone (even Super-mom) to be responsive and giving toward an infant or child when she is hurting inside.

Resist The Temptation To Rush Into Another Pregnancy Just To Do It "Right"

I often meet mothers who are unhappy with their birth experiences who quickly become pregnant again in order to make it a better experience "this time." Sometimes women will stay with their same practitioner who may have given them a hard time to give him or her another chance. (One woman I know stayed with her provider through five deliveries, even though she was unhappy with his care after each one.)
You need some time in order to put your experience into perspective, get to know the baby you already have, and physically recover. Adding another pregnancy to the equation makes things much more complicated and may not give you sufficient time to consider all of your options.

Likewise, I would encourage you not to make a decision about a planned repeat cesarean until you have some distance from your present experience. Far too often, I've seen women who are terrified of having another bad experience submit to a repeat cesarean birth that may not be necessary. Before you make this decision, read all you can about it and get a second (and third and fourth....) opinion if necessary.

In A Similar Vein, Resist Making Hasty Decisions About Not Becoming Pregnant Again

This is not the time to make a decision about a tubal ligation or other permanent method of birth control. Some women make this decision only to regret it later. Understandably, they never want to repeat what they've been through. If you decide to have a tubal ligation, it is much better to make this decision on solid ground rather than as a reaction to a negative birth experience.

Make A Conscious Effort To Forgive Yourself

At first you might balk at this suggestion. "I have nothing to forgive myself about." If you still feel this way after you've thought about it, great! However, I've talked with many women who feel at a deep level that they have somehow "failed." They blamed themselves for what happened and played the "if-only" game I described earlier. "If only I had been stronger...," "If only I had checked out the doctor/hospital more carefully....," "If only I had gone to a different prenatal class..." The list of "if onlys" is endless. Recognize that you did the best you could under the circumstances with the knowledge you had at the time, and let yourself off the hook!

In conclusion, I would encourage you to take good care of yourself and actively search for a supportive environment. Many mothers and babies have overcome difficult beginnings. I am confident that you can, too.

For Further Reading

There are a number of helpful books if you are struggling with a negative birth experience. The following is a listing of some of the better ones. Many can be obtained at your local library or bookstore.

Resources for Recovering from a Negative Birth Experience

These are three recent additions to the birthing literature that specifically address issues related to a less-than-perfect birth.

Freedman, L.H. 1999. *Birth as a Healing Experience.* New York: Harrington Park.

Madsen, L. 1994. *Rebounding from Childbirth: Toward Emotional Recovery.* Westport, CT: Bergin & Garvey.

Stern, D., Bruschweiler-Stern, N., & Freeland, A. 1999. *Birth of a Mother: How the Motherhood Experience Changes You Forever.* New York: Basic Books.

Web Sites on Negative Birthing Experiences

"Ask Dr. Gayle"--Gayle Peterson, author of Making Healthy Families
   www.askdrgayle.com
Baby Center
   www.Babycenter.com
BestFed.com--Nurturing children through progressive parenting
   www.bestfed.com
Birth-related E-mail Discussion Lists
   www.fensende.com
The Birth Trauma Association (Great Britain)
   http://www.patient.co.uk/showdoc/27000792/
Coalition for the Improvements of Maternity Services (CIMS)
   http://www.motherfriendly.org/
Gentlebirth.org
   http://www.gentlebirth.org/archives/brtrauma.html
International Cesarean Awareness Network
   http://www.ican-online.org/

Books About Cesarean Birth

These books specifically address cesarean births; although, there will be information useful to women who have had negative vaginal deliveries as well. I generally recommend that women wait to read these until you are ready to be angry because you will be angry after you read these books. They contain a number of practical suggestions about resolving your experience and planning for the next one.

Cohen, N.W., & Estner L.J. 1983. *The Silent Knife: Cesarean Prevention And Vaginal Birth After Cesarean.* Westport, CT: Bergin & Garvey.
Cohen, N.W. 1991. *Open Season: Survival Guide for Natural Childbirth and VBAC in the '90s.* Westport, CT: Bergin & Garvey.
Panuthos, C., & Romeo, C. 1984. *Ended Beginnings: Healing*

Childbearing Losses. Westport, CT: Bergin & Garvey.

Wolfe, S., & Jones, R.D. 1991. *Women's Health Alert.* Reading, MA: Addison-Wesley.

Books that Discuss the Historical or Cultural Implications of Various Birthing Practices

These books are very helpful if you are looking to understand your experience in a broader perspective. They are also useful in validating your experience.

Goer, H. 1999. *The Thinking Woman's Guide to a Better Birth.* New York: Perigee Trade.

Goer, H. 1995. *Obstetric Myths vs. Research Realities: A Guide to the Medical Literature.* Boston: Bergin & Garvey.

Kendall-Tackett, K. 2005. *The Handbook of Women, Stress and Trauma.* New York: Taylor & Francis.

Kendall-Tackett, K.A. 2005. *Depression in New Mothers: Causes, Consequences and Treatment Options.* Binghamton, NY: Haworth Press.

Mendelsohn, R.S. 1982. *Mal(e) Practice: How Doctors Manipulate Women.* Chicago: Contemporary Books.

Rothman, B.K. 1982. *Giving Birth: Alternatives in Childbirth.* New York: W.W. Norton (also published under the title: *In Labor: Women and Power in the birthplace*).

Wertz, R.W., & Wertz, D.C. 1989. *Lying-In: A History of Childbirth in America.* New Haven, CT: Yale University.

CHAPTER 8
So Tired:
Mothers and Fatigue

Fatigue is an excellent gauge of well-being because it is a very hard symptom to mask. The only way to get rid of fatigue is to treat the underlying causes. Fatigue has many faces, but they all say the same thing - the mental and physical load are too great. (Atkinson, 1985, p. 6)

Fatigue is epidemic among women in general and mothers in particular. Economist Juliet Schor in her book *The Overworked American* (1992) describes how mothers talked to her about sleep the way someone who is starving talks about food. Fatigue can overshadow your life, making everything seem like too much trouble. Lack of sleep can impact your ability to concentrate, handle stress, solve problems, and make decisions. You may become irritable with others and less productive. Eventually, lack of sleep has a negative effect on your health (National Sleep Foundation, 2000a), and can even make you fat (Vorona et at, 2005).

If you find yourself dragging through your day, read on. You can increase your energy level. When you are less tired, you benefit--and so do the people around you.

Why Are Mothers So Tired?

Fatigue is a common experience. But, we need to ask, why are mothers so tired? In this section, I describe some of the factors that may be contributing to your level of fatigue. In the section that follows, I'll offer some suggestions for what you can do.

Overwork

The most obvious reason mothers are tired is because they work so much. This can be true for mothers at home as well as those who are employed. In the classic *More Work for Mother* (1983), Ruth Schwartz Cowan writes that:

> With all her appliances and amenities, the status of being a working mother in the United States today is . . . virtually a guarantee of being overworked and perpetually exhausted (p. 213).

According to Schwartz Cowan, employed women typically work thirty-five hours per week in child and home care and forty hours per week in paid employment. That's seventy-five hours of work per week--a rate that few sweatshops can match. And, depending on the job, forty hours of paid work a week is probably conservative. It is easy to imagine an employed mother working eighty hours a week or more between home and office.

As I mentioned in earlier chapters, employment outside the home is not the only activity that can make you feel fatigued. Overwork can also come from shouldering the burden of housework alone; caring for multiple children, children with health or behavioral concerns, or children and aging relatives; or doing some combination of these activities.

Not Enough Sleep

Another obvious source of fatigue is sleep deprivation, which is rampant in the United States. According to the National Sleep Foundation 2000 Omnibus Survey, most adults in the U.S. get less sleep than they need. On average, adults sleep a little less than seven hours per night, with a third of those surveyed indicating that they sleep less than six and a half hours per night. Forty-five percent said that they give up sleep to get more work done. With employed mothers putting in approximately seventy-five to eighty hours a week, it should come as no surprise to learn that they are skipping sleep. But, this can be true for at-home moms as well, especially when they feel pressured to do it all. Crittenden

(2001) also noted that mothers were more likely to skip sleep than skimp on time with their children. The National Sleep Foundation (2000b) describes it this way:

> Sleep problems have become a modern epidemic that is taking a catastrophic toll on our bodies and our minds . . . In our twenty-four hour society; we steal nighttime hours for daytime activities, cheating ourselves of precious sleep. In the past century, we have reduced our average time asleep by 20%. In the past 25 years, we have added a month to our average annual work/commute time. Our national sleep debt is on the rise. Our society has changed, but our bodies have not, and we are paying the price.

Staying up too late is not the only reason we don't get enough sleep. Below, I've summarized some of the most common reasons why people don't get the sleep that they need.

Insomnia

There are few things more frustrating than insomnia. You're lying awake in the middle of the night, watching the clock: 2 a.m., 3 a.m., 4 a.m. You realize that you have to be up in a couple of hours, but you've hardly slept at all. Morning comes too quickly and you find yourself facing another day exhausted.

Shift Work

Shift work is notorious for causing sleep deprivation that results in daytime sleepiness. When someone works the night shift, she may try to sleep during the day. But, this can be difficult. It's light outside and there is usually a lot more going on. Similarly, someone who works a swing shift generally finishes work at 11 p.m. By the time she gets home and winds down, she may not get to sleep until 1 or 2 a.m. That doesn't leave much time to sleep if she needs to be up for the kids' morning routine.

On average, people who work swing or night shifts tend to sleep about four to six hours in a twenty-four hour period. Mothers will often take swing or night shifts so they can be home with their children during the day. Some families find that this works well for them. But, realize that it can be a major contributor to your fatigue. If you do decide to do shift work, it's best if you can stay on the same shift for at least three weeks. That's how long it takes the body to adjust.

Poor Sleeping Habits

Sometimes you don't get enough sleep because of bad sleep habits. These behaviors may not have caused a problem for you in the past. However, if you suddenly find that you are having difficulty getting the sleep you need, it might be helpful to take a look at your bedtime routine. Some poor habits include drinking caffeinated beverages, exercising, or drinking alcohol too close to bedtime. Alcohol can make you feel drowsy, but it interferes with the quality of your sleep and can make you feel groggy in the morning. Other habits that can contribute to poor sleep include using your bed as your office or a place to watch TV.

Sleep Disorders

Sleep disorders can also cause problems. Two of the most common types of sleep disorders are obstructive sleep apnea and restless leg syndrome (RLS). Obstructive sleep apnea refers to a condition where the throat closes during sleep and breathing is blocked. This causes people to waken many times throughout the night, making them very fatigued during the day. The person who suffers from this often snores loudly, making it difficult for his or her partner to sleep well.

Sufferers of RLS have the sensation that things are crawling under their skin whenever they lie down. They may find that their legs are in near-constant motion during the night. Not surprisingly, RLS interrupts sleep and is often difficult for partners to endure.

Infant and Child Care

Caring for an infant or young child can keep you up at night. Young babies, in particular, need to wake frequently during the night to feed since their stomachs are so small. There is increasing evidence that having interactions with their mothers during the night enhances their neurological development. But, sometimes this can disrupt your sleep. The National Sleep Foundation poll (2000a) found that taking care of children disrupted sleep for 21% women compared with 12% of men. Even as children move past infancy, they may still be poor sleepers, and it is more often mothers who tend to their nighttime needs.

When discussing infant or childcare and sleep, an issue that often arises is, should I sleep with my baby? This is ultimately an issue you will need to decide. Realize that approximately half of American parents share sleep with their babies either all or part of the night. Sharing sleep includes not only having your baby in your bed, but having your baby next to you in a crib, bassinet, or co-sleeper.

Where your baby sleeps is something I used to be more neutral about than I am now. Since working on the first edition of this book, I've had a chance to work with our state's Bureau of Maternal-Child Health on developing guidelines for safe co-sleeping. In the process, I've read much of the literature on co-sleeping and SIDS prevention. I've learned that having a baby sleep alone in another room doubles their risk of SIDS (McKenna, 2004; McKenna & Mosko, 2001). Anthropologist James McKenna has conducted groundbreaking research in this field and has demonstrated that the sleep cycles of mothers and babies actually synchronize when they sleep next to each other. This is thought to aid baby's brain and neurological development and protect them from SIDS. So I now always recommend that mothers keep their babies in their rooms for at least the first six months of their babies' lives. Your baby can be in a crib, bassinet, or co-sleeper beside your bed if that helps you sleep better.

Sometimes parents try to avoid co-sleeping with their babies, but may sleep with them on recliners, couches, or rockers. **Please don't do this** because you are greatly increasing the chance that your baby may fall or suffocate. Wherever your baby sleeps, make sure he or she is on a firm mattress with no fluffy bedding, pillows, or stuffed animals around that can cause suffocation. (See the list of resources at the end of this chapter for more information.)

As your children get older, you may still choose to handle your children's nighttime needs by bringing them into bed with you. This can be a great solution that lets everyone sleep better. But, at some point, you may find that having children in your bed disrupts your sleep. This can be especially true with older children who take up a lot more space. If you want your children near, you might consider having their bed next to yours with each of you retaining your own bed space.

Bedmates

A partner's snoring can become a serious source of sleep disruption, and women are more likely than men to have snoring partners. Twenty-two percent of women (versus 7% of men) reported that their partners' snoring interrupted their sleep (National Sleep Foundation, 2000a). Moreover, women in a recent study who slept with a partner who snored had twenty-one brief awakenings per hour and spent only 74% of the night actually sleeping. These women were losing about sixty minutes of sleep per night (*Health*, 2000).

Your pet can also disturb your sleep. You may have a cat that gets social in the middle of the night or a dog that comes to nudge you awake at first light. If you are feeling fatigued much of the time, you may have to temporarily or permanently banish your pets from your bedroom.

Stress

Stress can make it hard to sleep because even when your body is resting your overloaded mind is buzzing with what you need to do next. The National Sleep Foundation's 2000 poll found that 26% of women (compared with 16% of men) reported that stress interfered with their ability to sleep.

Depression

Fatigue is a symptom of depression, but it can also be a cause. Depression causes alterations in sleep. Particularly among people who are very depressed, sleep patterns differ compared with those who are not depressed. People who are depressed have long stretches of REM (rapid eye movement) sleep earlier in the night (Perlis et al., 1997). During REM sleep, the brain is in a highly active, almost awake state. This earlier occurrence of REM may explain one of the hallmark symptoms of depression: early-morning waking. Since the brain is so close to being awake during these times, it is easier to awaken. People who are depressed spend less time in deep sleep. This contributes to not only fatigue but pain since it is during deep sleep that muscles are repaired. If you are not getting enough deep sleep, this muscle repair cannot take place.

Post-Traumatic Stress Disorder (PTSD)

If you have suffered a major trauma or sustained a significant loss in your life, it may be contributing to your poor quality of sleep. PTSD is notorious for causing sleep problems. The culprit is often intrusive thoughts, which can occur during the day or at night in the form of nightmares. Even if you don't have enough symptoms for a full-blown diagnosis of PTSD, you may still be experiencing intrusive thoughts.

One study found that intrusive thoughts were directly related to levels of norepinephrine: the higher the levels, the higher the rate of intrusive thoughts (Lemieux & Coe, 1995). As you may recall, norepinephrine is one of the stress hormones. The traumatic event may have flipped a switch in your brain that has caused your body to be in a hyperaroused state. Consider using some mind-body techniques, such as relaxation training, to help counter the physiological reaction that the traumatic event created. You might find that as you process the trauma, your sleep improves. Medications can also be helpful if you are dealing with intrusive daytime thoughts or nightmares. These medications are part of a class known as SARIs (Serotonin-2 Antagonist Reuptake Inhibitors) and include the medications nefezodone and trazodone. Of the two, trazodone (Desyrel) is the choice most compatible with breastfeeding mothers (Hale, 2004).

In the following story, Teresa describes how grief and depression after losing a baby contributed to her almost daily feelings of exhaustion. Medication has helped, but has not completely eliminated her fatigue.

We lost our first child, Miranda, when she was three months old. She had Down syndrome and died as a result of complications during heart surgery. We purposely conceived right away. Gwen was born a year and two weeks after Miranda. I had a difficult pregnancy with both. Between our bereavement, Gwen's intensely high needs, and my history of depression, I soon was quite depressed. When Gwen was seven months or so, I sought counseling and medication and eventually pulled out of it. Gwen's little brother Duncan is now one year old. I have not gone off the Zoloft yet. I made the difficult choice to remain on medication during the pregnancy and ever since. (Several attempts to go off had poor results.) I don't feel guilty about it, especially since he and I are doing ever so much better than Gwen and I did. However, it seems that sleep loss and exhaustion are my perpetual companions.

Underlying Physical Conditions

In addition to the conditions described above, fatigue can be due to an underlying physical condition. In fact, fatigue may be the only symptom. The conditions with fatigue as a symptom are myriad and include anemia, hypothyroidism, diabetes, SAD, pregnancy, chronic fatigue syndrome, fibromyalgia, autoimmune diseases, and many others, even some cancers. If you are fatigued, a complete physical to rule out these conditions would be wise.

Iron-Deficiency Anemia

Anemia is one of the first conditions to consider as a cause of fatigue. It is remarkably common among women of childbearing age. Some 7.8 million women in America have low iron levels, and an additional 3.3 million have iron-deficiency anemia. Iron deficiency can have a variety of causes. The most common is a diet lacking in iron or a poor diet overall. Certain types of illnesses, especially those with chronic inflammation, can cause iron-deficiency anemia. Anemia may be due to bleeding from heavy menstrual periods, an ulcer, or, if you've recently had a baby, from a postpartum hemorrhage. Folic acid deficiency has also been linked to anemia. The symptoms of anemia are fatigue, pale or gray skin (including the linings of the eye and mouth), weakness, faintness, and breathlessness. Anemia can be diagnosed with a blood test.

Hypothyroidism

Hypothyroidism is another relatively common cause of fatigue in women. Thyroid hormones regulate our metabolism. Low levels can cause a wide range of symptoms, many of which are similar to those of depression. They include an inability to concentrate, tiredness, and forgetfulness. Low thyroid can also cause an intolerance to cold, persistently low body temperature, low blood pressure, weight gain, puffy face and eyes, constipation, and dry hair and skin.

Thyroid dysfunction can show up shortly after you've had a baby, and it is one possible contributor to depression in new mothers (Kendall-Tackett, 2005b). If you have diabetes, you are three times more likely to develop postpartum hypothyroidism (Weetman, 1997). As you age, you are at increased risk for developing hypothyroidism. By age sixty, approximately 20% of women have low thyroid function. Hypothyroidism is common in people with chronic fatigue syndrome, fibromyalgia, and some autoimmune diseases. Women with one or more of these conditions tend to experience a double or even triple whammy of fatigue. Hypothyroidism is diagnosed with a blood test.

Diabetes

Diabetes can cause significant levels of fatigue, and many with diabetes do not even realize that they have it. Other symptoms of diabetes can include frequent urination, thirst, blurry vision, weight loss, and hunger. But, fatigue may be your one and only symptom. Diabetes is diagnosed with a blood test, generally after consuming a concentrated amount of glucose.

Seasonal Affective Disorder (SAD)

Seasonal affective disorder (SAD) is a type of depression that occurs when there is less light available, such as during the winter. You may not experience SAD as depression per se, but you may notice a lack of energy in the winter. If you live in a part of the country with short winter days or where it rains a lot and is frequently overcast, you may have SAD without realizing it. Are you more energetic in the spring and summer? During the winter, do you find that you sleep more and crave foods loaded with carbohydrates? Do you tend to pack on an extra ten to twenty pounds during the winter and easily lose it when the days start getting longer? Any of these might indicate SAD which is easily remedied with light therapy (see Rosenthal, 1998, for further information).

Pregnancy

We don't often think of pregnancy as a contributor to fatigue, but fatigue is common in both early and late pregnancy. The more children you already have, the more likely you are to be fatigued during subsequent pregnancies. During a first pregnancy, you may have had plenty of time to rest when you felt tired or to nap during the day. This becomes much more difficult when you already have children at home. Recovery from birth may also be more challenging if you are coming home to other children. Like many American mothers, you might find yourself alone after a few days, not only to recover, but to care for your other children.

Chronic Fatigue Syndrome

Chronic fatigue syndrome (CFS) is a relatively new diagnosis, but accounts of CFS-like conditions have been documented since ancient times. CFS refers to a constellation of symptoms that include low-grade fever, persistent infection, sore throat, headaches, pain in muscles and joints, and tender lymph nodes. The hallmark symptom is overwhelming fatigue that worsens with activity. Depression and anxiety are both common in those with CFS (Friedberg, 1995).

CFS often starts with an infection or illness that doesn't seem to get better. Diagnosis of this condition is tricky since there are no laboratory tests that confirm its existence; although, the presence of the Epstein-Barr virus has been noted in some sufferers. Doctors typically make the diagnosis by eliminating other illnesses that could be causing the fatigue.

As with many other types of chronic illness, current stressors can trigger a relapse of CFS symptoms. Rose, who was diagnosed with CFS several years ago, saw her symptoms return with a vengeance after her husband was diagnosed with cancer. She had two young children at home, one with Down syndrome.

CFS is still a controversial diagnosis. Those who doubt whether it really exists have called it the "yuppie flu." Public skepticism makes those who suffer from it feel bad, and it reinforces their belief that no one understands what they are going through. But, researchers in the field feel that once its cause is officially documented, many people will hang their heads in shame over the way CFS sufferers have been treated in the health care system. People with CFS often do well with a comprehensive treatment program that includes light exercise, supplements, nutritional counseling (including identifying food sensitivities), and stress management.

Fibromyalgia

Fibromyalgia (FM) is a fairly new diagnosis and has many similarities to CFS. FM is a condition that causes diffuse soft tissue pain with fatigue as a common symptom. The people who suffer from it are overwhelmingly women. As with CFS, there are no laboratory tests that can confirm the diagnosis, causing some to dismiss its legitimacy. Diagnosis is made by pressing tender points at various places in the body. These locations are not tender among the general population, but are very painful for those who suffer from FM. Diagnosis is usually made by a rheumatologist, a physician who specializes in the treatment of arthritis and other rheumatic diseases. Although FM is not technically a form of arthritis, rheumatologists developed the diagnostic criteria and have been at the forefront in studying this condition. FM also tends to co-occur with certain types of inflammatory arthritis, such as rheumatoid arthritis and lupus.

Women suffering from FM can often point to a traumatic event that led to the onset of their symptoms, such as a car accident, an assault, or serious illness. Many of these women have family members who have similar conditions, indicating that there may be a genetic predisposition to FM.

FM also appears to alter sleep patterns (Roizenblatt et al., 2001). During slow wave sleep, alpha waves (which characterize an awake brain) intrude, causing FM patients to get insufficient slow-wave sleep. As I described earlier, the body needs slow-wave sleep to repair the microtrauma to muscles that occurs throughout the day. If this repair process is interrupted, the result is overall muscle pain.

Fibromyalgia tends to perpetuate both fatigue and pain because of muscle deconditioning. When you are exhausted, the last thing you want to do is exercise. Conversely, you can exercise too much, have a dramatic increase in pain for a week or more, and stop exercising. In either case, lack of exercise may contribute to deconditioning of muscles, which leads to more fatigue in the future. Fibromyalgia seems to respond well to comprehensive programs of diet, exercise, stress management, and supplements.

Autoimmune Diseases

Statistically, autoimmune diseases are fairly rare. However, I have included them because women of childbearing age are particularly vulnerable to many autoimmune diseases, and they experience overwhelming fatigue as a result. Autoimmunity is the process by which the body loses its ability to distinguish self from not self, and your immune system attacks your organs as it would an outside invader.

Autoimmune diseases include the 150 forms of inflammatory arthritis, two of the most common of which are rheumatoid arthritis and systemic lupus erythermatosus. Other less common diseases include sarcoidosis and scleroderma. Multiple sclerosis, while not a form of arthritis, is another autoimmune disease that strikes women of childbearing age. Women may have their first significant episode of an autoimmune disease while pregnant or shortly after giving birth. These illnesses can cause multiple miscarriages and infertility.

A recent article in the journal *Arthritis and Rheumatism* indicated that breastfeeding can trigger a flare of rheumatoid arthritis or other forms of inflammatory arthritis in women who are genetically vulnerable to it (Barrett et al., 2000). The authors speculated that the hormone prolactin was to blame. However, another study with a much larger sample found that breastfeeding actually lowered the risk of rheumatoid arthritis developing in the first place; the longer a woman breastfed, the lower her risk (Karlson et al., 2004). Surgery can also trigger an episode, so mothers who have had a cesarean birth are at increased risk. Finally, sleep deprivation can trigger an episode.

Not only do autoimmune diseases contribute to fatigue, but some treatments can as well. Prednisone and other corticosteroids are frequent treatments for autoimmune diseases, especially during periods of disease activity. Prednisone not only leads to rapid weight gain, but it can also cause muscle wasting. The lack of muscle tone and the additional weight can both contribute to a lack of energy.

Fatigue can trigger a flareup of symptoms. The body perceives that you are under attack when you are sleep-deprived. At the first sign of sleep deprivation, it fires up the immune system. People with autoimmune diseases already have an immune system that is too active, so sleep deprivation can increase their symptoms.

What You Can Do

Fortunately, there are many positive steps you can take to help alleviate some of the fatigue you feel. While you may not completely eliminate fatigue, overwhelming tiredness no longer has to be a way of life.

Determine Your Sleep Needs

Often, we feel we are getting enough sleep when we really aren't. So how can you tell? Here are a few questions to ask yourself.

- Do you need an alarm clock to wake you every morning?
- Do you roll over in the morning and catch a few more zs?
- Do you try to catch up on your sleep over the weekend?
- Do you feel drowsy after a big meal, in an overheated room, or during a long meeting?

If you are getting enough sleep, the answer to each of these questions should be no, according to the National Sleep Foundation (2000b). To determine how much you need, try this on your next vacation. Go to bed when you are tired, and get up when you are finished sleeping. For the first few days, you may need to get rid of your accumulated sleep debt. After that, you will have a pretty good idea of how much sleep you need to feel restored. When you return, make whatever adjustments you need to make to try to get that much sleep most nights.

Practice Good Sleep Hygiene

When you are having sleep problems, it's time to consider activities that might be interfering with your sleep. First, establish good bedtime rituals. Before bedtime, allow yourself some time to wind down. Try not to eat anything that is heavy or will upset your stomach at least two hours before bedtime. Also, avoid caffeine and more than one alcoholic drink in the evenings. Do not exercise in the two or three hours before bed. Exercise tends to rev you up, making it difficult for you to sleep.

Get out of the habit of doing anything in your bed, but sleeping and having sex. Often, people who suffer from insomnia spend non-sleeping time on or in their beds, watching TV, reading, catching up on work. If you are having sleep problems, it's time to stop this behavior, at least for now. When you have insomnia, get out of bed and do something boring. When you are feeling sleepy, try sleeping again. You want to associate your bed with sleep; lying there wide-awake gives you the opposite association. Similarly, your bed will lose its association with sleep if it becomes an extension of your office.

Make the Bedroom Pleasant

If you are having trouble sleeping, it's important that your bedroom be an oasis of comfort and calm. Since your bedroom is private, it may be the part of your home you ignore. Sometimes, all the clutter in your house ends up in your room. For the sake of your health, move everything out of your room that does not have to be there.

Your bedroom should be a comfortable temperature, neither too hot nor too cold. If your mattress feels too hard, consider either replacing it or getting a foam or feather mattress pad to make it more comfortable. Also, find a pillow that gives good support without putting a kink in your neck. Pay attention to anything you feel might be keeping you from sleeping. Are you sleeping in something comfortable? Do your legs get tangled in the sheets? Normally, you might be able to ignore these little annoyances, but when you are having trouble sleeping, you must consider them all.

If your bedroom is facing a noisy street or is next to noisy neighbors, consider getting a white noise machine or portable stereo to block some of these sounds. If the moon or streetlights shine in your face at night, use shades or reposition your bed to keep the light from disturbing your sleep.

Try not to have a home office in your bedroom. If it's unavoidable, cover your desk at night when you are not working. You might also find it stressful to have an end table overflowing with books and magazines you never get to, reminding you of work that you never seem to have time to finish. If you are having sleep troubles, stash your mound of reading materials out of sight.

Take Care of Your Body

You knew I would say this. As I've said elsewhere, you need to eat well, exercise, drink enough water, and reduce your stress. But, this is often easier said than done.

Diet

The current barrage of information on diet is very confusing. Should we eat a high protein or a high-carbohydrate diet? Proponents of both approaches think theirs is best and that the other will kill you.

So what are you supposed to do? I've come to a few conclusions. First, humans are pretty flexible. We can live well on protein or carbohydrates. The safest approach is probably somewhere in the middle. Eat carbohydrates, but mostly the unrefined kind found in whole grains, fruits and vegetables, and legumes. Drink plenty of water and eat an adequate amount of protein. You may have to experiment, especially with the amount of protein, to find what works best for you.

Second, what works well for you doesn't necessarily work well for your neighbor. Everyone has different eating histories, food sensitivities, and likes. You should honor those.

Third, eat food that tastes good and is of good quality. If you are going to have chocolate, have a small portion of quality chocolate. If you want a baked treat, have a piece of cake that you made yourself or got at a bakery rather than some fat-free concoction that was baked two weeks (or two months) ago.

Something else to consider with regard to carbohydrates and protein is timing. Protein gives you sustained energy, whereas carbohydrates can make you groggy. Carbohydrates might be more appropriate for an evening meal and protein better for lunch. Again, experiment and see what works best for you.

Exercise

In addition to watching your diet, you also need to exercise. I know that when you are tired, this is the last thing you feel like doing. But, exercise is energizing. If you haven't been exercising, start small with five minutes per day of walking or strength training with light weights. Gradually increase the time as you feel able. Being creative about when and where you exercise can help you add exercise to your day in a natural way so it doesn't feel like one more thing you have to do. While you're standing at the kitchen sink or talking on the phone, you can do calf raises. While you are watching TV, you can use exercise equipment. You can take a brisk walk during your lunch hours at work, even if you have only ten extra minutes. Exercise is one of the single most powerful things we can do to help ourselves. Be sure to make time for it.

If you have CFS, FM, or an autoimmune disease, you may need the assistance of your physical therapist. Take things slowly so that you don't overdo. You might also consider a program of gentle strength training to rebuild muscles that have wasted due to lack of use or medications.

Rest

A brief nap can be restorative, so think creatively about ways you can get some rest during the day. If you've been up caring for a child at night, do whatever you can to rest during the day. If at all possible, rest when your child rests. Don't use this time to catch up on chores. Napping may mean that other things don't get done--and that can be okay. Consider delegating these tasks or eliminating them from your list. Even if you are employed, you might be able to squeeze rest into your day. Companies are beginning to realize that workers who take brief naps are more productive and have fewer accidents at work. Investigate the possibility.

One caution about napping: Don't sleep too long or too close to your normal bedtime. This can interfere with your regular night's sleep.

Make Necessary Accommodations

If you have a chronic condition, you may have an ongoing battle with fatigue even after the condition has been identified and treated. You might need to exercise, but in a limited way. You might also need to limit other activities to conserve your energy. In a presentation at the 1999 American College of Rheumatology meeting in Boston, rheumatologist David Isenberg reported on his findings for lupus patients in his practice. He asked his patients to describe their worst symptom, fully expecting them to say fear of death, facial disfigurement, or some other life-threatening or disfiguring symptom. He was quite surprised to learn that his patients considered fatigue to be their worst symptom. His findings underscore one of the major challenges that women with chronic conditions face.

Ellen describes how she made accommodations for the physical disability that often left her very tired. She decided to quit her job so that she could have more control over her schedule:

Being a teacher was wonderful, but I loved being home with our three boys. It was good for me emotionally and physically not to have the pressures of a job. I had polio when I was a child and wore a brace or used crutches. I was able to do just about anything I wanted, but found stress was hard on me. Being in charge of my day with the boys made it easier to keep my activities in line. I did less and less as the boys grew since even getting into their school required more energy than I had, and I resisted getting a wheelchair or scooter for assistance. Years later, I found out that I have new physical problems from having had polio: my nerves and muscles are wearing out. I quit my job with the health department as a breastfeeding and nutrition educator. This led to sleeping a lot and depression. But, I keep active on the computer writing a nutrition column for polio survivors with post polio syndrome (PPS). My Web site helps me keep in touch with and help others who are discovering that PPS is affecting their health and lives in new ways, too. This feels good. My entire family is so supportive and that is so very helpful to me as I face new health problems. I'm just trying to take one day at a time and enjoying each one to the fullest. I'm resting a lot, but not giving up in any way! We just spent a month in Europe traveling by train. We planned it so I could rest, and we took a scooter to ride since I can't walk too far. I was able to see Rome on foot and to visit our oldest son and his wife in Sicily. They are expecting a baby in May: our first grandchild. Life is good!

If you have a physical disability but don't already have a handicapped tag for your car, you might consider getting one. I originally got one so I could limit my sun exposure (which can trigger a lupus flare). I was absolutely amazed at the difference it made in my fatigue level. Talk with you doctor about whether a handicapped tag would be appropriate for you.

Should You See a Doctor?

Fatigue is a very common complaint in primary care practice. Though it can be challenging for a doctor to track down its source, consulting a doctor may be a good idea if one or more of the following is true:

- The fatigue has lasted for more than three weeks.
- It is getting worse.
- It is interfering with your work or your relationships with your family.

When you see a doctor, request a complete blood count (CBC). This will tell your doctor if you are anemic or have too much iron in your system. If you had a postpartum hemorrhage within the past year, your blood iron levels may be low. A CBC (complete blood count) will also indicate if you have an infection. You might request thyroid and glucose tests. If you have a family history of an autoimmune disease or have some other symptoms such as joint pain, low-grade fevers, or frequent infections you might consider requesting an erythrocyte sedimentation rate or "sed rate." This is a general measure of inflammation. An elevated sed rate can indicate infection, autoimmune disease, or other illnesses and may cue your doctor to look further into the source of your fatigue.

You may have gone the medical route and not been satisfied. Another option is to consider herbal remedies that will help you sleep. Consult with a naturopath or physician trained in herbal medicine. With sedating herbs, it's best that you not try to treat yourself with the possible exception of an occasional cup of chamomile tea. Also, be sure to tell your regular doctor about any herbs you plan to take since these can interact with other medications you may already be taking.

Be Creative with Sleeping Arrangements

Americans, in particular, have pretty rigid ideas about where people should sleep. Parents are encouraged to keep children out of their room. Partners are encouraged to always sleep in the same room. If your current sleeping arrangements are working for you, by all means, leave them alone! But, if you are chronically fatigued, it may be time to put some of these shoulds aside--at least for the time being.

For example, you and your child (or children) might sleep better if you are in the same room. In many countries of the world, including industrialized countries like Japan, mothers and babies sleep together. As I described earlier, you might consider having your baby in bed with you or having your baby or child beside your bed in a bassinet, crib, or youth bed. This is also important for safety reasons, especially during the first six months of your baby's life.

A trickier issue is what to do about a snoring partner or one whose other sleep disorders keep you awake. The first approach is to talk to your partner about how his snoring is impacting you. Be extra careful here since this is not something your partner is doing deliberately. Try to frame this as a couple's problem that you want to find a solution for. Snoring may improve if your partner tries different positions for sleeping. Your partner can be checked for sleep apnea, and there may be an appliance that can help. There may be medication that will help with problems like restless leg movements. You can also try earplugs or sleeping in a different room or bed. You may find that an occasional night apart makes all the difference in how you feel the next morning. You may want to save this as a last resort. It can be hard for your partner not to take this as a rejection so approach the subject carefully.

Conclusion

Daily fatigue is something many mothers experience. Fortunately, you don't have to walk through every day feeling like one of the living dead. Getting enough good-quality sleep may be just what you need to face the challenges of mothering. And, there are steps you can take to get it.

For Further Reading

Many available books are helpful in identifying the multiple causes of fatigue. I've listed some of the better ones I've found below, along with some good Web sites.

Resources for Fatigue in General

Atkinson, H. 1985. *Women and Fatigue.* New York: Pocket Books.

Ford, N. 2000. *How to Get a Good Night's Sleep: 75 Natural Sleep Prescriptions.* New York: Barnes & Noble Books.

Monson, N. 1999. *Smart Guide to Boosting Your Energy.* New York: John Wiley and Sons.

Natelson, B.H. 1998. *Facing and Fighting Fatigue: A Practical Approach.* New Haven, CT: Yale University Press.

Smith, P. 1999. *The Energy Edge: Ten Simple Strategies to Soar Past Fatigue, Boost Energy, Shed Stress, and Reclaim Your Life.* New York: Harper Information.

Wade, C. 2000. *Natural Energy Boosters.* New York: Barnes & Noble Books.

Resources for Specific Conditions

Conly, E.J. 1998. *America Exhausted: Breakthrough Treatment on Fatigue and Fibromyalgia.* Flint, MI: Vitality Press.

Dement, W.C., & Vaughan, C. 2000. *The Promise of Sleep: A Pioneer of Sleep Medicine Explores the Vital Connection Between Health, Happiness, and a Good Night's Sleep.* New York: Dell Publishing.

Friedberg, F. 1995. *Coping with Chronic Fatigue Syndrome.* Oakland, CA: New Harbinger.

Goldberg, B. 1998. *Chronic Fatigue, Fibromyalgia, and Environmental Illness: 26 Doctors Show You How They Reverse These Conditions with Clinically Proven Alternative Therapies.* Tiburon, CA: Future Medicine Press.

Rosenthal, N.E. 1998. *Winter Blues: Seasonal Affective Disorder. What It Is and How to Overcome It.* New York: The Guilford Press.

Smyth, A., & Thompson, W.C. 1990. *Seasonal Affective Disorder: Winter Depression. Who Gets it? What Causes It? And How to Cure It?* London: Thorsons.

Shomon, M. 2004. *Living Well with Chronic Fatigue Syndrome and Fibromyalgia.* New York: Harper Resource.

Starlanyl, D.J., & Copeland, M.E. 1996. *Fibromyalgia & Chronic Myofascial Pain Syndrome: A Survival Manual.* Oakland, CA: New Harbinger.

Teitelbaum, J. 1996. *From Fatigued to Fantastic.* Garden City Park, NY: Avery.

Wolfson, A.R. 2001. *The Woman's Book of Sleep: A Complete Resource Guide.* Oakland, CA: New Harbinger Publications.

Sleep Disorders

National Center on Sleep Disorders Research, at National Heart, Lung, and Blood Institute: www.nhlbi.nih.gov

National Sleep Foundation: www.sleepfoundation.org

Chronic Fatigue Syndrome/Fibromyalgia

American Association for Chronic Fatigue Syndrome: www.aacfs.org

The CFIDS Association of America: www.cfids.org

Fibromyalgia Files: www.geocities.com/cfsdays/fmsfiles.htm

Healthtouch: search for fibromyalgia at www.healthtouch.com

Other Conditions

American Academy of Allergy, Asthma, and Immunology: www.aaaai.org

American Thyroid Association: www.thyroid.org

Resources for Child/Infant Sleep Problems/Safe Cosleeping

Safe cosleeping occurs all over the world. If you want to give cosleeping a try, look at these resources.

Gordon, J., & Goodavage, M. 2002. *Good Nights: The Happy Parent's Guide to the Family Bed.* New York: St. Martin's Press.

Pantley, E. 2002. *The No-Cry Sleep Solution: Gentle Ways to Help Your Baby Sleep through the Night.* New York: McGraw-Hill.

Sears, W. 1999. *Nighttime Parenting: How to Get Your Baby and Child to Sleep.* New York: Dutton/Plume.

La Leche League International: www.lalecheleague.org

The Natural Child Project:
   http://www.naturalchild.com/james_mckenna/
   (This site features several articles by noted cosleeping expert James McKenna.)

Mother-Baby Sleep Laboratory: http://www.nd.edu/~jmckenn1/lab/
   (This is Dr. McKenna's website.)

CHAPTER 9

The Long Shadow:
Adult Survivors of
Childhood Abuse and Adversity

We hear a lot these days about the dysfunctional family. These references are so common that they are almost a cliché. But, behind the cliché is the sad reality: some families are poisonous for children. Childhood abuse and adversity, particularly when severe, can cast a long shadow over your life, influencing your emotional state and how you relate to others. Even when not abusive, families can be dysfunctional in other ways. You may have had a chronically depressed, mentally ill, or substance-abusing parent. Whatever your experience, your upbringing may have left you poorly equipped to parent your own children. In this chapter, I describe how past abuse and family dysfunction may be affecting you now, and suggest some ways you can seek healing.

Types of Childhood Abuse and Trauma

Child maltreatment can take a variety of forms and range from mild to severe. Even non-abusive parents make mistakes that may have caused you harm. Abuse can occur both inside the family and with people who are not family members. By and large, however, the experiences I am describing occur within the home. And, you may have experienced more than one type. For example, someone who is sexually abusive is often physically abusive as well. In families where there is partner abuse, there is also likely to be parental depression and substance abuse. According to the latest thinking in the family-violence field, the cumulative effect of multiple types of abuse/pathology is more likely to have a negative impact than a single type of abuse (Edwards et al., 2004). Below is a listing of some of the more common types of abuse and adversity.

Sexual Abuse

One of the most highly studied forms of abuse is child sexual abuse. Experiences can include everything from fondling to oral, vaginal, or anal penetration. Approximately 20% of women (1 in 5), and 5 to 10% of men (1 in 10 to 20) have been sexually abused as children. The peak age of vulnerability is between seven and thirteen years of age, but children older and much younger have been abused (Finkelhor, 1994). According to the Third National Incidence Study of Child Abuse and Neglect, girls are three times more likely to be sexually abused than boys (Sedlak & Broadhurst, 1996).

Why does sexual abuse happen more often to girls? Two possible reasons have been offered, but neither completely explains this finding. One explanation is male dominance of women. In this framework, men are described as the abusers of women and girls, especially within the family. Research has, in fact, demonstrated that sexual abusers are overwhelmingly male and the majority of victims are female. But, this does not explain all sexual abuse. There are male victims and female perpetrators, too.

Access is another possible explanation for the sex difference in sexual abuse rates. Girls are more likely to be abused by family members, especially stepfathers, while boys are more likely to be abused outside the family. Girls may be more vulnerable to sexual abuse because the people most likely to abuse them are right in their homes. For girls, approximately half of perpetrators are family members; for boys only 10 to 20% are. While fathers and stepfathers are the most likely relatives to abuse, other family members can also be abusive, including brothers, uncles, grandfathers, and "friends of the family."

Mothers and other female relatives can also be sexually abusive. So far, we know little about female perpetrators. Some believe that this is because female sex offenders are rare. Others, however, including some adult survivors who were molested by their mothers, believe that female perpetration is the most secretive and closeted of all types of sexual abuse.

184

Physical Abuse

While sexual abuse is studied more often, physical abuse is actually more common for both boys and girls. However, unlike sexual abuse, boys and girls are equally likely to be physically abused (Sedlak & Broadhurst, 1996). Physical abuse ranges from spanking that crosses the line (and people are still arguing about where that line is) to torture and even murder.

Children are most vulnerable to physical abuse in the first three years of life, but it can occur at any time. When children are young, mothers are most likely to be the abusers. But, any family member can be abusive. And, as I describe in the next two chapters, children who have difficult temperaments or disabilities, especially ones that make them challenging to care for, are at higher risk for physical abuse (Sullivan & Knutson, 2000).

Recently, researchers have become interested in physical abuse among siblings. Sibling physical abuse is one of the most common forms of family violence. In most families, it is relatively mild. Because it occurs frequently, we tend to think of it as "normal." But, sibling abuse can be very severe and have many of the same consequences as parental abuse. In interviewing adult survivors of child sexual abuse, I have found that abuse by a brother or sister was often brutal and sadistic. (This seemed especially true when there was a substantial age difference.) I wouldn't be at all surprised to find something similar with regard to physical abuse.

Sibling abuse, especially in its more severe forms, often reflects an overall level of family pathology. Chances are, there are other types of maltreatment present as well. Parents may be abusive to their children or to each other, or at the very least, neglectful. Not surprisingly, being abused by multiple abusers makes the overall experience more severe.

Neglect

Neglect is by far the most common type of child maltreatment. Unlike physical or sexual abuse where something is actually done, neglect involves failure to do something. Types of neglect include not providing food,

185

clothing, or medical attention as well as failure to supervise, provide a safe environment, or a proper education. (Unfortunately, families who home-school are often harassed under the education portion of the neglect laws.)

Not surprisingly, families who neglect their children are often chaotic. And, while poverty accounts for some neglect, there is usually something else going on, especially in chronically neglectful homes. A classic paper entitled *The Psychological Ecology of the Neglectful Mother* was one of the first to address this issue. Norman Polansky and his colleagues (1985) gathered a group of mothers identified as neglectful by social services. They found another group of mothers who were not neglectful, but had the same income level, education, marital status, ethnicity, and even neighborhood as the neglectful mothers. What they found was illuminating. The mothers identified as neglectful were depressed, had few friends, and seemed unable to take advantage of the resources that were available to them in their communities. It wasn't just poverty that made them neglect their children. It was their inability to connect with others and receive support that was available to help.

Depression in mothers and fathers is also related to neglect. Recall from chapter 2 that depression influences a mother's ability to interact with her children. One interaction style of depressed mothers is avoidant. Avoidant mothers disengage from their children and ignore them much of the time. The other style, angry-intrusive, is a risk factor for physical abuse. (I'll discuss this in a minute.)

Neglect in more affluent families may happen in more subtle forms. Food and clothing may be provided, but the parents might be emotionally absent, showing little interest in their children. Neglect can also occur when mothers or fathers are so emotionally immature that their children have to care for them, rather than the other way around. Parents can be so uninvolved that they fail to notice when something really serious occurs in their children's lives. Marilyn and Sandy, two women I know, were raised in middle-class homes with neglectful, substance-abusing mothers. Both of these women were raped as teens by peers from their schools. Neither girl's family noticed the abrupt change in their behaviors after they were raped. These families never asked why their daughters were acting so strangely, and their lack of concern or acknowledgment simply compounded the problem.

Emotional and Verbal Abuse

A recent public service campaign in the U.S. reminded us that words can hit as hard as a fist. For many people, emotional abuse is the most damaging form of maltreatment, and it too can take a variety of forms. It can involve name-calling and saying hateful things. It can include constant comparisons between siblings or calling a child "stupid," "fat," "ugly," or a "loser." It can consist of mocking or holding a child up to shame, embarrassing her in front of her friends or even strangers. It can also include abandonment or threat of abandonment. Especially for young children, having a parent threaten to leave them someplace can be highly traumatizing. These types of experiences may be the source of many of the negative messages that replay in your mind.

Emotional and verbal abuse often accompanies other forms of family violence and child maltreatment. Some adult survivors recount how their mothers or fathers made them feel responsible for the abuse that was inflicted upon them. It can be especially devastating when girls are told that they are responsible for "seducing" someone who sexually abuses them. As adults, these women may end up in abusive relationships with adult partners who also blame their victims for the abuse: "If you would just keep the house clean, I wouldn't have to do this." Women in abusive adult relationships may have internalized these messages to such an extent that they stay since "no one else would want me."

Unfortunately, many forms of emotional abuse pass for "humor" in a family. Some parents find saying degrading things to be funny. Even some so-called family movies have very ugly examples of verbal and emotional abuse (the opening scenes of the movie *Home Alone* are an example). Sometimes, parents perpetrate this type of abuse. Other times, it is brothers and sisters. In most families, siblings will name-call and tease. But, as parents, we can either tolerate it or not.

A particularly heinous form of emotional abuse is when the abusive parent or sibling hits, tortures, or kills a child's beloved pet. Researcher Frank

187

Ascione of Utah State University has done groundbreaking research in this area (Ascione, 2005). In talking to women in battered women's shelters, he found that women often stayed in battering relationships because they feared for the life of a beloved cat or dog. When the pet was killed, it was often this event that made the woman finally leave. And, finally, he found that for women and children, watching their pets suffer was one of the most traumatic aspects of their entire abuse experience.

Parental Substance Abuse or Mental Illness

Families where there is substance abuse or mental illness bring many pressures to bear on their children. Children of alcoholics or substance abusers, especially the oldest girl, often find that they are the little adults in the family. If your parents were substance abusers, you may have been responsible for meeting your parents' emotional needs rather than the other way around. You may have also had to provide for the other children in the family, being the one who made sure that there was food in the house, your brothers and sisters had adequate clothing, and they did their homework after school. You might find that you are still taking care of lots of other people and that it's never reciprocal. Not surprisingly, parental substance abuse can increase the risk for physical or sexual abuse. This is not to say that alcohol or drugs cause parents to abuse. But, they can lower inhibitions and allow behaviors that might not have occurred in a sober state.

Parental depression and other mental illness can increase not only the risk of neglect, but also of physical abuse. Recall that one interaction style that depressed mothers exhibit is angry-intrusive. The interactions these depressed mothers have with their children tend to be hostile. The mothers, themselves, exhibit a lot of anger, perhaps crossing a line and physically abusing their children.

Substance abuse and mental illness are related to parents' failure to protect their children. A parent who is often high, drunk, or incapacitated may not be able to adequately keep children safe. They may bring people to their homes that abuse their children. Substance-abusing parents may also encourage their children to abuse substances, either by having them easily available or even by direct encouragement.

Children Witnessing Domestic Violence

Children who have watched a parent, usually their mother, being beaten often show many signs of disturbance even if they, themselves, were never actually abused. In one study, Catherine Koverola of the University of Fairbanks, Alaska, found that children who had witnessed their mothers being beaten were distressed, poorly adjusted, and showed signs of trauma that were the same or even worse than children who had been sexually abused (Koverola & Morohan, 2000). In the case of domestic abuse, staying together "for the sake of the children" is disastrous.

The kinds of domestic violence that children witness range from relatively mild to severe. Some children have even witnessed one parent killing another. Child witnessing tends to co-occur with other forms of maltreatment. For example, abusive partners may also abuse their children. Substance abuse and mental illness may afflict both parents. Children witnessing domestic abuse are at increased risk of experiencing partner abuse as adults. I know one particularly pathological family in which all four children witnessed their mother being beaten. The two boys grew up to beat their wives, and the two girls both married or lived with a series of abusive men. As the parents got older, the children would, on occasion, hit them, too. Not surprisingly, both parents and all four children were substance abusers as well.

Prolonged Separation, or Parent Illness or Death

Difficulties in childhood may have nothing to do with family dysfunction per se, but may be due to a child's prolonged separation from her parents. The effects of political strife, natural disaster, illness, or death are similar to those experienced by people who suffered abuse within their families.

If you were ill as a child, you may have been separated from your family and forced to undergo invasive and painful procedures. Children who have had multiple hospitalizations are at increased risk for depression and traumatic-stress reactions later in life. We're now realizing that even adults who endure painful medical treatments can suffer post-traumatic symptoms. These procedures are often worse for children, especially if they occurred in an era when parents were routinely separated from their sick children. Suzanne describes how her experience of forced separation from her family at age five influenced choices she made as a mother:

> I never really thought about why I chose to give up a promising career to stay home with my three children. It was made easier since it was economically feasible for us. But later, as I thought about my own mostly happy childhood, I found I am still saddened by the one dark time I encountered. When I was five years old, I contracted polio and was separated from my family for almost a full year in two separate hospitals. We were allowed occasional family visits, but only every other Sunday for two hours. It was just not enough time to get rid of those fears of abandonment. I knew deep down in my heart that I would go home, but was still fearful since I didn't have any idea when. It still haunts me today as I feel for that scared little girl.

Sometimes, the illness and death of a mother or father can change family dynamics and lead to some difficulties for the children. If your mother died during your childhood, you may have found it necessary to be the caregiver while you were still young. While this is understandable, it still could be influencing how you feel now. For many years, we've known that children whose mothers die, especially when the child is younger than age thirteen, are at increased risk of depression throughout their lives. Grief is certainly part of the reason, but there may also be something else going on. Researchers are now wondering if children's reactions could also be due to inadequate care prior to their mothers' deaths (Bifulco et al., 1992).

Long-term Effects of Past Abuse

While not true for everyone, the effects of childhood abuse can continue well into adulthood. This section summarizes some of the effects you might have experienced--or are experiencing now. Sometimes, parenting your own child will make memories of these past experiences very vivid. The long-term effects of past abuse can affect your psychological and physical health, both of which can influence how you mother your own children.

The symptoms adult survivors manifest are often logical extensions of dysfunctional coping mechanisms developed during childhood (Briere & Elliot, 1994). While these behaviors and beliefs may have helped you cope with ongoing abuse when you were a child, they are probably not working well now. From the hundreds of recent studies on the long-term impact of childhood abuse and adversity, we now know that these experiences can affect men and women in five key domains of functioning. These include:

- Physiological changes
- Harmful behaviors
- Dysfunctional beliefs
- Negative social relationships
- Emotional difficulties

These domains represent the range of what could happen. It doesn't mean you will manifest all or even most of these symptoms. But, this listing might help you recognize some reactions you've had, or are having, without realizing their possible connection to your past. I'm going to cover these only briefly here. If you want more information, I have many articles on my website (www.GraniteScientific.com).

Physiological Changes

Over the past 10 to 15 years, we learned a lot about how traumatic or chronically stressful experiences can influence a child's developing body and mind. Trauma can interfere with the quality of your sleep, lower your pain threshold, alter your immune system, and even make you more susceptible to memory and attention problems (Bremner, 2005). We know that adult survivors of childhood abuse tend to go to the doctor more often, have surgery more often, and have more chronic conditions than their non-abused counterparts (Kendall-Tackett, 2003a). In addition, abuse survivors are more vulnerable to stress-related illnesses, such as diabetes and other conditions ranging from cancer to skeletal fractures (Felitti et al., 1998; Kendall-Tackett, 2003a; Kendall-Tackett & Marshall, 1999).

Chronic pain is another commonly reported symptom among abuse survivors (Kendall-Tackett, Marshall, & Ness, 2003). The flood of stress hormones after a traumatic event sensitizes the body and actually appears to lower the pain threshold, making sensations more painful. Pain syndromes related to past abuse are irritable bowel syndrome, chronic pelvic pain, frequent headaches, and fibromyalgia (Kendall-Tackett, 2000; Kendall-Tackett et al., 2003).

Harmful Behaviors

Abuse survivors are more likely to engage in a wide range of harmful behaviors--ranging from smoking to eating disorders, substance abuse, and suicide attempts. All of these can impact you as a mother to a greater or lesser extent. In addition, high-risk sexual practices are more common in adult survivors--particularly of sexual abuse. For example, a relatively high percentage of teen mothers are abuse survivors. Even among married women, abuse survivors are more likely to have one or more unplanned pregnancies (Campbell & Kendall-Tackett, 2005).

All of these behaviors can influence your ability to mother your children effectively. But, each of these can be addressed and treated. You may find that it helps to address several of these problems at once.

Dysfunctional Beliefs

Cognitive distortions are some of the more common reactions to past abuse. There are two basic categories of cognitions that are affected by abuse: beliefs about self and beliefs about others. These are described below.

Shame and self-blame are two of the most common beliefs about self that are changed by abuse, and these can influence how well you cope. If you are ashamed or blame yourself (rather than the perpetrator), you are less likely to do well.

Self-efficacy is another belief that can be influenced by maltreatment. Self-efficacy refers to the belief that you are competent and can do things to improve your life. Unfortunately, abuse tends to undermine self-efficacy, and this can lead to depression. Self-efficacy is highly related to health behavior for you and your child. In one study, mothers low in self-efficacy were less likely to take care of themselves and were less able to care for their children--especially those with a chronic condition like pediatric asthma (Grus et al., 2001).

Past abuse can affect your beliefs about other people. Hostility and mistrust are two of the most common beliefs about others that abuse influences. Given your experiences, this is a completely understandable response. However, mistrust and hostility can create health problems for you as an adult. For example, you may be surprised to learn that hostility can suppress your immune system and make you more vulnerable to illness. It can also dramatically increase your risk of cardiovascular disease. (Remember the studies of "Type A" behavior and heart disease? Subsequent research found that it was hostility and not achievement that influenced people's cardiovascular risk.) In addition, mistrust and hostility can have a negative impact on your relationship with your partner, children, and friends. This is a classic example of a behavior that probably protected you when you were a child, but is now harmful to you as an adult.

Social Relationships

Adult survivors of past abuse may experience difficulties in relationships with others. Past abuse can influence your ability to trust others, make friends, and have relationships that are not exploitive. Adult survivors are often isolated and are less satisfied with their relationships than adults who were never abused. If you are an abuse survivor, you may find it difficult to find an adequate support network to help you cope with the demands of motherhood. You also have a higher risk for divorce and are more likely to be a single mother than women who have not been abused (Kendall-Tackett, 2003a).

That being said, this is not true for all abuse survivors. Women who have stable, loving partnerships as adults often find that these relationships can be quite healing. In a sample of incest survivors, those in stable or secure relationships as adults were significantly less likely to be depressed (Alexander et al., 1998).

On the more extreme other end, abuse survivors are more likely than average to end up in abusive relationships as adults. In fact, some of the beliefs about self (shame and self-blame) are related to increased risk. Learning to counter and grow beyond some of those negative beliefs about yourself is often a key way to heal and can often lead to more healthy, reciprocal, non-abusive relationships with adults.

Will You Abuse Your Own Kids?

A question I'm often asked is whether adult survivors are likely to abuse their own children. In a review of the literature, Anne Buist notes that many of the factors that make adult survivors vulnerable to depression, also increase their risk of abusing their own children (Buist, 1998). From my review of past studies, I find that adult survivors are at increased risk for abusing their children, but most abuse survivors don't.

Researchers have identified three *protective mechanisms--factors* that kept mothers from abusing their own children. These mechanisms are:

1) Emotional support from at least one non-abusive adult during childhood,
2) Participation in therapy at some point, and
3) A stable, satisfying relationship as an adult.

Mothers with one or more of these protective factors were able to break the cycle of abuse (Egeland, Jacobvitz, & Sroufe, 1988; Zuravin, McMillen, DePanfilis, & Risley-Curtiss, 1996).

Emotional Difficulties

Emotional difficulties that occur in the wake of childhood abuse are quite common and are woven throughout this book. Of these difficulties, depression is by far the most common. Childhood abuse and adversity can lead to a lifetime vulnerability to depression (Weiss et al., 1999).

However, vulnerability is not inevitable. Recognizing that you are at increased risk for depression particularly during times of stress can help you seek support during those times. If you are struggling now, it may be because of this prior vulnerability. Review chapter 2 for specific suggestions on how to cope with depression.

Post-Traumatic Stress Disorder (PTSD)

Another reaction is post-traumatic stress disorder (PTSD). This is a common reaction, but not as common as depression. To receive a formal diagnosis of PTSD, a person must have experienced a discernible traumatic event, such as past sexual abuse, and display symptoms in the following three domains:

1. **Intrusion.** Intrusion includes frequent re-experiencing of the event via nightmares or intrusive thoughts.

2. **Avoidance.** Avoidance includes numbing, or lack of responsiveness to or avoidance of current events. Avoidance can also include fear when faced with things that remind you of your experience, dissociation, and substance abuse (see below).

3. **Hyperarousal.** Hyperarousal includes persistent symptoms of increased arousal, including jumpiness, sleep disturbance, or poor concentration. This can include repetitive thoughts about what happened during the day and nightmares while you are asleep.

Briere and Elliot (1994) noted that many abuse survivors have symptoms of PTSD even if they do not meet the full criteria for a formal diagnosis. For example, they estimate that 80% of sexual abuse survivors have some post-traumatic symptoms.

Flashbacks of abuse experiences can be triggered by a variety of stimuli, including current abuse by another adult, talking to someone else about your abusive experiences, or learning of the abusive experiences of others. They can also be triggered by tactile or sensory stimuli associated with the abuse, such as smells (e.g., the scent of a particular cologne), tastes, textures, or sounds.

For some adult survivors of child sexual abuse, birth experiences can trigger flashbacks. Possible triggers related to birth include physical pain, callous treatment by caregivers, perceived loss of control, or the perineal pressure of second-stage labor. As noted in one qualitative study, birth can suddenly revive memories of sexual abuse that make it seem as if it was happening right then (Rhoades & Hutchinson, 1994).

Childhood abuse can also increase your vulnerability to stresses you may experience as an adult. In one study, Vietnam veterans who had been physically abused as children were found to be significantly more likely to develop post-traumatic stress disorder (PTSD) after combat than were veterans who had not been abused as children (Bremner et al., 1993). These findings were true even when the researchers compared veterans who had had the same amount of combat exposure.

What this means for you is that a previously abusive experience, of whatever type, may increase your risk for having a traumatic-stress reaction to something that happens to you in adulthood (Breslau et al., 2001). Experiences that could trigger this reaction include being mugged or assaulted as an adult, having a frightening birth experience, or the serious illness of someone in your family (including you or your child).

Avoidance

PTSD can be manifested as avoidance. Avoidance symptoms can occur because they help you cope by temporarily reducing emotional pain. One type of avoidance is dissociation. Dissociative symptoms often first appear during childhood when they become a way to escape from abuse or pain. Adult survivors often describe how they were able to numb body parts at will or how they would watch the abuse from outside their body. Some mothers can still use dissociation to cope with uncomfortable feelings of intense contact with their babies or children. Dissociation gets to be a problem for these mothers, however, when they have no control over when it happens.

196

Numbing of body parts and other types of dissociative reactions can also take place during birth. In a qualitative analysis of adult survivors during labor, Rhoades and Hutchinson (1994) described how some of the women they studied would remove themselves mentally and emotionally from labor. These women appeared to have easy labors in that they did not cry out or indicate that they were experiencing a great deal of pain. However, the nurses and midwives who attended them were concerned because the mothers appeared to be absent from their bodies. These types of dissociative responses may also be present when a mother breastfeeds.

Amnesia for abuse-related events is another type of avoidance response. Not everyone experiences amnesia, but many do. Linda Williams of University of Massachusetts, Lowell, conducted a prospective study (1994) of adults who, when they were children, had been treated for sexual assault in an emergency room of a large urban hospital. When she recontacted these women twenty years later, she found that 38% of the women she interviewed--all of whom had confirmed and documented sexual abuse experiences--had experienced total or partial amnesia regarding their abuse experiences. If you have large blocks of your childhood that you cannot remember, you may have had a traumatic experience in your life. It is normal to remember back to ages three or four. When someone tells me that they cannot remember anything before the age of thirteen, for example, I almost invariably find out later that they experienced some type of major childhood trauma.

The experience of mothering your child can trigger sudden memories of abuse. Gwen describes how memories of her abuse experience came flooding back once her child reached the same age she was when her abuse began:

> The first time I had issues with my abuse and raising my son was when he was five. This was the same age when I remembered my abuse beginning. I freaked out the entire year. I was afraid to give him a bath or touch him in any way. I would have thoughts about abusing him. At this time, I was in individual therapy and there I learned that all this was okay as long as I did not act on it. I believe if I ever get to that point I will commit myself somewhere for help.

197

Differences in Response to Past Abuse

Some people are deeply affected by past abuse, whereas others seem to show no symptoms at all. Your reaction could be anywhere in between. Not everyone who has experienced abuse will be traumatized. Researchers have identified several factors related to more severe reactions.

In general, abuse will be more harmful if the abuser was someone you knew and trusted. Your emotional attachment to the perpetrator and sense of betrayal can be more important predictors of harm than whether they are actually related to you. Another important factor is severity of the abusive acts. For sexual abuse, severity is defined by whether the abuse experiences included penetration (oral, vaginal or anal). For physical abuse, severity is described in terms of damage and degree of injury: the more severe the abuse, the worse the injuries. For neglect, severity is described in terms of the degree of deprivation.

Abuse that occurs often and lasts for years will typically be more harmful than abuse that happens only sporadically and over less time. The exception is the one-time violent assault (Kendall-Tackett, Williams, & Finkelhor, 1993). Not surprisingly, use of force has been shown to increase the severity of reaction to sexual abuse. Force may be more likely in a stranger and/or one-time assault, but this is not always true. While all sexual abuse is, by definition, non-consensual, sometimes the abuser will use trickery or mental coercion rather than force to gain compliance. In other situations, the abuser will hit, assault, or physically restrain his victim. Victims who experience this type of abuse are more likely to have symptoms as are victims who have experienced multiple types of abuse.

Childhood abuse can impact many aspects of the mothering experience. Claire describes how past sexual abuse affected her ability to mother her son. She experienced a whole array of feelings. In the immediate postpartum period and for the first year, she felt overwhelming sadness and grief. Later, she was very angry. Her story begins with her follow-up visits to her midwife:

Over the next days and weeks, I had several follow-up visits. Some were routine, but a few were because I just had a lot of trouble breastfeeding. Then too, I was glad of the contact with the midwives because I just couldn't stop crying. I felt bursting with pride at this incredible thing I'd done, and yet all I could feel when I looked at that perfect little one was grief, grief, grief. I could not understand it. The emotions were so intense that I could not sort them out or make them calm down. Eventually, I wore out. I wouldn't say I felt peaceful. I just felt like a dry autumn leaf. Resigned. Powdery. Lightweight. Just waiting to blow away or disintegrate. And, by turns, I began to feel normal things too, like fatigue, humor, boredom, longing for grown-ups to talk to, longing to go to work again, longing for a baby-sitter.

It is true that there was a sort of gap between how I'd envisioned myself mothering and how I was managing in reality. But, I think this is normal. I felt normal. Then, there came that time when they start to have a will of their own, and they sometimes cry in anger, asserting themselves. It terrified me. When he out-and-out cried like that, I'd fill with adrenaline as though my life were in danger, as though his life were in danger. I was afraid I'd hit him or shake him to get him to stop, so I'd find myself sitting outside on the front stoop while he wailed in the safety of his crib.

Other things start being obviously not right then, too. I sometimes would cry uncontrollably and feel nauseated. I'd spend whole days lying on my bed while he was at day care. I felt the gap between how I wanted to be with him and how I seemed to be as a mother widening. And then came some way, way stronger-than-usual reactions to things that were related to my memories of being molested: adrenaline rushes, strange sensations, panic, and dread. I started to feel as though I were losing it or worse. Maybe I was becoming mentally ill like my mother.

What You Can Do

Past abuse can influence every area of your life, including how you mother your children. But, there is much you can do to heal. Your past does not have to rule your future.

Should You "Just Get Over It"?

For many years, the prevailing wisdom encouraged trauma survivors to just forget about it. This advice still exists today in the form of the flippantly delivered admonition to "get over it." But, is that advice effective? Holocaust survivors are often used as examples of people who experienced horrifying events and yet put their pasts behind them. At first, they seemed to function well. However, as one study found, when these same survivors hit the milestones of middle and old age, their experiences started to haunt them. In a fascinating paper, researchers noted that as Holocaust survivors in their study aged, they had increasingly difficult experiences with their children leaving home and their own retirement and illness. The survivors had worse experiences with cancer than those their age who had not gone through the Holocaust. They had more pain. Hospitalizations were more traumatic. They experienced even political events, such as bombing during the Gulf War, more keenly than those who had not gone through the Holocaust (Solomon & Ginzburg, 1999). The researchers noted that as these people aged, their level of busyness decreased, allowing traumatic memories to surface again. In sum, the get-over-it strategy appears to work only temporarily, which leads me to my next suggestion.

Process Your Experience

In order to heal, you must find a way to process your traumatic experience. Professional therapy is one good way to do this. Remember that participating in therapy is one factor that prevented women from abusing their own children. Therapy can be either individual (just you and the therapist) or in groups (a small group of people with similar issues under a therapist's guidance). Be sure to seek out someone who has experience treating past abuse. State psychological associations can often give referrals. It's also important to find someone you like and have rapport with. Sharing your secret with someone can be remarkably healing in and of itself.

One area to specifically address in therapy is the presence of cognitive distortions. During your abuse experience, you may have internalized messages about being stupid, lazy, or dirty, and these thoughts could be influencing you today. Much of the harm that comes from past abusive experiences is directly related to what you tell yourself about it.

Another way to process traumatic events is through writing. The research of James Pennebaker demonstrates the powerful healing effects of expressing emotions in writing. Many of the men and women in his studies went through experiences similar to yours. Once they wrote about their experiences for a certain amount of time, they were able to put their traumatic pasts behind them. This resulted in measurable improvements in their psychological and physical health. If you want to give journaling a try, I'd encourage you to get Pennebaker's book, *Writing to Heal* (2004). It has many specific suggestions to help you get the most out of this activity.

Get Support

The process of recovery from traumatic events can take a long time. It's helpful if you have people in your life who understand that and will give you the space to heal. Having the support of others who have gone through similar experiences can also be important.

Support is especially important if you are irritable, withdrawn, or having difficulties controlling your anger. All of these reactions can be symptoms of depression, a common occurrence among adult survivors. If you feel like lashing out at your child or are feeling detached, you need to find someone to help you through these times. Be realistic about how much responsibility you take on. You may feel resentful when your children don't appreciate all the hard work you are doing on their behalf or how much better their childhood is than yours. When you are in danger of blowing your top, call someone. Most cities have chapters of Parents Anonymous or similar organizations. These numbers are in the front of your phone book; use them when you need them.

You might also consider seeking out one or more mothering mentors. Many times, adult survivors have no idea how to parent since their own upbringing was so difficult. We all tend to parent as we were parented. If you want to break the cycle of abuse, find someone who can help. To find a mentor, seek out women who have good relationships with their children and a positive view of mothering. Ask for their advice. If they offer their opinion in a way that makes you feel respected, continue to seek them out.

Special Considerations for the Breastfeeding Mother

Adult survivors of physical and sexual abuse face a whole range of additional challenges when they breastfeed. The intense physical contact of breastfeeding may be very uncomfortable for you. You might find breastfeeding painful because your abuse experience lowered your pain threshold. The act of breastfeeding may also trigger flashbacks.

Some mothers I've spoken with breastfeed because they think it's best for the baby, but they hate it the whole time. Other mothers find that the breast pump makes them very uncomfortable. I sometimes meet mothers who feel that they must do whatever their children want with regard to breastfeeding, even if it makes them cringe.

Several years ago, I gave one of my first talks on breastfeeding and the sexual abuse survivor. The next day a young woman approached me who had breastfed three children, two of whom were still nursing. She asked me if she would ever like it. Truthfully, I don't feel I gave her a great answer because I just didn't know. Since that time, many other abuse survivors have told me that while breastfeeding was never great, it became more tolerable over time. And, that might be a more realistic goal for you.

If you are an abuse survivor who is struggling with breastfeeding, I have some specific suggestions that might help. First, try to figure out what situations make you feel uncomfortable. Is it nighttime feeding? Is it your baby touching other parts of your body while nursing? Is it when your baby latches onto the breast? Pay attention to how you feel at different times of day and during the different phases of breastfeeding. Once you have identified some problem areas, see if you can make them better. If skin-to-skin contact is bothering you, can you put a towel between you and the baby? Can you avoid the feedings (perhaps nighttime feedings) that make you uncomfortable? Would you be more comfortable if you pumped and fed your baby with a bottle? Can you hold your baby's hand while nursing to keep him from touching other parts of your body? Can you distract yourself while nursing with TV or a book? (Many mothers have told me that this works well for them.) Experiment and find out what helps.

And third, remember that some breastfeeding is better than none--even if you must pump milk and use a bottle, or you are only nursing once a day. If you find yourself feeling rage while nursing, it's probably better for you and your baby if you stop. Mothering is not about martyrdom. If breastfeeding is something you loathe, don't do it. Remember, too, that you don't owe other people an explanation for the choices you make. It's none of their business (tell them I said so).

Set Some Boundaries

As a child, you had others violate your boundaries over and over. Now that you are an adult, you may have difficulties saying no to others. This may happen with your children, your partner, or other adults. Our culture pressures all mothers to do too much. But abuse survivors often feel a double portion of pressure since they are unable to place reasonable limits on how much time and energy they give to others. Learning to set such boundaries can have a major impact on the quality of your life.

Visualize Your Capacity for Wellness

I started studying family violence in 1983. At that time, I was an intern at one of the first treatment programs in the country for incest survivors. Many of the men and women there were very symptomatic, having endured the most extreme forms of abuse. During a training session, one of the senior clinicians said something that I'll never forget. She said that we must always see the capacity for wellness in our clients. We must see this and communicate it to them. The therapist who said this had seen people with very severe manifestations of past abuse, and yet she was able to hold out this hope.

203

Your experience of childhood abuse has most likely had at least some impact on you. But, what started as a difficulty can be turned into strength. Some adult survivors have reported that eventually something good came from their bad experiences (McMillen et al., 1995). They described how their abusive pasts made them more sensitive to the needs of others. They were motivated to be good mothers. Many felt compelled to help others who had suffered similar experiences. I've known many adult survivors who have not only broken the cycle of abuse, but have gone on to become terrific mothers. I'm confident that you can, too.

Conclusion

Reactions to past abuse vary from person to person. The responses of some survivors are relatively mild, while others experience severe reactions. Even when abusive experiences produce severe trauma, however, there is hope for healing. You can indeed become strong in the broken places, and life can be good. But, you must take the first step.

For Further Reading

There are many good books and other resources available to help you overcome the negative effects of past abuse. You are not alone.

Resources for Processing Your Traumatic Experience

This is a small sampling of materials that are available. Most books on the market are for survivors of sexual abuse, but there are also books on other types of maltreatment and family dysfunction.

Bowden, J.D., Gravitz, H.L., & Cruse, S.W. 1987. *Recovery: A Guide for Adult Children of Alcoholics.* New York: Fireside.
Copeland, M.E., & Harris, M. 2000. *Healing the Trauma of Abuse: A Woman's Workbook.* Oakland, CA: New Harbinger.
Courtois, C.A. 1996. *Healing the Incest Wound: Adult Survivors in Therapy.* New York: W. W. Norton.
Matsakis, A. 1996. *I Can't Get Over It: A Handbook for Trauma Survivors.* Oakland, CA: New Harbinger.

Matsakis, A. 1998. *Trust After Trauma: A Guide to Relationships for Survivors and Those Who Love Them.* Oakland, CA: New Harbinger.

Pennebaker, J.W. 1997. *Opening Up: The Healing Power of Expressing Emotions.* New York: Guilford Press.

Pennebaker, J.W. 2004. *Writing to Heal: A Guided Journal for Recovering from Trauma and Emotional Upheaval.* Oakland, CA: New Harbinger.

Salter, A.C. 1995. *Transforming Trauma: A Guide to Understanding and Treating Adult Survivors of Child Sexual Abuse.* Newbury Park, CA: Sage Publications.

Scixas, J.S., & Yoncha, G. 1986. *Children of Alcoholics: A Survivor's Manual.* New York: HarperTrade.

Sperlich, M., & Seng, J. *Survivor Moms Speak Out.*
(Mickey Sperlich is a midwife in Michigan who has been compiling a book for mothers who are abuse survivors. Her book was still in progress as this one went to press, but she said readers could contact her for ordering information. New Moon Midwifery, newmoonmid@aol.com)

Williams, M.B., & Poijula, S. 2002. *The PTSD Workbook: Simple, Effective Techniques for Overcoming Traumatic Stress Symptoms.* Oakland, CA: New Harbinger.

Information and Support for Past Abuse

Adult Survivors of Child Abuse: www.ascasupport.org

Healing Journey Chat Rooms for Adult Survivors of Trauma and Abuse: www.healing-journey.net

Rape, Abuse and Incest National Network: www.rainn.org

Granite Scientific Press: www.GraniteScientific.com
(Many articles on how abuse affects health of adult survivors.)

Adult Children of Alcoholics

Adult Children of Alcoholics World Service Organization: www.adultchildren.org

Children of Alcoholics Foundation: www.coaf.org

National Association for Children of Alcoholics: www.nacoa.net

Domestic Violence

National Organization for Victim Assistance: www.try-nova.org

Safe Horizon: www.safehorizon.org

Books about Psychological Trauma in General

These are great books to read if you want a broader understanding of psychological trauma in general. You may be surprised (and reassured) to discover that many of the emotions you are experiencing are predictable and normal for people who have experienced negative or traumatic life events.

Figley, C. 1985. *Trauma and Its Wake: The Study and Treatment of Post-Traumatic Stress Disorder.* New York: Bruner/Mazel.

Figley, C. 1986. *Trauma and Its Wake: Vol II. Traumatic Stress, Theory, Research and Intervention.* New York: Bruner/Mazel.

Herman, J.L. 1992. *Trauma and Recovery.* New York: Basic Books.

Kendall-Tackett, K.A. 2003. *Treating the Lifetime Health Effects of Childhood Victimization.* Kingston, New Jersey: Civic Research Institute.

Kendall-Tackett, K.A. 2004. *Health Consequences of Abuse in the Family.* Washington, D.C.: American Psychological Association.

Kendall-Tackett, K.A. 2005. *The Handbook of Women, Stress and Trauma.* New York: Taylor & Francis.

CHAPTER 10

Challenging Child I: Mothering a Child with Behavioral Issues

Several years ago, I was waiting for my son at a soccer camp. Soon, another mom joined me. As we chatted, she proceeded to tell me about her "hyper" son. On several occasions, she apologized in advance for her child's behavior, anticipating that he would soon be acting up. Although we had just met, she shared with me how mothering her challenging child had undermined her confidence, isolated her from other parents, strained her marriage, and kept her from having more children. And, she is not alone.

Children with behavioral issues can push parents to their limits. A recent article published in the journal *Child Abuse and Neglect* demonstrates the seriousness of problems that parents can face. In Sullivan and Knutson's study (2000) of over 50,000 children in the Midwest, they found that children with behavioral disabilities were *seven times* more likely to be maltreated (neglected and physically and emotionally abused) than were children without behavioral disabilities. Much of this abuse occurred in the children's own homes. Mothers were the abusers 67% of the time.

In this chapter, I describe two types of behavioral difficulties: the spirited temperament and attention deficit hyperactivity disorder (ADHD). While temperament and attentional difficulties are two distinct entities, they sometimes overlap and share many similarities in terms of how they make mothers feel. I focus on behavior because it is the most salient and challenging aspect of mothering these children.

The Spirited Temperament

From the start, babies come to us with their own personalities or temperaments, which range from easy to difficult. It is the difficult child who is the subject of this section. You may have noticed that I did not use "difficult" in the title for this section. Mary Kurcinka author of *Raising Your Spirited Child* (1998) points out that the word difficult emphasizes the negative aspects of this personality type without describing any of the positives. She prefers the term "spirited" because it honestly captures the challenges you face, while also describing the strengths of these children. It is a term that can give both you and your child hope. I prefer this term as well.

What Is a Spirited Child?

Children's temperaments include several dimensions: how much they cry, how well they adapt to new situations, how irritable they are, how active they are, and so on. Kurcinka (1998) lists nine dimensions that describe the spirited temperament; your child's temperament might exhibit one or more (or even all) of these dimensions:

1. **Intense.** Spirited children are intense. They often react negatively and tend to cry frequently. When they do cry, it is loud. Positive emotions are powerful (and loud), too.

2. **Persistent.** Spirited children are also persistent. Once they lock into an activity, they are reluctant to give it up.

3. **Sensitive.** These children are highly sensitive to sounds, smells, and the feel of their clothing. Crowds or lots of sensations at once easily overwhelm them. When their senses are overloaded, they have a tendency to overreact and have tantrums, both at home and in public places.

4. **Perceptive.** Spirited children notice everything and must often stop to observe whatever catches their attention. They may be on their way to do one thing when something else distracts them.

5. **Not easily adaptable.** Spirited children can be slow to accept new experiences. They do not enjoy surprises and often have difficulty transitioning from one activity to another.

6. **Irregular.** These children tend not to engage in regular routines. They are almost impossible to get on any kind of schedule. Many of them are almost super-human in their lack of need for sleep. This trait alone contributes to many of the bad feelings that mothers of these children experience.

7. **Energetic.** Children with spirited temperaments are often on the high end of the energy scale. Even if they are not running around, they are busy taking things apart, exploring, or making things.

8. **Tend to have a negative first reaction.** Spirited children will often receive new situations or activities negatively. Their first reaction is often no.

9. **Tend to have gloomy moods.** Spirited children can be very serious or even gloomy. They can also be pessimistic and are likely to focus on the negative aspects or flaws of a situation.

It's helpful to think of these dimensions as continua. Even among children with spirited temperaments, there is variation. Your child may have a personality that is mildly spirited, or your child may be on the other end--what some have called "explosive." Children with spirited temperaments can push mothers to their limits, even while they are still babies. Sheila Kitzinger studied 1,400 women in Australia and England. She compared mothers of babies who cried the most (more than six hours per day) to babies who cried the least (less than two hours per day). Among the mothers whose babies cried the most, she found that 80% were depressed, 57% described a desperate need to escape, 50% admitted that they were "itching to smack the baby," and 33% made negative comments about their partners. Common themes these mothers shared were of feeling trapped, guilty, useless, exhausted, inadequate, and bewildered (Kitzinger, 1990). In introducing these findings, Kitzinger made an interesting observation. She said that prior to working on this study, she couldn't understand how anyone could hit a baby. After the study, she was amazed that these women managed so much self-control.

As infants, spirited children need to be held a great deal of the time. They often will not separate from you. If you leave them with a sitter, they may cry the whole time you are gone. These needs can leave you feeling drained. They also open you up to criticism from others who assume that you made your child this way.

As your spirited child matures, she may not cry as much, but she will continue to exhibit behavior that exasperates you. Your feelings of frustration often will continue even with older children, as Lynn describes:

> I have a three-and-a-half-year-old spirited child. He is highly intelligent and very articulate. But, he has a very two-sided disposition. He can be the most thoughtful, generous, loving, helping child, and he can also be your worst nightmare. He bites other children to get his way. He must always win every confrontation. When he is in his bad mood, he will do anything to be difficult. He truly does not care what the cost will be. Once he is in this mode, I can't get him out of it. My husband has a particularly difficult time with him when he is this way.

Factors That Can Influence How You Feel

Spirited children are not all equal. Each child is a unique person in a unique family with unique circumstances. But, some types of situations are more difficult than others, making things more challenging for you.

Sleep Deprivation

A spirited temperament is often obvious from birth. These children can be poor sleepers and don't seem to require as much sleep as other children their age. If you have a baby or child who wakes several times during the night, this alone can wreak havoc on your emotional state. As I frequently tell mothers, prisoners of war are deprived of sleep as a means of torture. Therefore, you shouldn't be surprised when you fare poorly on limited sleep. (See chapter 8 for some specific suggestions to help you cope.)

Should You Let Your Baby "Cry It Out"?

Parents of spirited children are often advised to let their babies cry. If you respond to your child's cries the thinking goes, you are "reinforcing" it. If you have already tried letting your children cry, you already know that it doesn't work well for children with spirited temperaments. As Robert Wright (1997) describes in an article on parent-child co-sleeping, his first child could cry for two hours straight "without reloading." Spirited children can become overwhelmed by their strong emotions. For them, crying can last for hours rather than minutes. It's not unusual for spirited children to become so upset while they cry that they throw up.

But bottom-line, does letting spirited children cry work? Let's look first at whether responding to crying "reinforces" it. In its technical meaning, reinforcement refers to increasing the likelihood that the behavior will occur. So applied to infant crying, the idea is that if you respond to crying, the baby will be more likely to cry in the future. Interestingly, researchers have found the opposite to be true. When mothers in one study consistently responded to and tried to comfort their crying babies at three months (Crockenberg & McCluskey, 1986), the babies (including those with difficult temperaments) cried less at 12 months during separation and were more securely attached.

Excessive Disruptiveness

Your child's behavior is going to be more difficult for you if it includes tantrums, outbursts, screaming, running around, and aggression toward children or adults. These disruptive behaviors can draw unwanted attention to you and your child. Your child's disruptiveness can also be isolating for you.

Loss of Self-esteem and Confidence in Parenting

What you think about your child's behavior also makes a difference. Much of the anguish of mothering a child with a spirited temperament comes from inside your own mind. If you blame yourself for this

211

behavior, your experience of it will be worse than if you attribute it to your child's personality. Mothers with other, non-spirited children are more likely to recognize the influence of temperament than are mothers with only one spirited child. Similarly, mothers with a more laid-back style of mothering are going to be more comfortable than mothers who want to be on top of everything in their lives.

Lack of Support

Support makes a difference here, too. Mothers who have other people in their lives who encourage them and offer to help fare better physically and emotionally than mothers who have no one or, worse, lots of criticism. Finding support is going to be critical to your emotional survival.

In the next section, I describe the child with ADHD. There is a substantial amount of overlap between a spirited temperament and ADHD, and some children have characteristics of both. But, they are separate entities. ADHD is described below.

Attention Deficit Hyperactivity Disorder (ADHD)

You can spot them quickly: the kids who just can't sit still or pay attention. Parents and teachers say that these children are "hyper." Children with attention deficit hyperactivity disorder (ADHD) often do draw attention to themselves by acting up and getting in trouble, both at school and at home.

ADHD actually refers to several different chronic disorders and is estimated to occur in approximately three to five percent of school-age children. It is two to three times more likely to occur in boys (National Institute of Mental Health, 2000a). However, when hyperactivity is dropped from the list of symptoms, such as in ADD--Attention Deficit Disorder, the number of boys and girls is almost equal. The number of diagnoses of ADHD is on the rise, as is its impact on the health care system. In 1990, a survey of 2,400 practicing physicians indicated that there were 2 million patient visits associated with ADHD. By 1994, this number had reached 4.7 million (Sears & Thompson, 1998).

In the introduction to *The A.D.D. Book,* pediatrician William Sears describes three types of children he sees in his practice that have a diagnosis of attention deficit disorder (ADD). The first are children with a true biological anomaly that causes them to think, act, and learn differently. For these children, he recommends a three-pronged management approach that includes medication, behavioral strategies, and learning strategies. The second type of child has a situational type of ADD. These children's symptoms are manifest only in some settings (such as a classroom), and generally reflect a mismatch between the situation and the child's needs. Finally, there are children who are bright, energetic, and creative who act and learn differently, but do not have a disability. However, these children are often inconvenient for teachers with large classes and schools that value sameness. According to Sears, these children do not deserve a label, but need a learning environment that meets their needs. Along these lines, some more alternative-medicine-oriented physicians, such as Andrew Weil, wonder whether we are too quick to attach a label of ADHD to any child, usually a boy, who is active (Weil, 2000). Is it ADHD or just normal development?

Symptoms of ADHD

There are four core symptoms of ADHD. Your child may have any or all of these. The first is **inattention.** An inattentive child has difficulty concentrating and gets bored easily. Such children often have difficulty completing assignments and routine tasks because their attention wanders or they are easily distracted.

The second symptom is **selective attention.** Children with ADHD can become hyperfocused on one thing, ignoring everything else. Selective attention explains why children who have difficulty completing assignments can play video games for hours. As I will describe later, this hyperfocus can also be a strength. But, it can be a problem for your child if it is not properly channeled.

The next symptom is **hyperactivity.** Not all children with an attentional disorder have this symptom. Hyperactive children are always in motion. Even when these children are sitting, they are tapping their feet or a pencil. They wiggle and roam around the room, and have a tendency to talk incessantly. It can be one of the more difficult symptoms for you and others to cope with. Attentional difficulties without this symptom (ADD rather than ADHD) are often not diagnosed because the children are not disruptive in class. Some of their lack of attention might be misinterpreted as laziness or lack of motivation.

The final core symptom is **impulsivity.** Children with this symptom seem unable to control their behavior and often do not think before they act. They may hit, blurt out inappropriate information, have a hard time waiting for their turn in games, and grab toys from other children. They also have a tendency to lose or break things and can be accident-prone (National Institute of Mental Health, 2000b). These characteristics often make children appear less mature than their peers and can make them targets for bullies at school (Sears & Thompson, 1998).

Other traits that have been observed in children with ADHD are similar to traits described earlier regarding temperament. The first is intensity. Teachers and others often describe these children as "too emotional." Related to this are tendencies to overreact and to be unaffected by past consequences or future rewards. These children often have poor handwriting. They need frequent rewards and are more likely to find many things boring (Sears & Thompson, 1998).

Factors That Influence How You Feel

Life with a child with ADHD can present many challenges similar to those of parenting a spirited child. Here are some of the factors that can influence how you feel.

Disruptive Behavior

The more disruptive the behavior of a child with ADHD, the more challenging mothering will be for you. You may be embarrassed to take your child anywhere since you don't know how he'll act. Your child may grab toys from others and act up at relatives' homes. You may have difficulty getting your child through the school system and find yourself frequently meeting with school personnel. It may be impossible for you to just go somewhere without making extensive plans.

Strenuousness of the Treatment Regimen

Another factor influencing how you feel is the difficulty of your child's ADHD treatment regimen. You may find that a multi-pronged approach works best. This routine may include dietary modifications, medications, and behavior management. For example, your child might be sensitive to artificial colors, flavors, or sugar. Unfortunately, all of these things are in foods children love. It can be a challenge to identify dietary sensitivities and monitor these foods.

If your child is on medication, it may take several attempts to find the right medication or dose that works for your child. Older children may skip medications or start refusing them. Multiple daily dosings are going to be more complex than a single dose. You may also have to arrange for medication to be given at school.

Finally, behavioral management requires intense planning. You may have to anticipate situations that set your child off, design rewards for good behavior, and help your child navigate problem times.

Lack of Support

It will probably come as no surprise to you that support is important for mothers of children with ADHD. Mothers without support have a much harder time than mothers with support. You might blame yourself for your child's behavior, and others may assume it is your fault, too. You need people in your life who can counter some of this negative input and offer you concrete support and assistance.

Living with ADHD: One Mother's Story

Below is an excerpt from Brandi Valentine's story (2000) of life with a son with ADHD. You'll notice some of the themes described earlier in this chapter. Her son's behavior strained her relationships with her family of origin and her partner, who eventually left. Her son also had difficulties with other children and at school.

By the time James was three, he had a reputation. He had problems playing with other children. Older children, including his cousins and older sister, refused to play with him, so he spent much of his time playing alone. On the occasions he did play with other children, they were always younger than he was. James was often in trouble with the neighbors, and the fighting with his sister was nonstop. My father was the least understanding of all the family members, telling everyone that James was going to be the first family member ever to go to prison. He felt that if I just beat the kid, he'd straighten up. It got to be so that every visit to my parents deteriorated into a fight over my parenting skills and my lack of willingness to beat the child. My father hit James whenever James didn't conform to my father's wishes. Soon, the visits stopped. Things at home were not much better. The constant bickering between James and his sister was intense. James's father criticized me for my lack of ability to control the child and belittled me for my poor parenting skills. When James was four, I was able to get him into a preschool class offered by the public school system. His behavior problems became more apparent and new behaviors arose as he was put into a classroom setting. The diagnosis from his preschool teachers: Your child is psychotic. So I went to my pediatrician. He told me James was fine, but if I so desired he could put me on a waiting list for therapy. I was then sent home. At the age of five, James went to kindergarten. His ADD/ADHD behaviors became more pronounced. He could not perform such simple functions as cutting, drawing, or writing. He couldn't sit in his seat. He often spent his four hours a day in class either lying on the floor under the table or wandering aimlessly through the classroom touching everything. He was unable to stay on task no matter what he chose to do. The teacher overwhelmed with thirty children had no time for James, and as long as he didn't bother other students, he was allowed to wander through the class doing as he pleased. Due to the lack of funding in the school districts here, there was no aide for James' class, so I took on the role in order to help my son. It broke my heart to watch as he never got called upon to act out the little stories they learned. His papers were never placed on the wall, he was never invited to play with the other children, he was never chosen to take the attendance sheets to the office, and he was often left out of field trips because of his behavior. I now had something else to worry about--his self-esteem.

As Brandi's story indicates, ADHD can influence children's ability to make friends and do well in school. Such children's impulsiveness may lead to aggression with other children and may make them vulnerable to bullies. Other children may figure out how to make your child overreact, and he may end up in the principal's office--again!

Your child may start to feel like a bad kid. Not surprisingly, children with ADHD often have low self-esteem and are at higher risk for depression. If ADHD is unrecognized and untreated, children can have academic difficulties, increasing their risk for problems later in life, including problems with the law (Sears & Thompson, 1998).

Some Common Feelings

If your child has a spirited temperament or attentional disorder, you are probably working a lot harder than other mothers. Even day-to-day tasks are more challenging. Simply getting dressed for the day may turn into a battle of wills, as your child insists on wearing shorts in 38-degree weather. If you forget to give your child adequate preparation for an upcoming change, you might find that he is "off" for the whole day. Even cutting a sandwich into squares instead of triangles can cause a meltdown.

Mothers of children with behavioral concerns receive lots of unsolicited child-rearing advice. This can make you feel resentful, misunderstood, or inadequate as a mother. The responsibilities of caring for a child with behavioral concerns can be overwhelming, as Ellen describes: "At one of our recent visits to our son's clinical psychologist, I was informed that if I were in a paid profession, I could probably sue for burnout."

Depression

Mothers of children with behavioral concerns are at higher risk for depression, and this risk starts while their children are still infants. One study found a direct link between a difficult temperament in babies and depression in mothers (Cutrona & Troutman, 1986). These researchers also found that caring for a baby with a spirited temperament gradually eroded mothers feelings of self-efficacy, making them feel incompetent. Another study found that depressed mothers tended to blame themselves for their infants' behaviors. This occurred despite the fact that independent raters determined that the infants were, in reality, more difficult (Whiffen & Gotlib, 1989).

Similarly, having a child with an attentional disorder can increase your vulnerability to depression (McCormick, 1995). You may blame yourself for your child's difficulties and feel like you did something wrong. Even if you don't feel this way, others may openly speculate about what you did to bring about this condition in your child. Other families may not want you and your child around.

Without help and support, you might find yourself withdrawing from your baby or child and describing him in mostly negative terms. Unfortunately, if this cycle is not interrupted, you might find yourself unhappy with your child most of the time and sometimes resorting to harsh forms of punishment, which ties in with the next reaction I describe: anger.

Anger

Another common reaction to dealing with a spirited or attention-disordered child is anger, and this may also start early in your relationship. Children who have behavioral problems can embarrass parents in public with tantrums or outbursts. They may be asked to leave play groups, day care, or preschool. They may bite or hit other children. Other parents can also get quite angry with your child. You may resent how much your child seems to need to be with you and long for a break. Even during infancy, when these children don't sleep well, sleep deprivation may lead you to overreact to some of your child's behaviors. You might think about hitting your child as Barbara describes:

When the baby started throwing up, I felt terrible. I wouldn't go anyplace with her because I didn't want people to see her screaming. I wanted to be the perfect mother. My mother-in-law said, "You've got to relax. She's picking up on your cues." The baby had a difficult temperament. Even now, she's very stubborn and strong-willed. The control issue is big for me. I'm a perfectionist and always have been. I don't want the baby to experiment with food, even though I know its normal.

I wanted this baby so bad. When she came, I hated her. I thought of throwing her out the window. I just wanted her to die. I spanked her when she was three or four weeks old, and I'm still dealing with the guilt of it. I'd yell at her, right in her face, "I hate you. I wish you would die."

As I mentioned earlier, children with behavioral difficulties are the most likely to be abused and neglected. It is important that you realize that many other parents experience anger at their children. But, it is equally important that you get support and find safe ways to vent your anger so that it is not directed toward your child.

Guilt

Guilt is another common feeling among mothers of children with behavioral issues. Mothers tend to take a lot of responsibility for their children's behaviors. This may be especially true if the child with the behavioral issues is your first or only child. Mothers whose other children don't have behavioral concerns are often reassured that these behaviors are not their fault.

You may feel guilty because you harbor unpleasant feelings toward or even dislike your child. Sometimes, you might lose control and hit your child. When others talk to you about their warm feelings toward their children, you may begin to wonder what is wrong with you.

219

Isolation

Isolation is common among parents of children with behavioral issues. Parents may find that they are socially shunned. Family outings may need to be limited because your child is easily overwhelmed by too many people in the room, too much noise, or too much visual distraction. You might be embarrassed to go anywhere with your child because you don't know how she will act. People will often let you know that you need to "do something," but will leave you to cope alone.

Your Other Relationships

Having a child with behavioral issues can influence your relationships. Your partner may imply, or actually say, that you need to do a better job controlling "your" child. You may find that all your time together as a couple is dominated by taking care of your child, with no time left to nurture your relationship with each other. The cumulative effect of months of sleep deprivation may make both of you overreact to real or imagined offenses. The stress on your marriage or relationship is real; divorce is twice as common in families with a child with ADHD as it is in families with no ADHD (Sears & Thompson, 1998).

Caring for your child may severely limit other things you need to do. For example, if you are at home with your child, you may find it is difficult to take a shower, let alone clean the house or prepare dinner. This can lead to many misunderstandings between you and your partner. Your partner may return home and wonder what you did all day. Mary, whose son has a temperament on the extreme end of spirited, described how in her family, all other activities are on hold indefinitely. Her house is often in disarray and one time was so thrashed that the cleaning service she had hired had to call the office for help. The whole situation may feel so overwhelming that you seek employment outside the home just so you can escape. Of course, you may find you have difficulties trying to find someone who will care for your child while you work.

Raising a child with a spirited temperament or ADHD can leave you feeling drained. Right now, it's all you can do to cope day to day. It's impossible to even consider that there might be an upside. But, there are parents who have raised children just like yours and have lived to tell the tale.

Is There an Upside?

In the newest edition of the classic book *Parenting the Fussy Baby and the High-Need Child* (1996), William and Martha Sears open by describing their seventeen-year-old-daughter. She was their fussy baby and the inspiration for their book. Now she is a bright, talented young woman. Spirited children often are very perceptive, insightful, and sensitive. They see and experience things more deeply than do their more easygoing counterparts. The very characteristics that stress their parents actually turn into strengths.

Similarly, psychologist Lara Honos-Webb, in her book *The Gift of ADHD* (2005) notes that while many of the characteristics of children with ADHD seem negative on the surface, these traits may suggest positive underlying characteristics, such as a powerful imagination or searching insight. Children with ADHD are often very bright. Their ability to hyperfocus can actually be an advantage in certain situations, such as in sports. For example, it is a rare child who can concentrate so completely that she is not distracted by outside sights and sounds. The ability to hyperfocus actually gives such a child a competitive edge.

High energy is another trait that can be trying for teachers and parents. But, these children can become highly productive adults. Sears describes his own experiences as a child and an adult with ADD. Even during medical school, his professors were concerned about his high energy level. But, he points out that he has written twenty-three books and fathered eight children!

Finally, children with ADHD are often very creative because they are used to thinking about things differently. They can think fast and are good at focusing on the big picture. They can also be very tenacious and persistent. While they may have difficulty in school, they may excel at activities that require hands-on learning and creativity.

221

What You Can Do

Fortunately, there are a number of positive steps you can take to live more peacefully with your child. It is important that you take some positive action. Without it, the issues these children face become worse over time. Sears and Thompson (1998) noted that ADHD that is not recognized and managed can become a disability. If it is understood, accepted, valued, and shaped, it can be an advantage for your child and the people around him. A similar comment could be made about children with spirited temperaments.

Become the Expert on Your Child

If you haven't already done so, learn everything you can about your child's condition. This may mean reading parenting books, searching the Internet, or joining a support group. Also, learn from watching your child. When there is an episode, try to figure out what set things off after everything is calm again. You might find it helpful to keep a log. Look for patterns and try to figure out what the triggers are for your child. Sears recommends that parents do this because no one else will. Even if other people in your child's life care about him and want him to succeed, chances are they don't have the same investment you have. Learn so that you can become your child's advocate.

Design Situations Where Your Child Can Win

Once you know what sets your child off, you can start to design situations that bring out the best in your child, instead of the worst. For example, you might limit your child's exposure to situations where there are lots of people he doesn't know or where there is too much noise. You might start scheduling events, such as appointments or family outings, so that they occur during the time of day that is best for your child. Similarly, you might allow some acclimation time, or time between activities, so that you don't surprise your child with a sudden shift.

Sometimes, parents resent having to make all these accommodations for their children with behavioral challenges. Why must you go to all this extra effort on behalf of only one of your children? Others may have told you that your accommodations are silly or you will "spoil" your child. In considering whether these accommodations are a good idea, you might ponder what the alternative would be. You could try to force your child to behave, increase the amount and severity of punishment, or get into power struggles over everything. Chances are you have already tried this and found that it not only doesn't work, but dramatically increases the degree of unpleasantness in your home.

Anticipating your child's trouble spots and doing some prevention does not mean that you will never have another unpleasant day. But, you may find that the number decreases to a much more manageable level.

Avoid Power Struggles

A similar strategy has to do with avoiding battles over day-to-day activities by anticipating potential conflicts and having clear rules to deal with them. For example, you allow your child to select today's wardrobe, but you have only acceptable choices available. (If it is winter, store the shorts and tank tops elsewhere.) When asking what your child would like for breakfast, again offer only acceptable choices. You might offer cold cereal or oatmeal. This avoids struggles that might arise when your child selects candy for breakfast because she was asked an open-ended question.

Make Correct Attributions for Your Child's Behavior

Many of the problems you encounter as a mother of a child with behavioral issues are due to what our culture has to say about children. Ours is a culture that values children's independence from a very early age. From birth, children sleep in their own beds and are encouraged to be as separate from you as possible. Any baby or child who protests this forced separation is said to be manipulating you.

However, children with spirited temperaments often have a very high need to be with you. They may not separate easily and may cry until they make themselves sick. Parents put themselves and their children through these separations because they think it is in their children's best interests. Much of this cultural mandate has its roots in the behaviorism of the 1920s when John B. Watson encouraged mothers not to spoil their children with affection. While we rightly recognize the foolishness of much of his advice, pieces of it remain.

Other cultures that do not have this philosophical baggage consider some of our child-rearing tactics to be bizarre and even abusive. Kids with easygoing temperaments can often adapt to our culture's rigid approach. But, as you probably already know, children with spirited temperaments or ADHD do not. We need to retrain ourselves to think of our children's dependency needs as legitimate and not as attempts to manipulate us or get away with something. As I noted in the sidebar earlier in this chapter, children whose dependency needs have been met are generally more securely attached to their parents and cry less than children who have been forced to behave.

Get Support

I've said it throughout this book and I'll say it again: If you have a child with a behavioral concern, it can be very reassuring to talk to another parent who is struggling with the same issues. When you meet other parents whose children are acting the same way, it will be easier for you to believe that you are not the cause.

Children with behavioral issues can bring out the worst in their parents and teachers. Support is absolutely essential if you feel that you are losing control. These children are at very high risk of being abused, and to be truthful, it's not hard to see why. It is important that you find a person or group who will let you air your feelings in a safe way so that you do not take them out on your child.

Don't Make Any Permanent Decisions on Future Children Yet

In *Parenting the Fussy Baby and the High-Need Child* (1996), William and Martha Sears caution parents not to take any permanent steps to limit the size of their families until things are on a more even keel.

They describe how parents in their practice sometimes decided to get a vasectomy or tubal ligation, only to have their children grow out of their difficult stage. These parents often regretted their decision. If possible, wait until things settle down before making any permanent decisions.

Conclusion

Mothering a child who has behavioral issues can quickly swamp your coping abilities and bring you to your emotional knees. You might feel overwhelmed and totally alone. If you do, take heart. There are others who have gone before you and will show you the way. Take advantage of some of the resources listed at the end of this chapter and find the solution that works best for you.

For Further Reading

Reading the stories of other parents struggling with similar concerns can be very reassuring. These books and Web sites can offer a lot of assistance with any issue you are facing.

Resources for Temperament and ADHD

If you've never read a book about some of the issues you might be facing, these books are a great place to start. These are the ones that get passed from parent to parent. Each offers its own comforting advice.

Greene, R. 1998. *The Explosive Child.* New York: HarperCollins.

Honos-Webb, L. 2005. *The Gift of ADHD: How to Transform Your Child's Problems into Strengths.* Oakland, CA: New Harbinger.

Kitzinger, S. 1990. *The Crying Baby.* New York: Penguin.

Kurcinka, M.S. 1998. *Raising Your Spirited Child.* New York: Harper Perennial.

Kurcinka, M.S. 1998. *Raising Your Spirited Child Workbook.* New York: Harper Perennial.

Monastra, V.J. 2005. *Parenting Children with ADHD: 10 Lessons that Medicine Cannot Teach.* Washington, D.C.: American Psychological Association.

Sears, W., & Sears, M. 1996. *Parenting the Fussy Baby and High-Need Child.* New York: Little, Brown.

Sears, W., & Thompson, L. 1998. *The A.D.D. Book: New Understandings, New Approaches to Parenting Your Child.* New York: Little, Brown.

ADD Consultations: www.addconsults.com

ADDvance: www.ADDvance.com.
(For women and girls with ADHD)

ADD Warehouse: www.addwarehouse.com

Children and Adults with ADHD: www.chadd.org

Postpartum Education for Parents: www.sbpep.org

University of Illinois Extension: search for Nibbles, then Coping with the Spirited Child: www.urbanext.uiuc.edu

IVillage.com: http://parenting.ivillage.com/gs/gsbehavior/0,,45pv,00. html?iv_arrivalSA=1&iv_cobrandRef=0&iv_arrival_ freq=1&pba=adid=15207750
(Article on spirited children)

Books on Anger and Parenting/ Positive Discipline Strategies

Kurcinka, M.S. 2000. *Kids, Parents, and Power Struggles: Winning for a Lifetime.* New York: HarperCollins.

Nelsen, J., Erwin, C., & Delzer, C. 1994. *Positive Discipline for Single Parents: A Practical Guide to Raising Children Who Are Responsible, Respectful, and Resourceful.* Rocklin, CA: Prima Publishing.

Samalin, N. 1991. *Love and Anger.* New York: Penguin.

Sears, W., & Sears, M. 1995. *The Discipline Book.* New York: Little, Brown.

CHAPTER 11

Challenging Child II: Mothering a Child with Health Issues

For Mary, each day begins early as she must allow an extra two hours to get her daughter ready for school. Her days and weeks are filled with doctors' appointments, physical therapy, meetings with school personnel, and intense daily care of her child. By the end of the day, she is exhausted. She is inspired by her daughter's gentle spirit and quiet dignity. But, she sometimes wishes she had more help and just a little time off because the day-to-day living is so hard.

Mothering a child with a chronic illness or disability can be relentless and overwhelming. It can also be a source of personal growth and satisfaction. Your experience may contain elements of both. In this chapter, I describe some of the challenges of mothering a child with health concerns. Though there are a great number of health conditions that could be included in this chapter, I've focused on two broad categories: prematurity and chronic illness/disability. Many forms of chronic health issues are covered under these broad terms.

Prematurity

Every year in the U.S., approximately eight percent of babies are born either prematurely or with a low birth weight (National Center for Health Statistics, 2004). Fortunately, most of these babies now survive. However, babies born very early or very small are still at risk for a number of serious complications, including brain hemorrhages, chronic lung disease, respiratory distress, blindness or visual impairment, cerebral palsy, and language delays (American Association for Premature Infants, 2000), and their death rate is still substantially higher than babies who are full term.

A premature birth is almost always a surprise. Mothers and fathers are often overwhelmed by the emergency nature of the birth. The neonatal intensive care unit (NICU) can be intimidating. Today, NICU personnel are much better about involving mothers and helping them cope with the psychological fallout of having a baby born too soon. But, your baby may have been born before these changes were in place. Or, you may have encountered a hospital staff that didn't give you much attention, even recently.

Today's cost-consciousness in health care contributes to the challenges new mothers face. Health care providers are being forced to reduce hospital stays, so many fragile babies are being released from the hospital with little help and support for mothers. According to the American Association for Premature Infants, premature babies are falling through the cracks of our health care system. Many parents cannot find the services they need for their children, including occupational, physical, and/or speech therapy.

Mothers of premature babies are often anxious for the health and well-being of their babies. And, this anxiety can last long past infancy. Sandy, one of my former students, told me that she had been a very tiny premature baby at birth. As she was preparing to graduate from college with high honors, her mother said to her, "You're really okay, aren't you"? Sandy related the story with some exasperation, but it gives a glimpse into the fears and concerns her mother had. It was as if her mother had been holding her breath all these years, waiting to see if her child would be okay. Sandy's mother's reaction was not unusual. Linda, whose son was born at twenty-seven weeks and weighed two pounds, describes similar feelings:

> When my son was about sixteen months old, I began to have anxiety attacks. I don't think I ever dealt with all of the pain and heartache of the NICU. No matter how old or big our babies get, they will always be preemies to us.

Similar reactions have been noted in research studies, where mothers of preterm infants were less confident in their ability to parent than mothers of full-term infants, particularly if they had been denied contact with their babies. They also had difficulties learning to read their babies cues and were less likely to hold them, make eye contact, or smile. These problems vanished, or at least diminished, when mothers had access to their babies and were given help and support (Kendall-Tackett, 2005b). Patricia describes what it was like for her to give birth to a very ill premature baby:

> My first child was born at thirty-five weeks with severe hyaline membrane disease. He was in the hospital for five months: in the NICU for four months and in intermediate care for one month. The depression started around the time he was three or four weeks old. Up until that time, everything had been so urgent. He had had a couple of arrests. It was overwhelming. Suddenly, my son was doing better. Why was I feeling so bad? I had difficulties going to sleep. I was up several times during the night. It was difficult to wake up in the morning. I didn't want to do anything during the day except sleep and call the NICU to check in. I started to not eat well. I felt an impending sense of doom.

Your feelings after having a premature baby can be influenced by how early or sick your baby was at birth. They can also be influenced by your birth experience, how you were treated at the hospital, and how much support you had once your baby was released.

Level of Prematurity and Illness

If a baby was very premature (less than thirty weeks), very small (less than 1,500 grams), or very ill, you are more likely to be troubled than if your baby was healthy, relatively large, or only a couple of weeks early. Some babies even if they are not very premature have physical problems, including immature lungs, cerebral palsy, or intraventricular hemorrhage. Even babies who are not gravely ill may seem fragile and small. Not surprisingly, in a sample of mothers of premature babies, Blumberg (1980) found that the sicker the baby, the more likely the mother was to be depressed.

Circumstances of the Birth

Your baby's birth may have occurred under emergency conditions. You may have sustained an injury, such as a car accident or physical assault, which brought on premature labor. A complication of pregnancy, such as placenta previa, may have necessitated an emergency delivery. You may have been away from home when you went into labor, only to have your baby in an ambulance, cab, or emergency room away from your own doctor and family. Being separated from your baby may have been traumatic. Your baby may have been taken away before you could even hold her, as Helen describes:

> They took her away right after delivery. I never got to hold her. They brought her back, but my arms were tied to the delivery table. I wish they had released at least one arm. Leaving the hospital without the baby was really bad. I left early because I didn't want to leave at 11 a.m. with all the other moms and babies.

The Medical Situation

While care of babies in NICUs has greatly improved, you may have had your baby at a time when parents were excluded. Watching the staff perform medical interventions can be very difficult. For Jan, the worst part was watching the hospital staff put a tube down her baby's throat. She could hear her baby cry and gag and couldn't do anything about it. Even several years later, thinking about it makes her cry: "I shouldn't complain because she only had a few preemie problems. Others in the nursery were so sick. But, it was very stressful."

Medical personnel may have been insensitive and made comments that were hurtful or rude. Patricia described how the majority of doctors and nurses caring for her son were great. But, even after ten years, there was one comment that still rankles:

> A second-year resident said the worst thing to me. He said, "You see that baby over there? We called the parents" (which meant that the baby was going to die), "but your baby is the sickest one

on the unit." He was implying that our baby was sicker than the one who was going to die.

Anticipatory Grieving

Anticipatory grieving is another common reaction that can present some challenges for you. As you became convinced that your baby would not survive, you may have started to distance yourself from him in order to prepare for his eventual death. When your baby recovered and lived, your mourning was interrupted, and you had to readjust your focus. Having come so close to death, it may have taken some time for you to assimilate the reality that your baby would live.

The Transition to Home

The transition to home can be difficult for parents, especially after a lengthy hospital stay. Premature babies often act differently than full-term babies their same age. They are often more sensitive to stimulation and easily become overwhelmed. When babies withdraw, mothers may think their babies are rejecting them. Sometimes, mothers respond by withdrawing from their babies. This seems especially true in cases where the baby is very sick as was demonstrated in one research study (Jarvis et al., 1989). In this study researchers compared three groups of premature babies: those with no medical complications, those who were moderately ill (respiratory distress syndrome), and those who were very ill (bronchopulmonary dysplasia) at four and eight months of age. As predicted, degree of illness did influence the mother/infant interaction at both time points. Mothers of the sickest infants emotionally withdrew and became less responsive to them over time. But, mothers of moderately ill babies actually became more responsive over time.

Continuing health problems may have made your transition home more difficult. Although your baby was well enough to be released from the hospital, she was still not well. You may have had to scramble for services your baby needed. Andrea describes how medical mismanagement and her son's continuing illness filled her with anxiety:

> In his discharge conference, the pediatrician proposed that there may be something else going on. She thought maybe it was cystic fibrosis. I went crazy waiting for the results. She also tested for gammaglobulin, but never contacted us about the results. I assumed no news was good news. He was sick constantly the first year and a half. I found out the report on the gammaglobulin had been positive. No one did anything. He could have died. It was a nightmare.

Having been premature, your child is more vulnerable to chronic illness and disability. For many mothers with premature infants, this is phase two in the story of their children's health problems. But, there are many other mothers and children whose stories begin here. In the next section, I describe some of the challenges that mothers of children with chronic conditions face.

Chronic Illness and Disability

Myriad illnesses affect children. Common chronic childhood illnesses include asthma, diabetes, and autoimmune diseases such as juvenile rheumatoid arthritis and ulcerative colitis. Childhood cancer, once almost always fatal, is now being survived by many of the children who get it and is considered a chronic illness rather than a fatal disease.

Disability also covers a wide range of conditions. There are sensory disabilities such as blindness and deafness, motor impairments such as cerebral palsy, and developmental disorders including mental retardation, autism, pervasive developmental disorder (PDD), and Asperger's syndrome. There are emotional disabilities such as depression and post-traumatic stress disorder. Even learning disabilities and ADHD can be included in the list.

There is substantial overlap between the conditions described in this and the previous chapter. For example, a child who was born prematurely is at increased risk for cerebral palsy, ADHD, and learning disabilities. Some 20% of children with learning disabilities may also have ADHD.

Also, current thinking about developmental disorders places ADHD on the same spectrum as PDD, autism, and Asperger's syndrome; although, it is important to stress that ADHD will not progress to one of these more serious illnesses.

Mothers are often the ones who bear the full brunt of their children's health issues. In one recent study of parents in the year following the birth of a child with a congenital abnormality, mothers were significantly more likely to report personal strain than were fathers (Hunfeld et al., 1999). Similarly, in a study of parents of children with Asperger's Syndrome, Little (2002) found that a significantly higher percentage of mothers reported stress than fathers. A child with a chronic health condition can strain family finances, stress relationships, and cut families off from important sources of support (LaPlante et al., 1996).

Some parents are so overwhelmed that they do the unthinkable--abuse their children. Sullivan and Knutson (2000) studied more than 50,000 children in the Midwest. They found that children with disabilities were three times more likely to be neglected and physically, emotionally, or sexually abused compared with children who do not have disabilities. If you are struggling, it is important for you to recognize that you might respond to overwhelming stress by lashing out at your child. While most mothers have occasional angry feelings, you must find help and support so that you do not vent them on your child.

Certain factors influence how mothers feel in response to a child with health concerns, even when those illnesses and disabilities differ from one another. These factors will influence how challenging your child's condition is for you.

Seriousness of Health Concern

The higher the degree of risk for your baby or child, the more challenging a health concern will be for you. During the course of a life-threatening event, you might find that everything else goes on hold. Your life is reduced to day-to-day, or even hour-to-hour, functioning.

233

If your child's condition is serious but not life-threatening, you may still have many of the same concerns. Depending on how much help your child needs with the activities of daily living and whether she spends time at school or is home all day, your days may be filled with caring for your child and transporting her to and from appointments with physical or occupational therapists, doctors, and other health care providers.

Obviousness or Stigma of Impairment

The type and obviousness of your child's impairment can influence how others react to you and your child and also how you feel about yourself and your child. It might seem odd, but there is a hierarchy of acceptability of illness and disability. Some chronic conditions are likely to engender sympathy and support, while others can engender stigma and isolation. In summarizing the research literature, psychologist Rhoda Olkin (1999) notes that our judgments are influenced by the severity, visibility, and treatability of the condition; its effect on life expectancy; and whether the condition is perceived as contagious. In the hierarchy, conditions such as asthma or diabetes are not obvious and, therefore, more acceptable. Conditions that are more obvious are less acceptable and more stigmatized. Olkin indicates that the most highly stigmatized conditions are para- and quadriplegia, multiple sclerosis, cerebral palsy, and facial disfigurement.

In trying to explain why these stigmas exist, Olkin notes that all of us have ideas about how the body should appear, move, function, think, behave, and communicate. When people deviate from these standards, we stigmatize them. The more people deviate, the greater the level of stigma (Olkin, 1999). Even when there are no particular health consequences to an impairment, people may still shun your child if he or she looks different from other people.

Strenuousness of Managing the Condition

Some conditions require little effort from caretakers, while others require a great deal. The more strenuous the caretaking regimen, the more challenging it will be for you. For example, mothers of children with dietary restrictions must plan and be vigilant every day. Children

234

with peanut allergies can die from eating anything with peanuts, so their mothers may have to go to great lengths to ensure that their children are not exposed. Indeed, at mothers' insistence, some school districts have even gone so far as to request that all parents avoid the use of peanut butter if a child with a peanut allergy goes to a school. If your child has these types of allergies, some of these necessary measures can lead to social isolation for you and your child.

Another illness with dietary restrictions is diabetes: eating a forbidden food can bring on a coma or even death. Parents of a diabetic child must monitor the child's blood sugar levels and supervise his insulin injections. Managing this illness is a daily event.

Another type of condition that involves frequent management is orthopedic impairment, which may require daily exercises to strengthen muscles and protect joints. In addition, these exercises may need to be regularly supervised by a professional, such as a physical therapist.

Children in wheelchairs may also need a great deal of assistance in the activities of daily living, such as dressing, bathing, and toileting. Normal morning routines will tend to take longer so mothers will need to allow extra time for almost all activities. As children grow, managing these activities often becomes physically strenuous as well.

Beliefs About Why It Occurred

According to Gerry Koocher, pediatric psychologist and dean of Health Studies at Simmons College in Boston, parents may be either aided or hindered in coping with their children's illnesses by their beliefs about why it occurred. If parents believe they are responsible or that God is punishing them by making their children ill, coping will be much more difficult. On the other hand, if they believe that their children's conditions have brought some positives, they are in a better position to cope, as Elena describes:

> When I questioned why this terrible thing was happening, I kept in mind Billy's strong spirit and that something larger than myself was taking place. I thanked him for coming into our lives

and always felt pride at everything he accomplished and fought for. I am constantly amazed at the blessing of his presence in my life, what a gift it is to live this life in his company, as his mother.

Attempting to understand why something occurred is a natural part of coming to terms with a difficult event. However, when seeking a reason turns to guilt and blame, it ceases to be a helpful strategy for coping.

Suddenness

Illness or disability can happen suddenly with no warning. In *Healing the Child* (1996), Nancy Cain describes how her son became critically ill after being exposed to E. coli bacteria. He went from bright and healthy to deathly ill almost overnight. After he recovered from his infection, he developed seizures that were often life-threatening. This family's world was forever changed by their son's illness. Having no warning of these impending changes can make it more difficult to cope.

Cumulative Stressors

Families may be faced with multiple stressors at the same time, all contributing to a higher level of overall stress. Some types of stressors you may experience as the parent of an ill or disabled child include financial problems, strained relationships with your partner or other family members, single parenting, job pressures, and lack of support. Not surprisingly, the total number of children in a family can make a difference in the mother's stress level. Mothers are more able to cope with a child with health issues if they have only one child. Children with health issues born later into the family can be a greater source of stress because mothers have other children to care for as well.

Some Common Feelings

Parenting a child with a health concern tends to bring up certain feelings. I discuss some of the most common reactions below. It is important that you recognize and acknowledge your feelings, but it is also important that you get the help you need. According to Olkin (1999), there are two important tasks for parents of a child with a disability: accepting your child as a full member of the family and accepting the disability itself. These tasks will be easier for you if you are not struggling to take care of everything all by yourself.

Resentment and Anger

Resentment is a common feeling among parents whose children have health issues. If you have a child who is sick or has a disability, you may resent the changes you've had to make in your life. You may have had to quit your job. Outside activities may have been curtailed indefinitely. Your family may have needed to move to be closer to a medical facility. Having a medically fragile child may strain your finances to the limit.

You might also find that you are angry with others. If you are married, having a child with an illness or disability can strain your marriage. In fact, many marriages do not survive. If you have other, healthy children, you may resent their demands on your time, or even that they are healthy when your other child is sick.

The constant need to navigate the medical or educational systems may leave you feeling frustrated and angry much of the time. You may be mad at other mothers who just don't "get it." You may be mad at society because of its marginalization of families of children with special needs. And, you may be mad at God for allowing this to happen to you and your family.

Guilt

Guilt is common among mothers of children with disabilities or illnesses. Many mothers wonder if they somehow caused the problems their children are experiencing. Guilt may also come from your health care providers. Unfortunately, as the healthcare industry becomes more cost-conscious, you may find yourself feeling guilty for having a child that costs your insurer more. Many parents have related stories of being pressured into prenatal testing and into terminating a pregnancy when an anomaly was identified. If you chose not to have the testing or not to terminate the pregnancy, you might feel guilty for bringing a less-than-perfect child into the world. Even if you feel positive about your decision, others may question you and act horrified when they discover that you would "purposely" have a child with an abnormality. Not surprisingly, this is an issue of concern among many in the disability-rights' community.

You may feel guilty for not being able to meet everyone's needs or about spending time away from your partner and other children. Finally, you may feel guilty for failing to live up to expectations of yourself or others to be a perfect mother. According to Miriam Greenspan (1998), mothers are often pressured into silence about the difficulties of caring for children with disabilities. According to her, anything other than serenity and acceptance indicates that you still have unresolved feelings about your child's disability:

> Many mothers of children with disabilities prefer to keep their pain and exhaustion private, not wanting to fuel the argument that children with disabilities are a burden to their parents and to society. This is a self-enforced silencing that is part of what it means to be marginalized (p. 43).

If the job of mother often feels impossible for mothers of well children, it feels doubly so for mothers of children with special needs. And, as with any type of mothering, there will be good and bad days. To indicate that it is possible to get to a place of total acceptance where things never bother you is unrealistic and places an unfair burden on you.

Isolation

Isolation is another fact of life for families of children with health concerns. Other mothers may discourage their children from playing with your child because your child's condition makes them uncomfortable. You might find that you are no longer invited to functions as a family.

When talking with other mothers, you may find that the concerns they express seem minor compared to your experiences. This may increase your sense that others have no idea what you are going through. How in the world can you describe the relentless nature of your care giving responsibilities? How can you discuss feeding using a gastric tube, the daily care of an ostomy, or how to correctly fasten a leg brace? How do you explain that exposure to a normal childhood illness like chicken pox can have life-threatening consequences for your child? Margaret withdrew from volunteer work that she enjoyed because her son was out of control at meetings:

> My son has been assessed hyperlexic and diagnosed autistic and has a secondary diagnosis of ADHD. Before we made dietary changes (he is now casein- and gluten-free as per *Special Diets for Special Kids* by Lisa Lewis), he was either going to sleep around 1 a.m. or getting up and staying awake, running around in the night for a few hours. He sleeps regularly now unless he gets gluten, casein, or a Snickers bar. Chocolate once kept him awake for twenty-four hours. And me? After toughing it out with another special-needs child we lost in 1992 (Brian had leukemia from three until his death at three months short of thirteen), I am finally headed to my doctor to ask for some anti-anxiety medication.

Another isolating aspect of caring for children with special needs is the reaction (or lack of a reaction) of others in the wake of a life-threatening complication or episode. If your family has suffered a medical crisis, you may be taken aback by the sudden awareness that the world has continued on as before. You feel that the outside world does not acknowledge the dramatic change in your life. This type of experience further indicates the uniqueness of your situation.

Uncertainty

Your uncertainty can start with your knowing something is wrong, but not having any explanation. A correct diagnosis may be months or even years in the making. The condition you are trying to name may be elusive with symptoms that come and go and tests that come back as inconclusive. Your child may receive several different diagnoses before actually finding one that fits.

Uncertainty involves looking into the future and wondering what it will bring. Will she be the object of ridicule? Will he be able to get the services he needs? Will she be able to graduate from high school or college? Will she ever get married and have a family? What kind of life will he have? Will tomorrow bring a decline in functioning? Will she die? What will happen to him after you die?

Depression and Burnout

You may be so fatigued and burned out, that you lose touch with others and sink into depression or despair. Give yourself permission to acknowledge what you have accomplished just by living your life. But, also remember that you cannot do it alone. Everyone needs occasional nurturing--including you.

Sadness and Loss

Related to depression is sadness associated with the death of the dream child. Depending on the type and severity of the disability or condition, you may have to scale back your expectations about what your child will be able to do. Most of us start off wanting our children to be healthy, smart, athletic, attractive, and popular--even if we, ourselves, don't have these characteristics. As your child matures, there will be many times when you realize that your child is outside the norm. And, this may make you feel sad.

Recently, I attended a session for parents of special-needs children held at a conference for breastfeeding families. One of the more poignant moments was when these mothers acknowledged that a dream had died: the dream that if you breastfeed your baby, everything would be great. These women had breastfed their babies, yet all of their children had serious conditions.

Potential for Joy

The feelings I've discussed above help identify some of the challenges that parents of children with health concerns face. I wanted to voice

240

and validate these feelings. But, I don't want to leave you with the impression that this is the whole story. Parents of children with special needs acknowledge the difficulties, but also point to many positives.

For example, many of these children demonstrate great compassion for others. Miriam Greenspan (1998) described how her daughter would suddenly display flashes of insight about people that would take her breath away. Where, she would wonder, did her then six-year-old daughter learn that? Having a disability or chronic condition can mature other children in the family beyond their years. As adults, they may reach out to other families with children who are like them.

Parents themselves learn many things. Mothers often become extremely knowledgeable about whatever condition their children have. In some cases, they know as much as, or even more, than many of their children's doctors. Some, like the mother-activists described in chapter 4, have lobbied for changes that have affected hundreds or even thousands of other families with special needs.

Parents of children with health concerns often mention how they have become much more patient than they used to be. Having been through real crises, they are less likely to get rattled by events that would have bothered them earlier or that bother other parents. These parents have learned to focus on what's important rather than being so distracted by the cares of this world. In many cases, they've streamlined their lives and have achieved a level of simplicity others would like to imitate. Children with special needs can also display a grace that transcends their physical limitations as Miriam Greenspan describes:

> Esther herself is the best source of whatever courage and resistance I muster in the challenge of mothering her. She has taught me acceptance and gratitude for each moment in a way that has brought a very special kind of joy into my life. If there is a nightmare here, it is my fear that the world, when I leave it, will not be sufficient to hold her or to see her truly. The unanswered question is: Will her gifts find their place in a world not yet worthy of her, or of any of our children (p. 58-59)?

241

In writing about disability, psychologist Rhoda Olkin (1999) described how the research literature is often very one-sided in its presentation of families with children with disabilities. The studies emphasize the burdens of taking care of these children, but rarely discuss the positive aspects. While we must be realistic about the difficulties that families encounter and ensure that they get the help and support they need, we must also not adopt the attitude that these children are not worth it and that they only bring negative things to their families.

What You Can Do

Fortunately, there are some concrete things you can do to help break the isolation and ease the strain of mothering a child with a health concern. Perhaps the most important message I can give is that you are not alone.

Become an Expert on Your Child's Condition

As I suggested in the previous chapter, dedicate yourself to learning (or keep learning) everything about your child's condition. You and your partner are the ones who will have to advocate for your child through the educational and medical systems.

The information you gather is not only helpful in working with doctors and schools, but it is helpful for you as well. Children with health concerns often act differently than children who do not have these issues. By understanding their needs and limitations, you can start anticipating situations where they are likely to have difficulties. This can help you prevent some recurring problems that you encounter.

Join with Others and Get Support

In order to break free of isolation, you must find other parents who have had similar experiences. Fortunately, groups for almost any condition abound. And don't forget online support. There are chat rooms and email lists available on almost any subject. With these, you can access support twenty-four hours a day. This can be a boon for parents who are isolated geographically or who cannot get to a support group. Just reading the posts of other parents will let you know that you are not alone. You may also find that other parents are some of the best sources of information on what works and what doesn't.

When using any of these resources, however, one caution is in order. Sometimes support groups can be counterproductive if they are overly negative and interested more in complaining than in trying to do something constructive. While you must feel free to air some of your most negative feelings, too much time spent dwelling on the negative aspects of your situation can make it worse. If you find that you are walking away from sessions of support feeling worse than when you came in, its probably time to look for another group.

Continue to Nurture Relationships with Others

Parenting children with health concerns may leave you with little time for other relationships. You may feel so intent on meeting the needs of your child that you neglect the needs of your partner, family members, and friends. These people may seem like one more group that needs you, but you shouldn't forget that you need them, too. Having healthy, reciprocal relationships with others is a great buffer against all kinds of stress. While nurturing your relationships may feel like one more thing to add to your endless list, think of it as self-care.

Sometimes, the people closest to you say the most hurtful things. In their efforts to come to terms with what has happened to your child, other family members may try to assign blame for his or her condition. They may speculate about whether your family was the source of the "faulty genes" or whether you worked too much while you were pregnant. They may also be the ones to offer unsolicited child-rearing advice. In these situations, remember that you have a right to get the kind of help and support you need. If people make hurtful remarks, gently let them know that that kind of comment is hurtful and does not help. If they persist, you may have to distance yourself from that relationship.

243

Help Your Other Children Cope

Sometimes, your other children will feel pushed aside because it seems that all your energy is focused on caring for the child with a chronic condition. Their reaction is understandable, but everyone in the family will be happier if you make time for your other children as well. That may mean turning the care of your child with a chronic condition over to someone else for a while. Recognize that your other children may also resent how their sibling's difficulties impact them. They may feel embarrassed by the way their sibling acts in public or the stares they get. Your other children must also have a safe place to vent without harming the child with difficulties.

Even young children can be involved in caring and watching out for the needs of your child with health concerns. Their experiences with their brother or sister may make them more sensitive to the needs of others, and may even encourage their entry into the health care field as adults. While you do want to involve your other children, you must also be careful to let them be kids as well. You might also want to encourage them to develop relationships in your extended family or with other adults so that they will have plenty of adult time, too.

Learn How Much Information to Share

When dealing with any family issue that is outside the norm, you need to learn, usually through trial and error, how much information you should share with others. Sometimes, we mothers offer way too much explanation, usually in an apologetic way. On the other hand, a forthright, non-defensive request for the help your child needs can go a long way. For example, you might explain to the mother of a classmate that your child can't go to her house to play because the environment may not be accessible for your child, but that you would be happy to have her child over to play at your house.

I have learned to be forthright in asking for accommodations I need instead of assuming that others should know. Most people understand and are happy to do what I ask. But, there are still people who don't and who actually give me a hard time about making necessary accommodations and, occasionally, even about my using a handicapped tag for my car. While it would be nice if everyone were responsive, it's not always possible. In time, you will learn whom you can really share with and who would rather not hear it. It's also helpful to practice some non-defensive answers like, "that's what works best for our family." As you gain confidence, you'll feel more comfortable getting what you need without feeling it is necessary to explain your situation to people who refuse to understand.

By acknowledging your challenges and reaching out to others for help and support, you also become ready to embrace the positives that come with mothering a child with special needs. In closing, I'd like to share the words of Amy, the mother of a boy with Asperger's syndrome:

> Accepting your challenged child requires that you go through a grief process. You must mourn, in a sense, your vision of the child you expected your precious baby to become. Only then can you move on to accept the child you have been given. Eventually you will be able to look beyond your child's limitations and celebrate his or her uniqueness.

For Further Reading

Below is a listing of some of the books available for parents of children with health concerns. You should also contact some of the online sources for information about specific conditions.

Resources for Parents of Children with Health Concerns

Cain, N. 1996. *Healing the Child: A Mother's Story.* New York: Rawson Associates.

Finston, P. 1992. *Parenting Plus: Raising Children with Special Health Needs.* New York: Viking Penguin.

Gordon, S. 1993. *One Miracle at a Time: Getting Help for a Child with a Disability.* New York: Simon & Schuster.

Klaus, M.H., Klaus, P.H., & Kennell, J.H. 1996. *Bonding: Building the Foundations of Secure Attachment and Independence.* Cambridge, MA: Perseus Publishing.

Lavin, J.L. 2001. *Special Kids Need Special Parents: A Resource for Parents of Children with Special Needs.* East Rutherford, NJ: Berkley Publishing Group (Penguin USA).

Osborn, S.T., & Mitchell, J.L. 2004. *A Special Kind of Love: For those who Love Children with Special Needs.* Nashville, TN: Broadman & Holman.

Naseef, R. 1997. *Special Children, Challenged Parents.* Secaucus, NJ: Carol Publishing Group.

Sears, W., & Sears, M. 1995. *The Discipline Book.* New York: Little, Brown.
(See especially the chapter on parenting a child with special needs.)

Children's Disabilities: http://www.childrensdisabilities.info/

Federation for Children with Special Needs: www.fcsn.org

National Information Center for Children and Youth with Disabilities: www.nichcy.org

Social Security Administration: www.ssa.gov/pubs/10026.html

Special Child: For parents of children with disabilities: www.specialchild.com/index.html_

Preemies

Linden, D.W., Paroli, E.T., & Doron, M.W. 2000. *Preemies: The Essential Guide for Parents of Premature Babies.* New York: Pocket.

Ludington-Hoe, S. 1993. *Kangaroo Care: The Best You Can Do to Help Your Preterm Infant.* New York: Bantam.

Sears, J., Sears, M., Sears, R., & Sears, W. 2004. *The Premature Baby Book: Everything You Need to Know about Your Premature Baby from Birth to Age One.* New York: Little, Brown.

Children's Disabilities: www.childrensdisabilities.info/

Kangaroo Mother Care: www.kangaroomothercare.com/

Keep Kids Healthy: www.keepkidshealthy.com/newborn/premature_babies.html

Medline Plus: www.nlm.nih.gov/medlineplus/prematurebabies.html

Premature Baby, Premature Child: http://www.prematurity.org/

CHAPTER 12

Hello-Goodbye: Mothering and Childbearing Loss

> In a moment's time, our world shatters like fine china and the darkness comes. For some, it was a phone call from the doctor. Still others were all alone. Perhaps you found your precious baby lifeless in the crib, a heartbeat suddenly stopped. Or, maybe like me, it was in a cold, dark room that you felt life slip away as you watched a black, silent ultrasound. Our stories are all different, but our pain is the same (Linda DeYmaz, 1996, p. 1).

Childbearing loss is one of the greatest challenges mothers can face. Yet, it is far more common than you might believe. You may have lost your child through miscarriage, stillbirth, abortion, prematurity and neonatal death, or sudden infant death syndrome (SIDS). There may have been an accident at birth or a chromosomal anomaly. Your baby may have contracted a fatal infection.

You may wonder how you can go on after your precious baby has died. No matter how devastating your loss or deep your sorrow, there is hope for healing. In their poignant book *Ended Beginnings* (1984), Claudia Panuthos and Cathy Romeo describe the process this way:

> There are no shortcuts or quick fixes in these phases of healing for grief is relentless, and it will not be shortchanged. We cannot completely evade its presence in our lives no matter how desperately we may try. Yet, peace is possible in the mind and the heart when grief and pain are embraced, released, and openly expressed (p. xvi).

Types of Childbearing Loss

Loss is no respecter of persons. Women of all nationalities and income levels have suffered from childbearing losses. Some of you have experienced one type, while others have experienced two, three, or even more. Years of infertility treatments may have finally resulted in a pregnancy that ended in miscarriage. You may have had a baby born so early that he could not survive or lost a baby to SIDS only to miscarry on a subsequent pregnancy. The pain from each of these experiences is real. In this section, I describe some of the more common types of childbearing loss. Although the focus of this chapter is pregnancy and infant loss (for these are the most common types), much of what I share in this chapter can apply to the death of an older child as well.

Miscarriage

According to our most recent Census data, more than one million women miscarried in 2000, and these numbers probably underestimate the true incidence since they only included losses from pregnancies that had made it into official records (Ventura et al., 2004). Many miscarriages occur before women have even seen a doctor. Miscarriage is one of the most common and least acknowledged forms of infant loss. It is often experienced in private, leaving you to grieve alone.

Some women seem to take miscarriage in stride and are ready to "try again" in relatively short order. Many other women, however, feel a deep sense of loss after a miscarriage. A problem arises when people in your life assume that you have taken this event in stride and are then surprised by your sense of loss.

The physical aspects of miscarriage can be traumatic. Your first hint that you were about to lose your baby may have been a small amount of blood. You may have frantically called your doctor's office only to be told there was little that you could do. Or, they may have told you that spotting is normal for many pregnancies. Spotting might have continued for several days as you agonized over whether you would lose this pregnancy.

Rather than a little blood, there may have been a lot, either gradually or suddenly. Gushing blood and passing large clots are frightening, and in the case of miscarriage, they are harbingers of impending loss. Bleeding may have accompanied painful contractions that surprised you with their intensity.

Many women find the aftermath of miscarriage to be one of the most traumatic parts. It may have occurred at home or on a gurney in the emergency room. Hospital staff may have treated you in a callous or cavalier way. You may have found out that your baby was gone by looking at a black ultrasound screen. You may have had to undergo a D & C to make sure that there were no remnants of your pregnancy left behind. These surgical procedures can be frightening and painful and can reinforce your feelings of powerlessness. Even if the staff is kind, it does not completely take away from the invasive nature of these procedures.

The psychological and emotional impact of miscarriage is compounded for women who have had more than one. Your pregnancies may have been kept secret, meaning that you suffered alone when you miscarried. Each subsequent pregnancy is filled with fear as you wonder if this one will last. Kathleen Diamond (1991) describes her experience of multiple miscarriages this way:

> The mourning process became shorter after each miscarriage because I was resigned to failure and did not actually think each pregnancy was real. After each miscarriage, I went about business as usual. No one else could possibly feel as badly as I did, and besides, I had a sense of terrible shame and failure (p. 67).

Miscarriage might also occur in the midst of treatment for infertility. You may have endured months of hormone treatments, invasive exams, and daily temperature charts. Your pregnancy may have been the result of one or more sessions of in vitro fertilization. With each miscarriage, your odds of having a baby seemed to lessen, leaving you with an overwhelming sense of hopelessness. Getting and staying pregnant may have become the driving force of your life.

Whether you have had one or many miscarriages, you will find that there are few outlets for you to acknowledge your grief. You have probably had to mourn these loses alone (Panuthos & Romeo, 1984).

Infertility

Related to miscarriage is another form of childbearing loss: infertility. Infertility is also relatively common. In the 1995 National Survey of Family Growth, more than 6 million women reported impaired fecundity: difficulty in conceiving or carrying a child to term (Fidler & Bernstein, 1999). This is approximately 10% of women ages fifteen to forty-four. It is not unusual for women to have experienced miscarriage, sometimes several times, before, during, and after treatment for infertility. Indeed, some health programs won't even start a work-up for infertility until a woman has had her third miscarriage.

Infertility brings its own emotional repercussions. First of all, it interferes with a fundamental and highly valued human need. Fidler and Bernstein (1999) liken its emotional impact to that of cancer or heart disease. Some of the negative effects of infertility include isolation, depression, reduced job performance, and lower life satisfaction. Testing and treatment for infertility can consume your life. The testing is invasive, expensive, and often painful. The most intimate details of your life are laid bare. Sex loses its spontaneity and becomes mechanical. The onset of each period brings the realization that you are, once again, not pregnant. You may begin to wonder why this is happening to you when women who do not want children seem to get pregnant with ease.

There are also physical consequences of infertility that relate to childbearing losses. Women undergoing treatment for infertility are often given ovulation-enhancing drugs, which dramatically increase the likelihood of multiple births. Multiples are more likely to have any number of health concerns, including prematurity and low birth weight. The danger of death dramatically increases, especially for higher-order multiples (triplets and more). The mortality rate for these babies is fifteen times greater than it is for singletons (Kiely et al., 1992). You may find that you are faced with the challenge of mothering your surviving baby or babies while mourning the loss of one or more.

Multiple embryos may also be a result of in vitro fertilization. To increase the likelihood of pregnancy, healthcare providers may implant several embryos. This raises ethical dilemmas that parents of previous generations never had to face. One issue is that of selective reduction where the number of fetuses is reduced since fewer fetuses have greater chances of survival. On the other hand, mothers working very hard to become and stay pregnant are often not receptive to the idea of terminating any of their pregnancies. Some countries, such as Great Britain, are now limiting the number of embryos that can be implanted at one time to three, which may help prevent this dilemma.

It's also important to recognize that not all treatment for infertility ends with the birth of a baby. Couples may endure years of testing, treatment, and miscarriages before coming to the conclusion that they are unable to have a biological child. This is also experienced as a significant loss. Even when mothers go on to adopt, they may feel marginalized, though their path to motherhood is no less heroic than that of other mothers. Even after a woman becomes a mother through adoption, the sting of infertility may linger for years (Smith et al., 1998).

Abortion

Each year in the U.S. more than one million abortions are performed (Ventura et al., 2004). Although it is a fairly common procedure, it is one of the most politically divisive issues of our time. Since abortion is voluntary, you might wonder why it is included in this chapter. I didn't include it in the original edition of this book. But, in talking with mothers, I've realized that I needed to include it because it was influencing how they are feeling now. And, that may be the case for you.

The controversy surrounding abortion has influenced how it is studied, with some researchers anxious to show that it has no negative effect on women's emotional health and others wishing to show that it has a major negative effect because they want it to stop. The truth, as is often the case, is somewhere in between. Psychologist Nancy Adler and her colleagues, in two reviews of the literature (Adler et al., 1992; 2003) noted that abortion does not appear to cause psychological harm for most women. However, they did note that women who were ambivalent about having an abortion, did not have partner or parental support, or blamed themselves for the pregnancy were more likely to have a negative outcome.

In contrast, some studies have noted an increase in depression and/ or post-traumatic stress disorder following an abortion. One study, conducted in the former Soviet state of Belarus, found that 82% of women had post-traumatic stress symptoms following their abortions. This finding surprised the authors since abortion is the major form of birth control in that country and is a common procedure. Similarly, an American study found that women who aborted their first pregnancy were four to five times more likely to abuse drugs and alcohol compared with women who either carried their first pregnancy to term or had a miscarriage (Reardon & Ney, 2000).

One study from Australia (Allanson & Astbury, 2001) found that women who were seeking early abortions were more likely to have been abused as children and to have insecure attachments with current adult partners. In my experience, multiple abortions almost always indicates a history of past or current abuse. But, as Allanson and Astbury found, even one abortion can indicate a history of abuse. And, this past history can make you more vulnerable to both depression and post-traumatic stress disorder.

The net of all these studies indicates that abortion can, but does not always, cause psychological fallout for women who experience them. If you had an abortion, you may have felt traumatized by the experience right after it happened or you may have had a delayed response—feeling bad after another pregnancy loss or with the birth of a baby. You may find it difficult to discuss or even tell anyone about your previous loss through abortion, increasing your sense of isolation and despair.

Stillbirth

Stillbirth is another form of childbearing loss that refers to death of a baby at or near term. This occurs in approximately one percent of live births (National Center for Health Statistics, 2004). Stillbirth has a variety of causes. It can be due to an accident involving the cord or placenta, an infection, or toxemia in the mother.

In some cases of stillbirth, the baby dies before labor begins. Mothers often have a sense that something is wrong. They may have felt no movement or started to bleed and had sudden searing pains. Or, there may have been no warning at all. You may have learned of your baby's death during a routine examination when your doctor or midwife could not find a heartbeat.

Once you discovered that your baby was dead, you may have found yourself in the nightmarish scenario of needing to carry a dead baby for days or even weeks, awaiting labor. Unbelievably, you still needed to go through labor knowing that your baby would not be alive at the end. Since your baby was already dead, the staff may have given you strong pain medication, exacerbating your feeling that this was all happening to someone else.

Perhaps your baby died during labor. Things may have been going well, then suddenly the cord may have prolapsed or your uterus ruptured. Your baby may have contracted an infection during labor. Some type of chromosomal abnormality may have only allowed your baby to live for a brief time after birth.

In some situations, your baby may have died because of the incompetence or negligence of the medical staff. They may have left you alone when you had a complication. They may have ignored your pleas for help or misread the fetal monitor. This can be one of the most difficult deaths to accept because it might have been prevented. You may actually hate the people you feel are responsible, and even consider legal action.

Although your baby has died, your body may act like you have recently given birth to a living baby: your breasts fill with milk, you have lochia. Some mothers have described this experience as their whole body weeping for the lost child.

Prematurity and Neonatal Death

Birth weight and gestational age are the two most important predictors of infant survival (Mathews et al., 2004). Preterm birth (birth at less than thirty-seven completed weeks of gestation) is the second leading cause of infant mortality in the United States. Related to preterm birth is low birth weight (LBW) or having a birth weight that is less than five pounds or 2,500 grams. The babies at highest risk are those who are classified as very low birth weight or less than three and a half pounds or 1,500 grams. Approximately eight percent of babies born in the U.S. are low birth weight and approximately 1.5% are very low birth weight (National Center for Health Statistics, 2004).

As I mentioned in the previous chapter, the majority of premature babies in the U.S. survive, but babies who are premature or low birth weight have a drastically increased risk of death compared to their full-term counterparts. For babies born at full term, about seven babies die per 1000 live births. For babies under 2500 grams, 61 babies die per 1000 live births. For babies under 1500 grams, the rate is 253 per 1000 live births. And for babies between 500 and 999 grams, that rate of mortality is 863 per 1000 live births (National Center for Health Statistics, 2004). Similarly, babies born before 32 weeks gestation have a mortality rate nearly 75 times higher than babies who are born at term (Mathews et al., 2004).

No one knows for certain what causes preterm birth or low birth weight, but some risk factors have been identified. Teen pregnancy, poverty, and lack of prenatal care all contribute to low birth weight. Premature/LBW babies are twice as likely to be born to mothers who smoke. The birth of a previous premature baby increases the risk that you will have another baby who is premature. Having multiples also increases the likelihood of both prematurity and LBW. African Americans have approximately twice as many LBW babies as their white counterparts, a disparity that can't be fully explained by independent risk factors such as poverty (Matthews et al., 2004; National Center for Health Statistics, 2004). But, there are plenty of women who do not have any of these risk factors and yet give birth to premature and low birth-weight babies. You may have agonized over whether you did anything that caused your baby to be premature.

254

Mothers of premature babies find that they are faced with dilemmas about how much intervention to allow. Babies born too early or too small probably cannot survive. Yet, the line of too early is often blurry. Babies that are routinely saved today would have died even fifteen years ago. If your baby was born some time ago, you may face the realization that had your baby been born now, she may have survived.

You may have endured a week or a month (or longer) of wondering if your baby would survive, only to have him finally succumb. Your baby probably never left the hospital. He may have needed to be rushed from your side to a NICU that was far away, leaving you to drive many miles to be by your baby's side during your own recovery from birth. You may have needed to stay in a city far from home, returning each night to an empty hotel room. None of your family or friends may have ever even seen your baby, increasing the feelings of unreality surrounding her birth and death.

Sudden Infant Death Syndrome (SIDS)

Sudden infant death syndrome (SIDS) is the unexplained death of a baby less than one year of age that remains unexplained even after an autopsy, examination of the death scene, and a review of the case history. Approximately 90% of SIDS deaths occur by six months of age. SIDS affects approximately 1 in 700 babies born in the U.S., but the rate is lower in other countries (Sears, 1995). It is the third most common form of death for babies in the U.S., according to the Centers for Disease Control and Prevention (Matthews et al., 2004).

While we have been able to identify some risk factors for SIDS, its cause remains a mystery. Babies who are exposed to cigarette smoke, were born prematurely, sleep on their stomachs, or are formula-fed are at highest risk. However, there are many babies who have all these risk factors, but do not succumb to SIDS. Conversely, some babies who have none of these risk factors do.

Mothers whose babies die of SIDS are usually overwhelmed by the suddenness of the loss. Babies have died on the day they had a well-baby check. They have died at their mothers' breasts or while sleeping next to their mothers. In the next section, I share the story of one mother whose baby died of SIDS.

Jonathan's Song: One Mother's Story of SIDS

For Joan Valk, December 8, 1989, started like any day. But, the events of that day forever changed her life. When Joan went to check on her baby Jonathan in his crib, she made the heart-stopping discovery that he was not breathing. Her neighbor made a frantic 911 call, and the baby was rushed to the hospital. An hour later, the doctor came out to tell Joan and her husband, Henk, that their baby was gone. Jonathan, her second son, died that day of SIDS. He was three months old.

> All I could think of was that I needed to be with Jonathan. I said: "I want to see him. I've got to be with him." The nurse said, "Of course, of course." And, they brought us into the room where my little baby lay, wrapped in a white sheet on the gurney. When I reached the stretcher on which he lay, I pulled the white sheet open, exposing his pale little body. As I sobbed, "Oh, Jonathan, Jonathan, I loved you. I loved you so much." I caressed his naked body with my hand, touching every part, trying to etch into my mind what I soon would no longer be able to see. I looked up at Henk and he was weeping, tears streaming down his face, his head tipped back in disbelief. The nurses scurried to get chairs for both of us. I think they were afraid that one of us would faint. I covered Jonathan back up and picked him up to hold him. He had a tube sticking out of his mouth and a needle in his right shoulder. I asked the nurse if they could take them out, but she said no. As I held him, I stroked his coppery brown hair. I told the nurse that his hair had just started to grow in. Her eyes were red as she wept with us in our grief. I turned to Henk and said, "What can we do? I can't just walk away and leave him here." The nurses assured us that we could stay as long as we wanted to, and just hold him and be with him. I pulled his little hand out from underneath the sheet and held his fingers and stroked them. I touched his toes and his feet. I looked and looked at his face and hair. Even

with the tube and the discoloration around his eyes, he looked peaceful. I have always been afraid of death and dead bodies, but Jonathan did not frighten me. He was simply my son. Henk took Jonathan out of my arms and I didn't know what he was going to do. I was afraid that he was taking him away from me. But, he just wanted to pray. He committed our son back into the Lord's hands and thanked Him for the time we were able to have with Jonathan. Then he gave him back to me to hold. Before that, I was afraid to let go of Jonathan. After that prayer, I felt that it was time to leave him and go home. The nurse came in and I handed Jonathan to her. I kissed the top of his head and touched him one last time. Then we left the room and stepped out into the corridor.

Everything after that is after. This is about Jonathan and our story goes on. We said good-bye to him the best way we could and then tried to pick up the pieces. The great pain and emptiness are still quite real, but not as present every day. His name means God's precious gift and that's what we put on his tombstone, but I've come to realize that is what all children are. Children are precious, people are precious, each day is precious. That is what I learned from my son's short life and his death. We miss him so much. That will never fade. I know he is with my Father in Heaven and that helps, but there are times when I just want to hold him one more time, nurse him one more time, touch him, hear him just one last time. But, every time I feel that loss, that great void, I also feel grateful for the time we were able to have with one very special little boy, who gave us great joy for an incredibly short time and who we will never forget. No bitter grief could ever poison that, the wonderful sweet time we had with our son Jonathan Gerhard Valk.

Some Common Reactions

Everyone grieves in a different way and with a different intensity. Saul Bloom, a father whose baby died of SIDS, describes how you probably won't progress neatly through the stages of grief. The long-term process of grief is better described as two steps forward and one step back (Whelan,

257

2000). Below are some reactions that many mothers, fathers, and other family members experience.

Overwhelming Sorrow

Especially in the initial days and weeks after you lose your baby, you may feel overwhelmed by sorrow. Your loss may hurt so much that you wonder if you are losing your mind. Some mothers feel that they are being swallowed by grief and that they will never recover. Even when it stops being an almost constant presence, sorrow can come again in waves that sweep over you.

This deep sadness can also affect how you go about your day-to-day life. You may have trouble eating and sleeping or find yourself seriously considering suicide. Even if you are not actively planning to take your own life, you may fantasize about going to sleep and not waking up or about getting sick and dying so you can be with your baby.

Some mothers describe clinging to reminders of their babies, such as a favorite toy or a photograph, or continuing to wear maternity clothes. In your sorrow, your mind might start to play tricks on you. You might hear the baby crying or expect to see him lying in his crib. Your arms might ache to hold her and your breasts may fill with milk. You may grieve with your whole body.

Numbness and Denial

Numbness and denial are two other common reactions. In the initial days and weeks after your baby dies, you may feel like you are in a fog or that you are floating, watching this happen to someone else. You may not be able to even cry. It may feel like a dream from which you'll soon wake up and find your baby back with you.

Numbness and denial do serve a useful purpose. They temporarily shield you from pain and give you time to contemplate the unthinkable. Unfortunately, this reaction may also send the wrong message to people around you. Those closest to you may interpret your lack of tears or another strong reaction as an indication that you are handling it well.

When then numbness wears off in a few days or weeks, these same people may be surprised by your reaction and view this sudden display of emotion as backtracking. Or, the people who have gathered to support you may have gone home and back to their normal lives, leaving you alone to deal with your strongest feelings.

A Feeling of Unreality

In the days and weeks following the death of your baby, you may have a sense of unreality. You may feel surprised that life continues as before when you have been forever changed. This sense of unreality may be especially troubling if no one knew you were pregnant or if your baby never left the hospital. You may have bonded with the hospital personnel who knew your baby. But, once your baby has died, you don't see the hospital personnel anymore. They now have other families to care for.

When you go back to your normal life, you are a different person. People in your life who want to spare you from pain may avoid talking about your baby. But, you are in pain anyway and not being able to talk about your baby just reinforces the unreality of the situation.

Others in your life may remove any trace of your baby before you even return from the hospital. Unfortunately, this may compound the problem for you. You may have wanted to smell the scent of your baby one more time in his clothes or sit in the rocker where you planned to hold him. These things may be the only tangible connections you have with your baby. Even if you never brought your baby home, making your own decisions about the baby's things can help make this loss real to you, giving you an opportunity to say good-bye in your own time.

Anger and Rage

Anger can be one of the most persistent feelings you have. In the weeks, months, and even years following your baby's death, you may find that you are really, really angry. You may be mad that your partner did so little to support you when you needed him or at his apparent lack of grief. You may be mad at things he said or did or that he couldn't prevent the loss of your baby. Or, your grief may be manifesting itself as anger and your partner is simply a convenient target.

You may also find that you are mad at your mother, father, and siblings, or at other children you have. The stress of losing a child may bring other issues to the surface. Why are the other children all so healthy when your baby is gone? Why do they seem to need you so much? Why are they acting up now?

You may also be mad at God. He could have protected your baby; why didn't he? You may wonder why this happened to you, especially when you've always tried to be a good person. Why would God take a baby that you really wanted when He gives babies to people who abuse them? How could a God of love allow you to suffer so much?

You may have been treated badly by medical personnel. The police may have insensitively implied that you had something to do with your baby's death. The hospital may have been more interested in your insurance information than in the fact that your baby just died. Your doctor or others may have tried to comfort you by saying: "You can have another one," or "At least this baby died before you got attached." Comments like that may actually destroy relationships you had prior to the loss of your baby. Realize that most people say such things out of ignorance. Their lack of experience and discomfort with strong emotions can manifest itself in ways that are inadvertently hurtful to you.

While anger may feel energizing and positive after being overwhelmed by grief, you must still be careful to express it in safe ways. Your anger is understandable and legitimate. But, you can permanently damage your relationships with your partner, friends, family, or surviving children by lashing out at them. Deidre had a twin sister who died shortly after birth. One day in a fit of anger, Deirdre's mother told her that she wished that Terry had been the one who survived. Deidre has carried the pain of those angry words for many years, and it has created a permanent rift between her and her mother.

Saul Bloom whose son died of SIDS suggests that you seek some form of physical release that will not harm you or others. He sought his by splitting wood and replacing plantings in his yard (Whelan, 2000). On those days when you feel overwhelmed by grief and anger, you might find that it helps to take a vigorous walk, throw rocks in your backyard, or hit a pillow. Writing in a journal or sharing with a support group can also be safe ways to vent your anger.

Isolation

Mothers who experience childbearing loss often find that they are left alone to grieve much of the time. People might avoid you because they don't know what to say. They may have children the same age that your child would have been, or they might be obviously pregnant or have a new baby and worry that seeing their children may make you sad. They might even be afraid to associate too closely with someone whose baby has died because they fear it might happen to them.

You may find that the people in your life are supportive--to a point. At some time in the future, friends and family will expect you to get on with your life and may be surprised that you are still grieving.

Finally, you may find that you cannot talk with other mothers who haven't lost children. Hearing them complain about their busyness makes you wish you could have even one more day of that kind of life. How can these women complain when they still have their precious children with them?

Guilt

Another very common reaction is guilt. Many mothers feel a profound sense of guilt and wonder if they shouldn't have been able to do something that would have prevented their babies' death. Did activities during pregnancy contribute to your miscarriage or premature birth? Could your ambivalent feelings about being pregnant somehow have caused this to happen? You may have had an abortion earlier in your life, and with the loss of this baby, you are grieving for both.

You might feel guilty that you let your baby sleep, never dreaming that she was dead in her crib. If only you had checked on her sooner! Thinking back, you might remember every harsh word or thought. You remember the times when you finished what you were doing before going to get him or the times when you were distracted, exhausted, and not enjoying every minute of time with your baby. If you had only known, you would have let the housework wait.

As you begin to work through your grief, you will start to have some good days. You may laugh occasionally and have times when you feel lighthearted. You'll have times when you enjoy the feeling of sun on your face or the company of your partner, your children, or your friends. And, then the guilty thought comes: "If I'm enjoying myself, does that mean I don't care about my baby"?

Depending on the circumstances surrounding your baby's death, you may feel guilty or regretful about other things that happened at the hospital. You may wish you had been there when your baby was removed from life support or died. You may wish that you had held him just one last time, taken pictures, saved a lock of her hair, or had a chance to say goodbye.

Mothers may be called upon to make decisions about how much intervention they wanted for their babies. These decisions are typically made for people at the end of life, rather than the beginning. Should my baby be placed on a ventilator or life support? Is this causing my baby pain? Should I just let her go? If you decided to take your baby off of life support, you may feel responsible for her death. If you decided to keep your baby on life support, you may feel responsible for the pain that he suffered.

Fear

If you have other children who are still living, you may find that you are fearful for them as well. You may stand and watch them for hours as they sleep to make sure that they are breathing. If you have subsequent children, you may be fearful through the entire pregnancy and even until they are past the age when your first child died. Each childhood illness can cause you to hold your breath in apprehension. Once you've become personally aware of the fragility of life, you know that any moment you can lose someone else you love, as Kathy Whelan (2000) describes:

> Struck by tragedy once, I live waiting for the other shoe to drop. The first time Anna had a cold, I curled up in a fetal position, sure she would be dead by morning. The first time we took Michelle to the hospital for stomach pain, I was sure it was cancer. Every time Steve travels for business, I worry he will never return. I am emotionally tender. Unlike bones, which become stronger when broken, the heart gets weaker, the muscle tender (p. 191-192).

It may be years until you can approach others in a less fearful way.

Powerlessness

Powerlessness is another common reaction. You may have known that you were having a miscarriage and realized that there was nothing you could do. Similarly, there was nothing you could do to keep your baby from dying. Sometimes you will assume guilt that is not yours because it is a way to counter powerlessness. Although guilt feels bad, it may seem preferable to the feeling that things were completely beyond your control. Powerlessness is often compounded by events that occur during or after the death of your baby. Hospital routines can be overwhelming. You may have had an emergency cesarean, under general anesthetic. There may have been no time for the doctor and nurse attending you to even explain what was happening, or you may perceive that the hospital staff was incompetent and allowed your baby to die.

After your baby's death, you may have been swept into the world of law enforcement. There may be an autopsy to determine the cause of death. You may even have been questioned as a suspect.

Loss of Identity

When a child dies, part of your identity gets lost, too. If your first baby miscarried or died, are you still a mother? You may have had a miscarriage before you told anyone that you were pregnant. Do you tell people now that you had a miscarriage? On the other hand, can you carry on as if nothing has happened when part of you longs to scream, "My baby died!"?

Even when mothers have other children at home or have children after one dies, there is often awkwardness about what to tell people when they ask how many children you have. Do you acknowledge the child who died? You may not want to tell strangers that you lost a child. But, to not acknowledge this child may make you feel deeply sad. Do you tell people that you have three children when you really have had four--or none when you have had one?

Depression

In the weeks and months following your baby's death, you may find that you are quite depressed and are having trouble eating, sleeping, or even getting through the day. You might contemplate suicide. If you are depressed, it is important for you to get help soon. Don't try to go it alone. You might need a support group, one-on-one support from a counselor experienced in grief work, or both. Some mothers find it helpful to take antidepressants until they feel like they can function again. This might be a good idea for you, too.

Your Other Children

Childbearing loss does not exist in a vacuum. It can affect how you feel about the children you already have and those you have after your loss.

Children You Already Have

The loss of one child may make you fearful for your other children as well. You may find yourself being overprotective of them. You may also have days when you are overwhelmed by caring for them. They may provide a glimpse of life the way it used to be or a sad reminder of what you have lost. Well-meaning friends and relatives might not know how to help you: Is it better to try to keep your other children away from you or allow them to be near?

In the midst of your own grief, it can be hard to think about the needs of others. But, your other children are grieving too, though they may express it in ways that seem inappropriate. Or, they may be too young to fully understand why everyone seems so sad and why their brother or sister is never coming home. They may sense the tension in the air and begin to act up, or they may be feeling guilty. Perhaps they had wished that the baby had never come to your family and now feel responsible for his death. Your living children need to be able to express these kinds of concerns. While it is understandable that you might not feel up to meeting their dependency needs, recognize this and get some help. Bring in other caring adults so that your other children have one-on-one time to help them cope.

Should You Have Another Child?

This, of course, is a very personal decision. Some parents are too fearful to contemplate conceiving again quickly--or ever. You may decide not to have any more children. If you do make that decision, try not to take any permanent steps while you are in the midst of your grief. After grief recedes, you may find that you very much regret it. Conversely, you might decide to get pregnant very soon after your baby dies. Your body may ache to hold another child. But, it may be better to wait until the grief is not so raw before trying to get pregnant again. Consider also whether you are physically ready to conceive again. Your body may not have sufficiently recovered from your previous pregnancy.

It is important that you realize that any subsequent child will never replace the child you lost. Your new baby will be his or her own person, and you cannot expect this new child to be just like your child who died. That is a heavy burden for a child to bear, and in the long run, it is not really fair for either of you.

Loss of a Multiple

Twins and higher-order multiples (triplets and more) are at increased risk for dying. One of your babies may have been weaker or smaller than the other(s) and did not survive. The baby may have died in utero or after a stay in the NICU. You may find yourself in the unusual position of grieving while also caring for your surviving babies, as Tammy (2000) did:

> Everyone just expected me to be happy that I had a survivor. And, I was and I still am. I endured (and am still enduring) both joy and grief in one. I am thrilled to have Matthew and have him doing well, but I am incredibly saddened that I don't have Mark. Everyone around me expected me to just go on and not truly grieve for Mark. Even family members.

There are physical challenges associated with the loss of a multiple. You may have one or more preemies to mother at home, while needing to also be at the NICU. It should come as no surprise that you spend your first few weeks or months in a state of perpetual exhaustion. (See the resource list at the end of this chapter for Web sites that address the loss of a multiple.)

What You Can Do

There is nothing you can do that will bring your baby back. But there are steps you can take that will help you heal and bring some closure to your experience.

Take Care of Yourself Physically

In the aftermath of any significant loss, your body becomes more vulnerable to illness. As I described in chapter 2, a flood of stress hormones suppress the immune system. Unfortunately, in the wake of a baby's death, you may find that you cannot sleep or eat and that you are up most of the day taking care of other people's needs. Suddenly, you become quite ill, too.

Even though you don't feel like doing it, it is important that you take care of your health. Physical self-care is an important part of your grief work. You might also consider incorporating regular massage into your self-care regimen. We often carry severe grief in our bodies as well as our hearts and minds. Massage will help dissipate some of the stress your body carries and will also boost your immune system.

Take Care of Yourself Emotionally

You also need help and support as you grieve. Finding support may be harder than it first appears. Family members may be supportive at first, but then expect you to get on with your life.

The stress of a baby's death may put a significant strain on your relationship with your partner. Your partner may be grieving in a very different way than you. Men and women have very different culturally sanctioned ways of dealing with feelings. For example, you may need to talk about what happened as a way to process your feelings and make what happened seem more real. Your partner may find that talking about it makes him feel worse, and that for him, the most effective strategy is just not to think about it. It is easy to fall into a situation where each partner feels that the other is being insensitive to his or her needs. Each family member needs permission to grieve in his or her own way.

That being said, you need to give yourself permission to seek support outside of your family or your relationship with your partner if you cannot get what you need inside your family. A support group for parents who have experienced similar losses may be lifesaving for you, as can a therapist who specializes in grief work.

Don't forget the Internet as a possible source of support and healing. There are many sites dedicated to all types of infant loss. Even if you choose not to share your story online, you may find it helpful to read about the experiences of others. This support is available twenty-four hours a day--a boon if you are having trouble sleeping.

Finally, although this is not technically support, you might find it helpful to write about your experiences. Writing offers you a safe place to vent some of your feelings and can help you understand and gain perspective on your experience. If you have never journaled before, you might want to check out *Writing to Heal,* by James Pennebaker (2004). This book is based on his research that demonstrates the psychological and emotional benefits of writing things down. Journaling provides the opportunity for you to process difficult experiences in writing, and Pennebaker's book gives specific suggestions for getting the most benefit out of this activity.

Find a Way to Memorialize Your Baby

One of the difficulties of pregnancy loss or infant death is that there is little left to memorialize your baby's life. The experience will seem more real to you if you can find a concrete way to remember your baby. If you haven't done so already, you might consider holding a memorial service. Some people remember their babies by planting a tree, making a donation, or setting up a charitable fund. Even putting together a scrapbook or photo album can mark your baby's time with you, however brief. One of my neighbors lost a little girl at the age of four. Every year, she puts up a Christmas tree with only angel ornaments on it to commemorate her daughter.

Work toward Acceptance

Be realistic about how much recovery you can expect. You can adapt to what has happened, but it is not something you get over or forget. Your experience has most likely changed the way you look at the world, and you will never be the person you were before. But, you can learn to live again, experience joy again, and love other children. Many women have turned their personal sorrows into strengths and have used their experiences to reach out to others. Ten years after the death of her baby to SIDS, Kathy Whelan (2000) describes her journey toward healing this way:

> The hardest part of survival is acceptance. Accepting who I am, a mother who has lost a son. Accepting that Mikey was here and that I lost him. I can no longer mother Mikey, but I can mother other people who have had similar losses. And so, almost 10 years after losing my son, I am surviving. No, I am thriving. I faced the fears of having children again. I lived through five pregnancies, one miscarriage, and three first years of worry. I am raising three beautiful children. They are loving, affectionate, and creative. I have used my pain to write meaningful stories and poems that have touched other people's hearts. I have used my creativity as an outlet for the love of my dead son, a son who may never see my work, but who lives in my heart because of my work. I have been an example of survival to other parents who

268

are just beginning their grief journeys. I have used my pain to show my children the depths of my love for them. I love how my Dad explained grief. With time, grief would find a place in my heart where it could live peacefully. And every now and then, I could take out my grief and feel its overpowering sadness. The feelings would be similar to those I first felt, but they would not take control of my every waking thought. And, so I bear my grief for Mikey in my heart, close to the surface of my soul. And every once in a while, my grief, my love pours out, reminding me of the passion I had for my first-born son. And, I can live with that (p. 192).

Surviving the death of your baby will be the hardest thing you ever do. But, as the mothers who have shared their stories in this chapter will tell you, there is hope. You can go on. In closing, I'd like to share the words of Linda DeYmaz, from her remarkably touching book, *Mommy, Please Don't Cry* (1996):

Someday, Mommy, we will hold each other tight! Then, you will cradle me in you arms, And stroke my hair . . .And once again, our hearts will beat together. Mommy, please don't cry . . .I'll wait right here for you.

For Further Reading

There are some excellent resources available to mothers and fathers who have experienced childbearing losses. You'll have times when you want to read everything you can find, and other times when you don't want to read anything at all. Give yourself permission to grieve at your own pace and in your own way. There is also a lot of information available on the Internet. If you are not the type of person who likes support groups or you do not live in a place where there is one nearby, these sites may become lifelines to you.

Resources for All Types of Infant Loss

These books and Web sites describe all types of infant loss. All are good. You may find them especially helpful if you have experienced more than one type of loss.

Davis, D.L. 1996. *Empty Cradle, Broken Heart: Surviving the Death of Your Baby.* Golden, CO: Fulcrum Publishing.

DePuy, C., & Dovitch, D. 1997. *The Healing Choice : Your Guide to Emotional Recovery After an Abortion.* New York: Fireside.

Douglas, A., Sussman, J.R., & Davis, D.L. 2000. *Trying Again: A Guide to Pregnancy After Miscarriage, Stillbirth, and Infant Loss.* Lanham, MD: Taylor Trade Publishing.

Kendall-Tackett, K.A. 2005. *The Handbook of Women, Stress and Trauma.* New York: Taylor & Francis.
(For a more academic discussion of trauma and loss.)

Lanham, C.C. 1999. *Pregnancy after a Loss: A Guide to Pregnancy After a Miscarriage, Stillbirth or Infant Death.* East Rutherford, NJ: Berkely Trade.

O'Keefe Lafser, C. 1998. *An Empty Cradle: A Full Heart. Reflections for Mothers and Fathers after Miscarriage, Stillbirth, or Infant Death.* Chicago: Loyola.

O'Neill, J. 2005. *You're Not Alone: Healing Through God's Grace after Abortion.* Deerfield Beach, FL: Faith Communications.

Panuthos, C., & Romeo, C. 1984. *Ended Beginnings: Healing Childbearing Losses.* Westport, CT: Bergin and Garvey.

A Place to Remember: www.aplacetoremember.com

International Stillbirth Alliance: www.stillbirthalliance.org/

March of Dimes Foundation: www.marchofdimes.com/pnhec/572.asp

Mommies Enduring Neonatal Death: A Christian support organization. www.mend.org/

Mothers 35 Plus: www.mothers35plus.co.uk/losing2.htm

Silent No More (helping women who have had abortions): www.operationoutcry.org

Stillbirth and Neonatal Death Society: http://www.uk-sands.org/

Resources for Loss of a Multiple

Center for Loss in Multiple Births (CLIMB): www.climb-support.org
Multiple Angels Network: www.angels4ever.com
Parents of Multiples Forever: www.erichad.com

Resources for Sudden Infant Death Syndrome

Sears, W. 1995. SIDS: *A Parent's Guide to Understanding and Preventing Sudden Infant Death Syndrome.* New York: Little, Brown.

Whelan, K. A. 2000. *Grief Songs: Stories, Letters, and Poems That Chronicle the Recovery and Survival of a Community after the Sudden Death of a Baby.* Boston: Massachusetts Center for Sudden Infant Death Syndrome.
(Available from the Massachusetts Center for SIDS, Boston Medical Center, One Boston Medical Center Place, Boston, MA 02118; 800-641-7437.)

National SIDS/Infant Death Resource Center: www.sidscenter.org
SIDS Alliance: www.sidsalliance.org

Resources for Miscarriage and Infertility

Allen, M., & Marks, S. 1993. *Miscarriage: Women Sharing from the Heart.* New York: Wiley.

Diamond, K. 1991. *Motherhood after Miscarriage.* Holbrook, MA: Adams Media.

Hygeia Foundation and Institute for Perinatal Loss: www.hygeia.org
InterNational Council on Infertility Information Dissemination: www.inciid.org
IVF.com: www.ivf.com
Resolve: The National Infertility Association: www.resolve.org
Women's Health Information: Search for recurrent miscarriage at www.womens-health.co.uk

DeYmaz, L. 1996. *Mommy, Please Don't Cry.* Sisters, Ore.: Multnomah Publishers. (This amazing little book deserves some special comment. It looks like a children's book, but is written for mothers from the baby's perspective. Many mothers have been touched by this book. It is written from an explicitly Christian point of view.)

Epilogue

In the opening chapter, I encouraged you to make positive changes in your life. But, you may not know where to begin. In this last brief chapter, I want to bring some of the threads together and help you find a starting place.

Identify the Positives in Your Life

Throughout this book, I've described the difficulties you face as a mother. To help you identify problem areas, I needed to focus on the negatives. Now I want you to refocus. Take a minute and think about what is going well.

I learned this principle from two unlikely sources. The first was in Julie Morgenstern's *Organizing from the Inside Out.* Julie is a professional organizer. The very definition of her job is to help people recognize problem areas in their lives. Yet, she states that when you are looking to make a change, you should first consider what is working for you now. That way, you build changes on strengths you already have.

Jon Kabat-Zinn, in *Full Catastrophe Living,* teaches the same principle. Jon teaches mindfulness meditation to patients at the University of Massachusetts Medical Center. Many of his patients are critically, or even terminally, ill. Yet, he encourages them to see that no matter how sick they are, more is right with their bodies than wrong. I first read this at a time when I was very ill, and it really struck me. When you are sick, there is a tendency to focus on what's not working. He provided the broader picture and made me see beyond my immediate health crisis.

You can apply the same principle. Right now, you may feel overwhelmed by your life. You may see only problems. But, if you can identify even one strength, you can start by building on that.

Take Time Out for Self Care

This is also a good time to start treating your body right. You may think that you have "no time" to exercise, eat well, and relax. But, think of it this way. If you had a total break down of your health, somehow your work would still be there. Mothering is a marathon, not a sprint. If you are going to be there for the long haul, you must start investing in your future health now.

Change Your Daily Work

Start by paying attention to your daily tasks: ones you like and ones you don't. Focus on the tasks you dislike. Can you change them? For example, if you're employed and your job is the source of stress, think about how to make it better. Can you change jobs? Can you reduce your hours or work out a more flexible arrangement? Can you take some classes to increase your skills? Elaine St. James, in *Living the Simple Life*, has a lot of practical suggestions on how you can change your daily work. You may not be able to make changes now; but you can make a plan. Knowing that you have a way out, even if it is several years down the road can help make the present situation more tolerable. By identifying the particular trouble spots, you can start to think of solutions, rather than writing off your whole life as difficult.

Start Laughing Again

I talk with mothers all the time and can't help but notice that we can be a grim bunch. We take ourselves much too seriously. King Solomon wrote, "a merry heart does good like medicine" (Proverbs 17:22). Science is finally catching up and confirming what he knew. Laughing and a lightness of spirit enhances the immune system and makes us feel better. When we are stressed, our sense of humor often vanishes.

If you are out of practice, here are some suggestions. Rent or borrow funny movies. Read funny books. Keep a stash of humorous materials on hand and pull them out whenever stress starts getting the better of you. Learn to appreciate the natural joy of children. Many things that happen in our every day lives are quite comical. We have to stop being so intense and learn to see the joy and humor around us.

Seek a Mothering Mentor

When we are in the midst of our own daily struggles, it is easy to lose sight of the big picture. You may wonder if what you are slaving for each day makes any difference. A mothering mentor can be a tremendous source of encouragement. When you are in the midst of day-to-day childcare, you may believe that this stage will last "forever." Talking with older women can help you realize how quickly this time goes by when looked at from the perspective of a whole life. My one caution would be for you to seek the advice of women who had positive mothering experiences. Just because a woman is older, you cannot assume that she enjoyed her time as a mother. A mother who is bitter about her mothering experience can reinforce some of the negative self-talk you are trying to eliminate. Someone can be honest about the difficulties and challenges of mothering, but still have an overall positive experience. Seek these women out.

Learn to Pace Yourself

So often we wear ourselves out thinking that everything needs to be done now. We labor under the false belief that if we only work hard enough, we can do it all. Recognize that this is a lie. There will always be stuff to do, but it doesn't all have to be done today. Besides, people who learn to take breaks and pace themselves are actually more productive.

Cultivate a Spiritual Life

Like many of you, I have specific religious beliefs and am not entirely comfortable recommending a generic "spirituality." On the other hand, I would be remiss if I did not mention the amazing health benefits of faith, prayer, and meditation. People with religious beliefs typically live longer, are in better health, and have more positive relationships with family members. Don't let the busyness of everyday life crowd out the needs of your spirit.

Surround Yourself with Beauty

My final suggestion has to do with nourishing your soul. Do this for yourself and your family. We often labor under the mistaken belief that beauty is for the rich alone. We think of great works of art or lovely pieces of furniture. Fortunately, beauty is something that we all can have for very little cost.

Sometimes, you can dramatically increase beauty with things you already have. Can you group items more attractively? Can you bring out some family heirlooms or other things you love? Can you attractively frame some of your photographs? Can you bring more color to a room? Reducing clutter can dramatically improve the looks of a room. Look around your home. Do you love the stuff that is there? If not, why are you keeping it? If you can't improve it, consider moving it to another location, selling it, or giving it away. Learn to make conscious choices about what you have around you.

Beauty is not limited to our sense of sight. Our other senses can experience beauty, too. Listen to music that nourishes your soul. It doesn't have to be "classical," although, there are some very good collections available. It should be music that makes your spirit soar. Many public libraries have great collections of tapes and CDs you can borrow for free. Or, perhaps you can swap with a friend. Fortunately, music is a very inexpensive source of beauty.

Think also of smell. Our sense of smell has been capitalized on in a big way in the last few years. It is great to have a home or work place that smells good. Different scents can increase your alertness (peppermint), improve your mood (citrus), promote relaxation (lavender), or invoke images of a cozy home (baking bread, cinnamon). Think about ways you can incorporate nice smells into your every day life.

Taste is another way that you can incorporate beauty. Learn basic cooking techniques that can help you eat good food. Often, simply prepared food is best. Glenna Matthews, in *Just a Housewife*, describes the "dumbing down" of the American palate with the mass production of convenience foods. We've lost our taste for fresh vegetables, succulently prepared meats, and fresh fruits. As we create workspaces in our kitchens that are more pleasant, perhaps we can once again enjoy the delights of a home-cooked meal.

Finally, don't forget beauty that is experienced through our sense of touch. Do you have a comfortable place to sit in your home? Home furnishings can be pretty uncomfortable. Don't sacrifice comfort purely for looks. Also, be sure to have places where people can sit comfortably together. Many times, families don't have enough seating for everyone to be together at the same time. This small change can yield big dividends for your family.

Conclusion

And so, my friends, we've come to the end of our journey together. Mothering is a tough job, but can be one of your proudest lifetime achievements. The work you are doing is vital to the next generation. In closing, I'd like to leave you with the following thoughts by Alexandra Stoddard in her book *Mothers: A Celebration* (1996b).

> The word mother conjures up more than a person. A mother is a life force, a spirit. She is living, loving energy channeling abundance into all of our lives. Being a mother is about having children, but her influence extends far beyond her own offspring. She is a universal person. Her strength comes gently. What makes her strong is her inherent maternal instincts. A mother is the greatest force in the world.

> All females are part of this universal generous energy. Collectively, women nourish, guide, and provide continuity.

> Mothers mother. That's what we do. That's who we are. Bless you (p. 269-270).

References

Abramowitz, J.N., & Mattoon, A.T. 1999. *Cutting the Costs of Paper: Saving Forests, Water, Energy, and Money.* Worldwatch Institute. From www.worldwatch.org.

Adler, N.E., David, H.P., Major, B.N., Roth, S.H., Russo, N.F., & Wyatt, G.E. 1992. Psychological factors in abortion: A review. *American Psychologist.* 47: 1194-1204.

Adler, N.E., Ozer, E.J., & Tschann, J. 2003. Abortion among adolescents. *American Psychologist.* 58:211-217.

Affluenza. 2000. From www.pbs.org.

Alexander, P., Anderson, C.L., Brand, B., Schaeffer, C.M., Grelling, B.Z., & Kretz, L. 1998. Adult attachment and long-term effects in survivors of incest. *Child Abuse and Neglect.* 22:45-61.

Allanson, S., & Astbury, J. 2001. Attachment style and broken attachments: Violence, pregnancy, and abortion. *Australian Journal of Psychology.* 53:146-151.

Allen, S. 1998. A qualitative analysis of the process, mediating variables, and impact of traumatic childbirth. *Journal of Reproductive and Infant Psychology.* 16: 107-111.

American Association for Premature Infants. 2000. From www.aapi-online.org

Armour, S. 2003. U.S. workers feel burn of long hours, less leisure. Employees pay cost of rising productivity. *USA Today,* December 17, 2003, 1B.

Ascione, F.R. 2005. Children, animal abuse and family violence: The multiple intersections of animal abuse, child victimization and domestic violence. In *Child Victimization*, edited by K. Kendall-Tackett and S.M. Giacomoni. Kingston, NJ: Civic Research Institute.

Aslett, D. 1984. *Clutter's Last Stand.* Cincinnati, OH: Writer's Digest Books.

Aslett, D. 2000. *No Time to Clean.* Pocatello, ID: Marsh Creek Press.

Atkinson, H. 1985. *Women and Fatigue.* New York: Pocket Books.

Avissar, S., Nechamkin, Y., Roitman, G., & Schreiber, G. 1997. Reduced G protein functions and immunoreactive levels in mononuclear leukocytes of patients with depression. *American Journal of Psychiatry.* 154:211-217.

Babyak, M., Blumenthal, J.A., Herman, S., Khatri, P., Doraiswamy, M., Moore, K., Craighead, W.E., Baldewicz, T.T., & Krishnan, K.R. 2000. Exercise treatment for major depression: Maintenance of therapeutic benefit at 10 months. *Psychosomatic Medicine.* 62:633-638.

Baker Miller, J. 1995. *Toward a New Psychology of Women.* Boston: Beacon Press.

Barrett, J.H., Brennan, P., Fiddler, M., & Silman, A. 2000. Breastfeeding and postpartum relapse in women with rheumatoid arthritis and inflammatory arthritis. *Arthritis and Rheumatism.* 43: 1010-1015.

Beck, C.T. 2004a. Birth trauma: In the eye of the beholder. *Nursing Research.* 53(1): 28-35.

Beck, C.T. 2004b. Post-traumatic stress disorder due to childbirth. *Nursing Research.* 53(4): 216-224.

Beecher Stowe, H. 1853/1997. *Uncle Tom's Cabin.* New York: Dutton Signet.

Beecher Stowe, H. 1852. *Letter to Eliza Cabot Follen December 16, 1852.* From www.xroads.Virginia.edu.

Bergeron, L.R. 2005. Abuse of elderly women in family relationships: Another form of violence against women. In *Handbook of Women, Stress and Trauma,* edited by K.A. Kendall-Tackett. New York: Taylor & Francis.

Bifulco, A., Harris, T., & Brown, G.W. 1992. Mourning or early inadequate care? Reexamining the relationship of maternal loss in childhood with adult depression and anxiety. *Development and Psychopathology.* 4: 433-451.

Blum, N. 2005. How busy is too busy? *Contemporary Pediatrics (online).* Retrieved February 2, 2005 from www.contemporarypediatrics. com/contpeds/article/articleDetail.jsp?id=128424.

Blumberg, N.L. 1980. Effects of neonatal risk, maternal attitude, and cognitive style on early postpartum adjustment. *Journal of Abnormal Psychology.* 89: 139-150.

Brady, D. 2000. Martha Inc.: Inside the growing empire of America's lifestyle queen. *Business Week Online. Retrieved* January 17, 2000 from www.businessweek.com.

Brandt, A. 1998. *Understanding and Acknowledging Negative Emotions.* From www.ec-online.net.

Bratman, S., & Girman, A.M. 2003. *Handbook of herbs and supplements and their therapeutic uses.* St Louis, MO: Mosby.

Breathnach, S.B. 1995. *Simple Abundance: A Daybook of Comfort and Joy.* New York: Warner Books.

Bremner, J.D. 2005. The neurobiology of childhood sexual abuse in women with posttraumatic stress disorder. In *Handbook of Women, Stress and Trauma,* edited by K.A. Kendall-Tackett. New York: Taylor & Francis.

Bremner, J.D., Southwick, S.M., Johnson, D.R., Yehuda, R., & Charney, D.S. 1993. Childhood physical abuse and combat-related posttraumatic stress disorder in Vietnam veterans. *American Journal of Psychiatry.* 150: 235-239.

Breslau, N., Davis, G.C., Peterson, E.L., & Schultz, L. 1997. Psychiatric sequelae of post-traumatic stress disorder in women. *Archives of General Psychiatry.* 54: 81-87.

Briere, J.N., & Elliot, D.M. 1994. Immediate and long-term impacts of child sexual abuse. *The Future of Children.* 4: 54-69.

Buck, P.S. 1941. *Of Men and Women.* New York: John Day.

Buist, A. 1998. Childhood abuse, postpartum depression and parenting difficulties: A literature review of associations. *Australian and New Zealand Journal of Psychiatry.* 32: 370-378.

Burns, D. 1999. *Feeling Good: The New Mood Therapy.* New York: Avon.

Cain, N. 1996. *Healing the Child: A Mother's Story.* New York: Rawson Associates.

Campbell, J.C., & Kendall-Tackett, K.A. 2005. Intimate partner violence: Implications for women's physical and mental health. In *Handbook of Women, Stress and Trauma,* edited by K.A. Kendall-Tackett. New York: Taylor & Francis.

Cardozo, A.R. 1996. *Sequencing: A New Solution for Women Who Want Marriage, Career and Family.* San Bernardino, CA: Borgo Press.

Cassidy, A. 1999. Time squeeze: Can working moms beat the clock? Results from our exclusive survey. *Working Mother.* November: 48-54.

Cloud, H., & Townsend, J. 1992. *Boundaries: When To Say "Yes," When To Say "No." Take Control Of Your Life.* Grand Rapids, MI: Zondervan.

Collegeboard.com (2005). *The extracurricular edge: Quality over quantity.* Retrieved on February 2, 2005 from www.CollegeBoard.com/parents/article/0,3708,703-704-0-21282,00.html.

Covey, S.R. 1989. *The 7 Habits of Highly Effective People.* New York: Fireside.

Crittenden, A. 2001. *The Price of Motherhood: Why the Most Important Job in the World is Still the Least Valued.* New York: Owl Books.

Crockenberg, S., & McCluskey, K. 1986. Change in maternal behavior during the baby's first year of life. *Child Development.* 57: 746-753.

Cutrona, C.E., & Troutman, B.R. 1986. Social support, infant temperament, and parenting self-efficacy: A mediational model of postpartum depression. *Child Development.* 57: 1507-1518.

Dacyczyn, A. 1998. *The Complete Tightwad Gazette.* New York: Villard Books.

Davidson, J. 1991. *Breathing Space: Living and Working at a Comfortable Pace in a Sped-Up Society.* New York: MasterMedia.

Diamond, K. 1991. *Motherhood after Miscarriage.* Holbrook, MA: Adams Media.

DeNavas-Walt, C., Proctor, B.D., & Mills, R.J. 2004. *Income, Poverty, and Health Insurance Coverage in the United States: 2003.* Washington, D.C.: U.S. Census Bureau.

DeYmaz, L. 1996. *Mommy, Please Don't Cry.* Sisters, OR: Multnomah Press.

Doherty, W., & Carlson, B. 2002. *Putting Families First.* New York: Henry Holt & Co.

Dominguez, J., & Robin, V. 1992. *Your Money or Your Life: Transforming Your Relationship with Money and Achieving Financial Independence.* New York: Viking.

Durik, A.M., Hyde, J.S., & Clark, R. 2000. Sequelae of cesarean and vaginal deliveries: Psychosocial outcomes for mothers and infants. *Developmental Psychology.* 36: 251-260.

Earle, A.M. 1898/1992. *Home Life in Colonial Days.* Stockbridge, MA: Berkshire House.

Edwards, V.E., Anda, R.F., Felitti, V.J., & Dube, S.R. 2004. Adverse childhood experiences and health-related quality of life as an adult. In *Health Consequences of Abuse in the Family*, edited by K.A. Kendall-Tackett. Washington, D.C.: American Psychological Association.

Egeland B., Jacobvitz, D., & Sroufe, L.A. 1988. Breaking the cycle of abuse. *Child Development*. 59: 1080-1088.

Felitti, V.J., Anda, R.F., Nordenberg, D., Williamson, D.F., Spitz, A.M., & Edwards, V. 1998. Relationship of child abuse and household dysfunction to many of the leading causes of death in adults. *American Journal of Preventive Medicine*. 14: 245-258.

Fidler, A.T., & Bernstein, J. 1999. Infertility: From a personal to a public health problem. *Public Health Reports*. 114: 494-511.

Fields, J. 2004. *America's Families and Living Arrangements: 2003*. Washington, D.C.: U.S. Census Bureau.

Figley, C. 1985. *Trauma and Its Wake: The Study And Treatment Of Post-Traumatic Stress Disorder*. New York: Bruner/Mazel.

Finkelhor, D. 1994. Current information on the scope and nature of child sexual abuse. *Future of Children*. 4: 31-53.

Fisher, D.G. 1996. Mothers at home. *New Beginnings*. Sept.-Oct.:132-135.

Fisher, J., Astbury, J., & Smith, A. 1997. Adverse psychological impact of operative obstetric interventions: A prospective longitudinal study. *Australian and New Zealand Journal of Psychiatry*. 31: 728-738.

Friedan, B. 1963. *The Feminine Mystique*. New York: Dell.

Friedberg, F. 1995. *Coping with Chronic Fatigue Syndrome*. Oakland, CA: New Harbinger.

Fritz, H.L., & Helgeson, V.S. 1998. Distinctions of unmitigated communion from communion: Self-neglect and overinvolvement with others. *Journal of Personality and Social Psychology.* 75: 121-140.

Fuller, J.A., & Warner, R. 2000. Family stressors as predictors of codependency. *Genetic, Social, and General Psychology Monographs.* 126: 5-22.

Galea S., Vlahov, D., Resnick, H., Ahern, J., Susser, E., Gold, J., Bucuvalas, M., & Kilpatrick, D. 2003. Trends of probable post-traumatic stress disorder in New York City after the September 11 terrorist attacks. *American Journal of Epidemiology.* 158(6): 514-524.

Genevie, L., & Margolies, E. 1987. *The Motherhood Report.* New York: Dell.

Greenspan, M. 1998. "Exceptional" mothering in a "normal" world. In *Mothering Against the Odds: Diverse Voices of Contemporary Mothers,* edited by C. Garcia Coll, J.L Surrey, and K. Weingarten. New York: Guilford.

Gromada, K. 1999. *Mothering Multiples.* Schaumburg, IL: La Leche League International.

Grus, C.L., Lopez-Hernandez, C., Delamater, A., Appelgate, B., Brito, A., Wurm, G., & Wanner, A. 2001. Parental self-efficacy and morbidity in pediatric asthma. *Journal of Asthma.* 38: 99-106.

Hale, T.W. 2004. *Medications and Mothers' Milk.* Amarillo, TX: Pharmasoft Medical Publishing.

Hammonds, K.H. 1998. There really aren't enough hours in the day. *Business Week Online,* from www.businessweek.com.

Health. 2000. The alarming truth about his snoring. *Health.* Jan/Feb: 22.

Helgeson, V.S., & Fritz, H.L. 1998. A theory of unmitigated communion. *Personality and Social Psychology Review.* 2: 173-183.

Helgeson, V.S., & Fritz, H.L. 1999. Unmitigated agency and unmitigated communion: Distinctions from agency and communion. *Journal of Research in Personality.* 33: 131-158.

Helpguide.org. 2004a. *Stress Burnout: Signs, Symptoms and Prevention.* From www.helpguide.org/mental/burnout_signs_symptoms.htm.

Helpguide.org. 2004b. Burnout: Signs, *Symptoms and Prevention.* From www.helpguide.org/mental/signs_symptoms.htm.

Hochschild, A., with Machung, A. 1989. *The Second Shift.* New York: Avon Books.

Hochschild, A.R. 1997. *The Time Bind: When Work Becomes Home and Home Becomes Work.* New York: Metropolitan Books.

Holden, C. 2000. Global survey examines impact of depression. *Science.* 288: 39-40.

Holliday, C. 1922/1999. *Women's Life in Colonial Days.* Mineola, NY: Dover.

Honos-Webb, L. 2005. *The Gift of ADHD: How to Transform Your Child's Problems into Strengths.* Oakland, CA: New Harbinger.

Humphrey, S. 2003. *The Nursing Mother's Herbal.* Minneapolis: Fairview Press.

Hunfeld, J.A., Tempels, A., Passchier, J., & Hazebroek, F.W.J. 1999. Parental burden and grief one year after the birth of a child with a congenital anomaly. *Journal of Pediatric Psychology.* 24: 515-520.

Infoplease. (2005a). *Average number of vacation days around the world per year.* Retrieved February 2, 2005 from www.infoplease.com/ipa/A0922052.html.

Infoplease (2005b). *Percent of households with Internet access, 2001. Retrieved* February 2, 2005 from www.infoplease.com/ipa/A0880773.htm.

Isenberg, D.A. 1999, Nov. *Complicated Systemic Lupus Erythematous: How to Assess It, How to Treat It.* Invited address at the annual meeting of American College of Rheumatology, Boston, MA.

Jarvis, P.A., Myers, B.J., & Creasey, G.L. 1989. The effects of infants' illness on mothers' interactions with prematures at 4 and 8 months. *Infant Behavior and Development.* 12: 25-35.

Johnson, S.K. 2000. Chore wars. *Ladies' Home Journal* Online March. From www.lhj.org.

Kabat-Zinn, J. 1991. *Full Catastrophe Living: Using the Wisdom of Your Body and Mind to Face Stress, Pain and Illness.* New York: Dell Publishing Company.

Karlson, E.W., Mandl, L.A., Hankinson, S.E., & Grodstein, F. 2004. Do breastfeeding and other reproductive factors influence future risk of rheumatoid arthritis: Research from the Nurses' Health Study. *Arthritis and Rheumatism.* 50:3458-3467.

Kendall-Tackett, K.A. 2000. Physiological correlates of childhood abuse: Chronic hyperarousal in PTSD, depression and irritable bowel syndrome. Invited review. *Child Abuse and Neglect.* 24: 799-810.

Kendall-Tackett, K.A. 2003a. *Treating the Lifetime Health Effects of Childhood Victimization.* Kingston, NJ: Civic Research Institute.

Kendall-Tackett, K.A. 2003b. *The Well-Ordered Home: Organizing Techniques for Inviting Serenity into your Life.* Oakland, CA: New Harbinger Publications.

Kendall-Tackett, K.A. 2005a. *The Handbook of Women, Stress and Trauma.* New York: Taylor & Francis.

Kendall-Tackett, K.A. 2005b. *Depression in New Mothers: Causes, Consequences and Treatment Options.* Binghamton, NY: Haworth Press.

Kendall-Tackett, K.A. 2005c. *The Well-Ordered Office: How to Create an Efficient and Serene Workspace.* Oakland, CA: New Harbinger Publications.

Kendall-Tackett, K.A., & Marshall, R. 1999. Victimization and diabetes: An exploratory study. *Child Abuse and Neglect.* 23, 593-596.

Kendall-Tackett, K.A., Marshall, R., & Ness, K.E. 2003. Chronic pain syndromes and violence against women. *Women and Therapy.* 26: 45-56.

Kendall-Tackett, K.A., Williams, L.M., & Finkelhor, D. 1993. The impact of sexual abuse on children: A review and synthesis of recent empirical studies. *Psychological Bulletin.* 113: 164-180.

Khalsa, K.P.S. 2000. Don't take your herbs for granted. *Herbs for Health.* July/August: 52-55.

Kiely, J.L., Kleinman, J.C., & Kiely, M. 1992. Triplets and higher-order multiple births: Time trends and infant mortality. *American Journal of Diseases of Childhood.* 146: 862-868.

Kirkland, K. 2000. On the decline in average weekly hours worked. *Monthly Labor Review.* July: 26-31.

Kitzinger, S. 1990. *The Crying Baby.* New York: Penguin.

Klaus, M., Kennell, J., & Klaus, P. 1993. *Mothering the Mother.* Reading, MA: Addison-Wesley.

Koverola, C., & Morahan, M. 2000, July. *Differential Impact of Exposure to Domestic Violence and Child Sexual Abuse: Maternal Functioning as a Meditating Variable.* Paper presented at "Victimization of Children and Youth: An International Research Conference." Durham, NH.

Kuhn, M.A., & Winston, D. 2000. *Herbal Therapy and Supplements: A Scientific and Traditional Approach.* Philadelphia, PA: Lippincott.

Kurcinka, M.S. 1998. *Raising Your Spirited Child: A Guide for Parents Whose Child is More.* New York: Harper Perennial.

LaPlante, M.P., Carlson, D., Kaye, H.S., & Bradsher, J.E. 1996. *Families with Disabilities in the United States: Executive Summary. U.S.* Department of Health and Human Services. From www.aspe.os.dhhs.gov.

Lehmkuhl, L. 1999. *Health effects of long work hours.* 32 Hours: Action for full employment. From www.web.net/32hours/health%20Effects%20v2.htm

Leman, K. 1987. *Women Who Try too Hard: Breaking the Pleaser Habits.* Grand Rapids, MI: Fleming H. Revell.

Lemieux, A.M., & Coe, C.L. 1995. Abuse-related post-traumatic stress disorder: Evidence for chronic neuroendocrine activation in women. *Psychosomatic Medicine.* 57: 105-115.

Lesperance, F., & Frasure-Smith, N. 2000. Depression in patients with cardiac disease: A practical review. *Journal of Psychosomatic Research.* 48: 379-391.

Lewis, D.S., with G. Lewis. 1989. *Motherhood Stress.* Dallas, TX: Word Publishing.

Little, L. 2002. Differences in stress and coping for mothers and fathers of children with Asperger's syndrome and nonverbal learning disorders. *Pediatric Nursing.* 28: 565-570.

Mack, D. 1997. *The Assault on Parenthood: How Our Culture Undermines the Family.* New York: Simon and Schuster.

Maranjian, S. 2004. Shocking credit card facts. *The Motley Fool. Commentary,* Retrieved September30,2004 from www.fool.com/news/commentary/2004/commentary04093001.htm?logvisit=y&source.

Marco, C.A., Schwartz, J.E., Neale, J.M., Shiffman, S., Catley, D., & Stone, A. 2000. Impact of gender and having children in the household on ambulatory blood pressure in work and non-work settings: A partial replication and new findings. *Annals of Behavioral Medicine.* 22: 110-115.

Martin, J. 2004. For many teens, after-school activities make the grade. *The Daily Herald.* Posted May 16, 2004. Retrieved February 2, 2005, from www.dailyherald.com/oped/col_martin.asp?intID=38123143.

Mathews, T.J., Maenacker, F., & MacDorman, M.F. 2004. *Infant Mortality Statistics from the 2002 Period Linked to Birth/Infant Death Data Set*. National Vital Statistics Report, Vol. 53, Number 10. Washington, D.C.: U.S. Department of Health and Human Services.

Matthews, G. 1987. *"Just a Housewife": The Rise And Fall Of Domesticity In America*. New York: Oxford University Press.

McCormick, L. 1995. Depression in mothers of children with Attention Deficit Hyperactivity Disorder. *Family Medicine*. 27: 176-179.

McGrath, E., Keita, G.P., Strickland, B.R., & Russo, N.F. 1990. *Women and Depression: Risk Factors and Treatment Issues*. Washington, D.C.: American Psychological Association.

McGuire, P.A. 1999. Worker stress, health reaching critical point. *APA Monitor Online* May from www.apa.org/monitor.

McKenna, J.J. 2004. Sudden Infant Death Syndrome (SIDS or Cot Death): Infant sleep, breastfeeding, and infant sleeping arrangements. In *Encyclopedia of Medical Anthropology*, edited by C. Ember and M. Ember. New York: Academic/Plenum Publishers.

McKenna, J.J., & Mosko, S. 2001. Mother-infant cosleeping: Toward a new scientific beginning. In *Sudden Infant Death Syndrome: Problems, Progress, Possibilities*, edited by R. Byard and H. Krous. New York: Arnold Publishers.

McMillen, C., Zuravin, S., & Rideout, G. 1995. Perceived benefit from child sexual abuse. *Journal of Consulting and Clinical Psychology*. 63: 1037-1043.

M.C. 1893/1995. *Everybody's Book of Correct Conduct, Being The Etiquette of Every-day Life*. London: Saxon and Co.

Mintz, S., & Kellogg, S. 1988. *Domestic Revolutions: A Social History of American Family Life*. New York: Free Press.

Mohrbacher, N., & Kendall-Tackett, K.A. 2005. *Breastfeeding Made Simple: Seven Natural Laws for Nursing Mothers.* Oakland, CA: New Harbinger Publications.

Moran, V. 1997. *Shelter for the Spirit: Create Your Own Haven in a Hectic World.* New York: Harper Perennial.

Morgenstern, J. 1998. *Organizing from the Inside Out.* New York: Henry Holt and Company.

Murray, B. 2000. Family income predicts children's postdivorce well-being. *Monitor on Psychology.* June: 14.

Murray, M.T. 1996. *Natural Alternatives to Prozac.* New York: William Morrow and Co.

National Academy on an Aging Society. 2000. *Caregiving: Helping the Elderly With Activity Limitations.* From www.agingsociety.org.

National Center for Health Statistics. 2004. *Health, United States, 2004.* Washington, D.C.: U.S. Department of Health and Human Services, Centers for Disease Control and Prevention.

National Institute of Child Health and Human Development. 1999. Chronicity of maternal depressive symptoms, maternal sensitivity, and child functioning at 36 months. *Developmental Psychology.* 35: 1297-1310.

National Institute of Mental Health. 2000a. *NIMH Research on Treatment for Attention Deficit Hyperactivity Disorder (ADHD): The Multimodal Treatment Study.* From www.nimh.nih.gov.

National Institute of Mental Health. 2000b. *Attention Deficit Hyperactivity Disorder.* www.nimh.nih.gov.

National Sleep Foundation. 2000a. *2000 Omnibus Sleep in America Poll.* From www.sleepfoundation.org.

National Sleep Foundation. 2000b. *The Nature of Sleep.* From www.sleepfoundation.org.

Olkin, R. 1999. *What Psychotherapists Should Know about Disability.* New York: Guilford.

O'Neil, J.R. 1993. *The Paradox of Success: When Winning at Work Means Losing at Life.* New York: G.P. Putnam's Sons.

Panuthos, C., & Romeo, C. 1984. *Ended Beginnings: Healing Childbearing Losses.* Westport, CT: Bergin and Garvey.

Pennebaker, J.W. 2004. *Writing to Heal.* Oakland, CA: New Harbinger Publications.

Pearson, A. 2002. *I Don't Know How She Does It.* New York: Anchor Books.

Perlis, M.L., Giles, D.E., Buysse, D.J., Thase, M.E., Tu, X., & Kupfer, D.J. 1997. Which depressive symptoms are related to which sleep electroencephalographic variables? *Biological Psychiatry.* 42: 904-913.

Polansky, N.A., Gaudin, J.M., Ammons, P.W., & Davis, K.B. 1985. The psychological ecology of the neglectful mother. *Child Abuse and Neglect.* 9: 265-275.

Potter, B. 1998. *Overcoming Job Burnout: How to Renew Enthusiasm for Work.* Berkeley, CA: Ronin.

Preston, J., & Johnson, J. 2004. *Clinical Psychopharmacology Made Ridiculously Simple.* Miami, FL: MedMaster, Inc.

Radke-Yarrow, M. 1998. *Children of Depressed Mothers.* Cambridge, U.K.: Cambridge University Press.

Raskin, V. 1997. *When Words Are Not Enough: The Women's Prescription for Depression and Anxiety.* New York: Broadway.

Reading, R., & Reynolds, S. 2001. Debt, social disadvantage and maternal depression. *Social Science and Medicine.* 53: 441-453.

Reardon, D.C., & Ney, P.G. 2000. Abortion and subsequent substance abuse. *American Journal of Drug and Alcohol Abuse.* 26: 61-75.

Rhoades, N., & Hutchinson, S. 1994. Labor experiences of child sexual abuse survivors. *Birth.* 21: 213-220.

Robins, V. 1994. *A Declaration of Independence from Overconsumption.* New Road Map Foundation. From www.newroadmap.org.

Roizenblatt, S., Moldofsky, H., Benedito-Silva, A.A., & Tufik, S. 2001. Alpha sleep characteristics in fibromyalgia. *Arthritis and Rheumatism.* 44: 222-230.

Rosenthal, N.E. 1998. *Winter Blues: Seasonal Affective Disorder. What it is and how to Overcome It.* New York: The Guilford Press.

Ryding, E.L., Wijma, K., & Wijma, B. 1998. Experiences of emergency Cesarean section: Aphenomenological study of 53 women. *Birth.* 25: 246-251.

Sapolsky, R.M. 1996. Why stress is bad for your brain. *Science.* 273: 749-750.

Sapolsky, R.M. 2000. Glucocorticoids and hippocampal atrophy in neuropsychiatric disorders. *Archives of General Psychiatry.* 57: 925-935.

Schor, J. 1992. *The Overworked American: The Unexpected Decline of Leisure.* New York: Basic Books.

Schwartz, F.N., with Zimmerman, J. 1992. *Breaking with Tradition: Women and Work, The New Facts of Life.* New York: Warner Books.

Schwartz Cowan, R. 1983. *More Work for Mother: The Ironies of Household Technology from the Open Hearth to the Microwave.* New York: Basic Books.

Sears, W. 1991. *Christian Parenting and Childcare.* Nashville, TN: Thomas Nelson.

Sears, W. 1995. *SIDS: A Parent's Guide to Understanding and Preventing Sudden Infant Death Syndrome.* New York: Little, Brown.

Sears, W., & Sears, M. 1996. *Parenting the Fussy Baby and High-Need Child.* New York: Little, Brown.

Sears, W., & Thompson, L. 1998. The A.D.D. Book: *New Understandings, New Approaches to Parenting Your Child.* New York: Little, Brown.

Sedlak, A., & Broadhurst, D.D. 1996. *Third National Incidence Study of Child Abuse and Neglect.* Final Report. Washington, D.C.: U.S. Department of Health and Human Services.

Solomon, Z., & Ginzburg, K. 1999. Aging in the shadow of war. In *Posttraumatic Stress Disorder: A Lifespan Developmental Perspective,* edited by A. Maercker, M. Schutzwohl, and Z. Solomon. Seattle: Hogrefe & Huber.

Smith, B., Surrey, J.L., & Watkins, M. 1998. "Real mothers": Adoptive mothers resisting marginization and re-creating motherhood. In *Mothering Against the Odds: Diverse Voices of Contemporary Mothers,* edited by C. Garcia Coll, J.L. Surrey, and K. Weingarten. New York: Guilford.

St. James, E. 1999. *Living the Simple Live: A Guide to Scaling Down And Enjoying More.* New York: Hyperion.

Stan, A. 2000. Woman on the verge: On the eve of her run for the Senate, Hillary Rodham Clinton reflects on a very public life in transition. *Working Woman.* Sept.: 60-63.

Stoddard, A. 1992. *Creating a Beautiful Home.* New York: Avon Books.

Stoddard, A. 1996a. *Gracious Living in the New World: Finding Joy in Changing Times.* New York: Avon Books.

Stoddard, A. 1996b. *Mothers: A Celebration.* New York: Avon Books.

Sullivan, P.M., & Knutson, J.F. 2000. Maltreatment and disabilities: A population-based epidemiological study. *Child Abuse and Neglect.* 24: 1257-1273.

Swindle, R., Heller, K., Pescosolido, B., & Kikuzawa, S. 2000. Responses to nervous breakdowns in America over a 40-year period. *American Psychologist.* 55: 740-749.

Talbot, R. 2005. *Debt facts and figures.* Retrieved February 2, 2005, from www.creditaction.org.uk/debtstats.htm.

Tammy. 2000. *Personal story of loss of a multiple.* From www.angels4ever.com.

Taylor, S.E., Klein, L.C., Lewis, B.P., Gruenewald, T.L., Gurung, R.A.R., & Updegraff, J.A. 2000. Biobehavioral responses to stress in females: Tend-and-befriend, not fight-or-flight. *Psychological Review.* 107: 411-429.

Trowell, J. 1983. Emergency caesarian section: A research study of the mother/child relationship of a group of women admitted expecting a normal vaginal delivery. *Child Abuse and Neglect.* 7: 387-394.

Twenge, J.M. 2000. The age of anxiety? The birth cohort change in anxiety and neuroticism, 1952-1993. *Journal of Personality and Social Psychology.* 79: 1007-1021.

U.S. Census Bureau. 2005a. *Median and average square feet of floor area in new one-family houses completed by location.* Retrieved February 1, 2005 from www.census.gov/const/C25Ann/sftotalmedavgsqft.pdf.

U.S. Census Bureau. 2005b. *Number of bathrooms in new one-family houses completed.* Retrieved February 1, 2005 from www.census.gov/const/C25Ann/sftotalbaths.pdf.

U.S. Department of Labor, Bureau of Labor Statistics. 1997a. Workers are on the job more hours over the course of the year. *Issues in Labor Statistics,* Feb. 1-2.

U.S. Department of Labor, Women's Bureau. 1997b. *Women of Hispanic Origin in the Labor Force.* From www.dol.gov.

U.S. Department of Labor, Women's Bureau. 1997c. *Black Women in the Labor Force.* From www.dol.gov.

U.S. Department of Labor. 1998. *Work and Elder Care: Facts for Caregivers and Their Employers.* From www.dol.gov.

U.S. Department of Transportation, Bureau of Transportation Statistics. 2004a. *State Transportation Profiles 2004*, Table 5-14: Average daily trips and miles per person by age: 2001. Retrieved February 2, 2005, from www.bts.gov/cgi-bin/breadcrumbs/PrintVersion. cgi.

U.S. Department of Transportation, Bureau of Transportation Statistics. 2004b. *State Transportation Profiles 2004*, Table 4-1: Commuting to work: 2000. Retrieved February 2, 2005 from www.bts.gov/cgi-bin/breadcrumbs/PrintVersion.cgi.

Valentine, B. 2000. *Personal Story of ADHD*. From www.adhdnews.com. Used with permission.

Van Gurp, G., Meterissian, G.B., Haiek, L.N., McCusker, J., & Bellavance, F. 2002. St. John's wort or sertraline?: Randomized controlled trial in primary care. *Canadian Family Physician*. 48: 905-912.

Ventura, S.J., Abma, J.C., & Mosher, W.D. 2004. *Estimated Pregnancy Rates for the United States, 1990-2000: An Update*. National Vital Statistics Reports, Vol. 53, Num. 23. Washington, D.C.: U.S. Department of Health and Human Services.

Vorona, R.D., Winn, M.P., Babineau, T.W., Eng, B.P., Feldman, H.R., & Ware, J.C. 2005. Overweight and obese patients in a primary care population report less sleep than patients with a normal body mass index. *Archives of Internal Medicine*. 165: 25-30.

Weetman, A.P. 1997. Fortnightly review: Hypothyroidism: Screening and subclinical disease. *British Medical Journal*. 314:1175-1178.

Weiss, E.L., Longhurst, J.G., & Mazure, C.M. 1999. Childhood sexual abuse as a risk factor for depression in women: Psychosocial and neurobiological correlates. *Archives of General Psychiatry*. 156: 816-828.

Weisse, C.S. 1992. Depression and immunocompetence: A review of the literature. *Psychological Bulletin*. 111: 475-489.

Weil, A. 2000. ADHD: Are we overmedicating children? *Self Healing.* Aug.: 8.

Whelan, K.A. 2000. *Grief Songs: Stories, Letters, and Poems that Chronicle the Recovery and Survival of a Community After the Sudden Death of a Baby.* Boston: Massachusetts Center for Sudden Infant Death Syndrome.

Whiffen, V.E., & Gotlib, I.H. 1989. Infants of postpartum depressed mothers: Temperament and cognitive status. *Journal of Abnormal Psychology.* 98: 274-279.

Williams, L.M. 1994. Recall of childhood trauma: A prospective study of women's memories of child sexual abuse. *Journal of Consulting and Clinical Psychology.* 62: 1167-1176.

Woodbury, R.M. 1925. *Infant Mortality and Its Causes.* Baltimore, MD: Williams and Wilkins.

Wright, R. 1997. Go ahead…sleep with your children. *APA Monitor.* June: 16-17.

Wurtman, J.J., & Suffes, S. 1997. *The Serotonin Solution to Achieve Permanent Weight Control.* New York: Fawcett Columbine.

Zuravin, S., McMillen, C., DePanfilis, D., & Risley-Curtiss, C. 1996. The intergenerational cycle of child maltreatment: Continuity vs. discontinuity. *Journal of Interpersonal Violence.* 11: 315-334.

Kathleen Kendall-Tackett, Ph.D., IBCLC

Dr. Kendall-Tackett is a health psychologist, International Board Certified Lactation Consultant, Research Associate Professor of Psychology at the Family Research Lab, University of New Hampshire, and a Fellow of the American Psychological Association. She is a La Leche League leader, chair of the New Hampshire Breastfeeding Taskforce, and member of the La Leche League International Board of Directors.

Dr. Kendall-Tackett is author or editor of 12 books including *Treating the Lifetime Health Effects of Childhood Victimization* (2003, Civic Research Institute), *The Health Consequences of Abuse in the Family* (2004, American Psychological Association), *Depression in New Mothers* (2005, Haworth), *Breastfeeding Made Simple*, co-authored with Nancy Mohrbacher (2005, New Harbinger), and *The Well-Ordered Home* and *The Well-Ordered Office* (2003; 2005, New Harbinger).

Dr. Kendall-Tackett received a Bachelor's and Master's degree in psychology from California State University, Chico, and a Ph.D. from Brandeis University in social and developmental psychology. She has won several awards including the Outstanding Research Study Award from the American Professional Society on the Abuse of Children, and was named 2003 Distinguished Alumna, College of Behavioral and Social Sciences, California State University, Chico.

Dr. Kendall-Tackett lives in New Hampshire with her husband Doug Tackett, her sons Ken and Chris, and quite a few pets.

Ordering Information

Pharmasoft Publishing, L.P.

1712 N. Forest St.

Amarillo, Texas, USA   79106

8:00 am to 5:00 pm CST

Call...806-376-9900

Sales...800-378-1317

FAX...806-376-9901

Online Web Orders...

http://www.iBreastfeeding.com